INSIDE EDUCATION

DEPTH PSYCHOLOGY
IN TEACHING AND LEARNING

by

Clifford Mayes

ATWOOD PUBLISHING
MADISON, WI

Inside Education: Depth Psychology in Teaching and Learning
By Clifford Mayes
© 2007 Atwood Publishing
All rights reserved.
Printed in the United States of America.

Atwood Publishing
Madison, WI
www.atwoodpublishing.com

Cover design by TLC Graphics, www.tlcgraphics.com

Library of Congress Cataloging–in–Publication Data

Mayes, Clifford.
  Inside education : depth psychology in teaching and learning / by Clifford Mayes.
     p. cm.
  Includes bibliographical references and index.
  ISBN 978–1–891859–68–7 (pb : alk. paper)
  1. Psychoanalysis and education. 2. Archetype (Psychology) 3.
Teaching—Psychological aspects. 4. Learning, Psychology of. 5. Jung, C. G. (Carl
Gustav), 1875–1961. I. Title.

LB1092.M39 2007
370.15—dc22

                                    2007023968

ACKNOWLEDGMENTS

Few, indeed, are the books that come into existence merely on the strength of a single author's efforts. An author must rely upon the insights and encouragement of loved ones, friends, and colleagues in the course of his or her work. I am no exception to that rule. Hence, I would like to offer here my thanks to people who have been instrumental in the creation of this volume.

I want to thank my wife and best friend, Pam—the kindest, brightest, and most creative person I have ever known. Without her nurturing love and example of a life lived in pursuit and service of what is good and true, I could do nothing of any consequence. Our children—Lizzie, Josh, and Dana—bring energy and joy into our lives.

I am indebted to Professor Edward Pajak, Chairman of the Department of Teacher Development and Leadership at Johns Hopkins University. In his innovative work, Ed has blazed the trail for so many of us in the last two decades in defining the methods and horizons of psychoanalytic inquiry into teaching. Despite his many and varied accomplishments, Ed is a humble man of faith—one who is always ready to give of his time in order to be of service to researchers, teachers, and students.

Professor Robert Boostrom, Chairman of the Department of Teacher Education at the University of Southern Indiana and the U.S. Editor of *The Journal of Curriculum Studies*, has offered sagacious council, professionally and intellectually, over the years. I will always thank my lucky stars for the day I met him when we were on a discussion panel at a meeting of the American Educational Research Association in Chicago in 1998. Bob's intellectual acumen and organizational gifts are matched only by his personal authenticity and dedication to solid scholarship and humane educational practices.

I am grateful for the privilege of associating with Professor Robert Bullough, Jr., Professor of Teacher Education and Associate Director of the Center for the Improvement of Teacher Education and Schooling at Brigham Young University. His friendship and advice are precious to me professionally and personally. More than just a friend, Bob is an older brother. Best of all, he never remembers any of my jokes. This means that I can tell him the same ones over and over again and he always finds them funny.

Like all of those who teach, research, and study in BYU's McKay School of Education, I have been blessed by the wise governance and generous encouragement of our dean, Richard Young. Dean Young's leadership in the Peaceable Schools movement is instrumental in creating the kind of school environments where the pedagogical principles for which I advocate in this book can flourish.

It is an honor to know and work with the students in the McKay School of Education at BYU. Very often, I am the student and they are the teachers. Virtually every class, they convey to me invaluable truths about what it means to think, feel, and act from one's intellectual, emotional, and spiritual depths. In our class discussions, they have patiently helped me work out the ideas presented in this book.

Gene Gillespie, my dear friend of over forty years, is not only a superb poet and musician but has an understanding of archetypal psychology which rivals that of some of the best scholars in the field. Being able to "kick ideas around" with him has been an integral part of my evolving understanding of Jung since I started reading him thirty-five years ago. Gene also thought of the title for this book.

Linda Babler, the head of Atwood Publishing, has been enthusiastically supportive of this project since it first reached her desk in the tentative form of an unpolished manuscript. Her wisdom, humor, professionalism, and integrity have made it a delight to carry this project through to its conclusion. I also express my gratitude to the administrative assistant of the Department of Educational Leadership and Foundations at BYU, Bonnie Bennett, who unfailingly provides me with both practical support and words of wisdom to help me in my work. Thanks also go to my research assistant Bryan Blair for both technical and conceptual help in completing the final drafts of this manuscript. I have also benefited from stimulating conversations with other Jungian-oriented researchers and counselors during our monthly meetings of the C.G. Jung Fellowship of Salt Lake City.

Above all, I wish to thank my Father in heaven for His tender mercies in my life. It has been my experience that even (and perhaps especially) during the hardest times and darkest seasons, His arm is always stretched out to pick me up and move me gently on.

TABLE OF CONTENTS

FOREWORD

Clifford Mayes is an associate professor of education in the Department of Educational Leadership and Foundations at Brigham Young University and a Jungian-oriented counselor. He has published numerous articles and several books relating various aspects of depth psychology, especially Jungian psychology, to education. His book *Jung and Education: Elements of an Archetypal Pedagogy*, published in 2005, was, as far as I am aware, the first book-length study in English to focus exclusively on the implications and applications of Jungian thought to education.

In this present book, *Inside Education: Depth Psychology in Teaching and Learning,* Mayes expands on the ideas that he introduced in *Jung and Education* in a variety of new and exciting ways. He also folds in terms and techniques from such post-Freudian theorists as Heinz Kohut, D.W. Winnicott, and W.R.D. Fairbairn in order to cull those elements out of psychoanalytic theory that are most relevant to teaching and learning. His weaving together of both classical Freudian and Jungian as well as neo-Freudian and neo-Jungian thought makes this an original and important book. Its importance is far greater, however, because it offers a view of education that runs directly counter to prevailing national policy and explicitly addresses many of the fundamental problems underlying public education today.

Anyone who regularly reads the newspapers is well aware that public education in the United States is supposedly in a state of crisis, evidenced by the poor performance of American students on standardized tests as compared with students in other countries. The response of policy makers, particularly at the national level, has been a concerted attempt to make schooling more literal, more linearly rational, and more reliant on computers and other technology. Mayes' book addresses the less widely recognized but true crisis in American public education today, the fact that classrooms and schools are relentlessly becoming less human, less symbolic, and less spiritual places—trends that are manifested in increasing numbers of student drop outs, rising levels of violence by students against themselves and others, high rates of teacher turnover, and shortages of principals and other administrators.

In the three chapters that comprise the first half of his book, Mayes clearly, concisely, and accurately introduces educators to basic elements of post-Freudian thought, such as Kohut's mirroring and idealizing transference; Winnicott's "good-enough mothering," holding environments, and transitional objects; and Fairbairn's distinction between healthy and pathological intellectualization. He also presents the essential elements of Jungian thought, such as, persona, shadow, anima and animus, archetypes, the collective unconscious, the Self, the transcendent function, and individuation. His description of transference and counter-transference as they play out in the classroom between teachers and students is especially enlightening and contrasts sharply with the technical descriptions of instruction that are typically found in education textbooks. Mayes draws on illustrations from his own teaching and bravely analyzes the roots of his successes and failures. Throughout, his style is erudite and eloquent, yet simultaneously playful and entertaining.

The second half of Mayes' book applies original applications of depth psychology to schooling more fully than any other book in print. Chapter four, for example, "New Horizons in Archetypal Pedagogy," fundamentally challenges the underpinnings of reforms inherent in recently enacted policies, such as the Bush administration's hallmark legislation, *No Child Left Behind*. While the ideas Mayes puts forth might seem obvious assertions to anyone who has examined his or her internal psychic life, they are likely to seem subversive to most policy makers. Several examples include:

- The teacher–student relationship is archetypal.
- Education should not be reduced to technical rationality.
- Education should not be confused with mere "intellectualism."
- The symbolic domain and intuitive function are crucial to the educational enterprise.
- Failure can be constructive.

These principles represent antidotes to the business-driven obsession with technical-rationality that currently dominates public education. Together, they comprise a new way for understanding what education is and should be about.

A concern with spirituality pervades the book, no doubt a result of the author's own religious beliefs, which he readily shares. This concern is expressed in several places, from consideration of the question whether Jung himself was "religious" and recognition of the importance of teachers embracing a sense of "calling," through the conclusion that the most important implication of Jungian psychology for education is that there is a certain sanctity in the acts of teaching and learning which must always be embraced and defended in the face of corporate reform that would turn education into mere technical training and uncritical acceptance of a prevailing political *status quo*.

In later chapters, Mayes explores various archetypes of teaching, including the student as hero and the teacher as sage and shaman, shadow projections of both students and teachers, and the teacher and the eternal return. He addresses archetypal transference in the classroom, the presence of *Eros*, the Great Mother, the classroom as a sacred precinct, and how culture and archetype may intersect in the psychosocial dynamics of a teacher's sense of calling and classroom practices. He even employs Jung's understanding of alchemy as a psychospiritually symbolic practice to help a veteran teacher reflect on the course of her career as a teacher.

The final chapter, though brief, is one of the most valuable contributions of this unique and remarkable book. Here, Mayes succinctly summarizes yet also amplifies themes from Jung's writings about education. While most contemporary authors focus attention on how Jungian psychology contributes to our understanding of adult development, Mayes reminds us that we must not lose sight of the beginnings of each human's heroic journey and suggests new directions in what could become a Jungian pedagogy. Students, after all, need a caring adult to inspire them with a love of learning, to lift and exalt their spirits, to open new horizon's of understanding, to help them transcend mundane experience, and to help them mature into fully functioning adults.

Ed Pajak, Ph.D.
Professor and Chair
Teacher Development and Leadership
School of Professional Studies in Business and Education
Johns Hopkins University

INTRODUCTION

THE PSYCHOSPIRITUAL DIMENSIONS
OF TEACHING AND LEARNING

There is no scarcity of books on teaching and learning. So why another one? Quite simply because only a small handful of those books consider teaching and learning from the viewpoint of depth psychology.

Behaviorists, in the tradition of Skinner, study how to teach in such a way as to get quantifiable results from students on standardized instruments of assessment. Constructivists, in the tradition of Piaget, attempt to identify universal cognitive structures developing in more or less invariant sequences of maturation in the individual in order to determine the categories and procedures involved in logical thinking. Social constructivists, in the tradition of Vygotsky, are concerned with how thought, as internalized language, is fundamentally dialogical, social, and therefore political in its origins and purposes. All of these approaches—especially the cognitive and social constructivist ones— tell us important things about teaching and learning. None of them, however, typically has a great deal to say about the emotional and spiritual side of teaching and learning. It is *those* aspects of education that concern me in this depth psychological approach to teaching and learning.

By "depth psychology" I mean any view of the psyche that takes seriously the idea that *personal subconscious* processes and *collective unconscious* processes (a distinction that will become clear in the course of this study) affect how one consciously experiences and intentionally acts in the world. As Ira Progoff (1959) has put it:

> *Depth is the dimension of wholeness in man.* It is not a level in the psyche literally and spatially; but it is indeed a level in the human organism *in principle*. It is present and it is *deeper* down in the psyche in the sense that it is more fundamental than those mental contents that are in closer relation to sur-

face consciousness and to sensory contact with the outer world. (p. 8. Emphasis in original)

I believe that the depth psychologies of Freud and Jung (in their classical forms as articulated by those two masters themselves) as well as their more recent forms (after nearly a century of having been considerably refined, deepened, and even substantially altered by second-, third-, and even fourth-generation depth-psychology scholars and practitioners) offer powerful ways of framing and answering questions in the deeper domains of pedagogy. This book thus asks some important depth-psychological questions, and tries to offer at least a few suggestive answers, regarding what Salzberger–Wittenberg (1989) has so aptly called "the emotional experience of teaching and learning."

For instance, I ask: What are some of the deeper psychological and spiritual reasons that a particular person has decided to become a teacher? How do these psychospiritual factors relate to other dynamics in the person's psyche and soul? How might those psychospiritual issues affect the emotional climate of the classroom, which is so largely determined by how the teacher approaches her subject matter and interacts with her students? What are some of the psychological and spiritual issues that get stimulated in a student in learning situations? How, if at all, should a teacher identify and deal with these things in students, considering the fact that she is not a therapist, and how should she do so in a way that is most psychospiritually and educationally productive for herself and her students? Are there ways that she can examine her own interior life so that she can grow as a teacher, and as a human being?

The classroom is a place where both teachers and students often experience love and anger, acceptance and anxiety, excitement and boredom, hope and frustration—powerful feelings all, and rooted in the teacher's and students' interior landscapes of psyche and spirit. We cannot approach the depths of teaching and learning if we do not consider such things. That is the purpose of this book. I believe that it is an especially important thing to do in a political climate which so obsessively focuses on standardized approaches to teaching, learning, and assessing that the student's emotional and spiritual nature and needs not only get lost in the shuffle but get violently attacked in the name of "higher test scores" and "international competitiveness"—those perennial political rationales in the history of American educational rhetoric for running roughshod over our children's hearts and souls in order to serve someone else's military–industrial goals.

To say that the depth-psychological domains of teaching and learning have been relatively unexamined, however, is not to say that there has not been some very good work along these lines over the last several decades. However, most (although by no means all) of them have been written by psychiatrists, not educationists.[1] Furthermore, virtually all of these studies deal with personal psychological issues involving sex, power, and personal identity—vital issues, to be sure, and ones which I certainly address in the present book. However, my primary focus is on that aspect of depth psychology that is called "transpersonal psychology." What is transpersonal psychology?

It is a "family" of approaches to psyche and spirit which—although it recognizes the importance of such personal issues as sex, power, social functionality, and identity—also goes beyond them in accessing and working with other, "higher" elements in the person's total interior economy. Transpersonal psychology began to establish itself as a discipline in the mid-1960s when Abraham Maslow, whose "hierarchy of needs" model of the psyche was built entirely upon personal issues of drives and identity, came to feel that model was incomplete.

Above and beyond primal drives and self-actualization needs, Maslow came to see the central importance of the inherent human need to go higher than just one's own individual world, to discover within oneself "the naturalistically transcendent, spiritual, and axiological," to establish some sort of inner contact with the Divine. He called this religion with a little "r" since, on one hand, it obviously revolved around a person's spiritual commitments but, on the other hand, it neither required nor excluded formal religious commitments in that person. Transpersonal psychology, said Maslow, is "centered in the cosmos rather than in human needs and interest, going beyond humanness, identity, self-actualization, and the like.... Without the transpersonal, we get sick, violent, and nihilistic, or else hopeless and apathetic"

---

1 Perhaps the most notable of these since the 1960s (although we could take this lineage back to the opening decades of the 20th century (which, in fact, is precisely what is done in Chapter 1) include Kubie's (1966) *Contemporary Educational Psychology*; Ekstein and Motto's (1969) *From Learning for Love to Love of Learning: Essays on Psychoanalysis and Education*; Fox's (1975) *Freud and Education*; Kirman's (1977) *Modern Psychoanalysis in the Schools*; Salzberger–Wittenberg's (1989) *The Emotional Experience of Teaching and Learning*; Field, Cohler, and Wool's (1989) *Learning and Education: Psychoanalytic Perspectives*; Block's (1997) *I'm Only Bleeding: Education as the Practice of Social Violence Against Children*; Appel's (1996) *Positioning Subjects*; Britzman's (2003) *After-Education: Anna Freud, Melanie Klein, and Psychoanalytic Histories of Learning*; Barford's (2002) *The Ship of Thought: Essays on Psychoanalysis and Learning*; and Todd's (2003) *Learning from the Other: Levinas, Psychoanalysis, and Ethical Possibilities in Education.*

(1968, iii–iv). Depth psychological models of the psyche which attempt to unite both the personal and transpersonal are called *psychospiritual*, and that is my orientation in this book. Jungian psychology—the basic principles of which I outline for the reader in Chapters 2 and 3—is one of the family of psychospiritual psychologies. Indeed, it is perhaps the most important foundation upon which the psychospiritual psychologies arose in the last half of the 20th century (Ferrer, 2002).

In this book, I use a Jungian lens to look at the inner life of the teacher and student in the classroom since Jungian psychology is, in my estimation as a professor of education as well as a counselor in private practice, the best of all of the depth, psychospiritual psychologies. Except for my earlier book, *Jung and Education: Elements of an Archetypal Pedagogy,* which is the first book-length study in English of the educational implications and applications of Jungian thought, there have, as far as I can determine, been no book-length studies regarding Jung and education (Mayes, 2005a). *Inside Education* presents my latest thinking on some of the basic principles and practices in Jungian pedagogy that I presented in a more preliminary form in *Jung and Education.*

Inside Education is also (again, as far as I can determine) the first book on teaching and learning to consider in a sustained way *both* the personal *and* transpersonal domains—and thus attempt to address the *complete* range of "depth psychology"—not just its personal *or* transpersonal domains. Just as there have been some excellent studies in Freudian and selfobject approaches to education, as mentioned above, there have also been admirable texts on the transpersonal realm in education.[2] *Inside Education,* however, is the first book that, despite its essentially transpersonal focus, attempts to synthesize the personal and transpersonal in its examination of pedagogical theories and practices.

THE ORGANIZATION OF THIS BOOK

Chapter 1 offers an historical overview of what psychoanalytic theorists and practitioners have had to say about pedagogy over the last eight decades. This is important both because of its inherent historical interest and because there has been no such overview offered to teachers and educational scholars for at least 30 years. But it is important mostly

2 The following sources are classics in the field of transpersonal education: Roberts, 1979, 1981, 1985; Roberts & Clark, 1975; Whitmore, 1986.

because it lays the conceptual and technical foundation for the theory and practice of depth pedagogy in general, both in its personal and transpersonal aspects.

Chapter 1 introduces some of the basic precepts of classical psychoanalysis for the reader who does not know them well or would like to review them. More importantly, though, this chapter examines three of the major interpreters and revisers of psychoanalysis in the second half of the 20th century: Heinz Kohut, D.W. Winnicott, and W.R.D. Fairbairn. Each has contributed in his own way to what is called self-object psychology. In Chapter 1 especially, but throughout the book, I attempt to tease out what seem to me to be some of the major educational implications and applications of their theories and practices. Thus, Kohut's ideas of "mirroring," "empathy," and both functional and dysfunctional "narcissism" appear throughout the book as do Winnicott's notion of "holding environments," "good-enough mothering," and "transitional objects/environments" and also Fairbairn's explorations into the schizoid nature of over-intellectualization.

Chapters 2 and 3 are an introduction to the psychology of C.G. Jung—variously called Jungian psychology, analytical psychology, or archetypal psychology throughout the book. These chapters provide the reader with an overview of Jungian thought that draws upon all of the 20 volumes of Jung's *Collected Works* as well as from the works of a great many of the leading Jungian writers, past and present. By the time he or she has finished this introduction, the reader will have quite a serviceable grasp of many of the major theoretical concepts and therapeutic techniques of Jungian psychology, which then applied to education in further chapters.

Chapter 4, "New Horizons in Archetypal Pedagogy," speculates about some of the major principles, practices, problems, and potentials that an archetypal approach to teaching and learning engenders.

Chapter 5 is "The Teacher as Shaman"; Chapter 6, "Archetype, Culture, and Gender: A Maori Professor Reflects on her Academic Career"; and Chapter 7, "Alchemy and the Teacher." These chapters offer the reader three concrete examples of what I have called "psycho-spiritual reflectivity" (Mayes, 2001) and "archetypal reflectivity" (Mayes, 1999) for teachers.

Teacher reflectivity—a movement in teacher education in which I have been involved for the last decade—emphasizes the usefulness to both prospective and practicing teachers of reflecting deeply on the psy-

chological as well as the cultural and political forces and factors that have led one to become a teacher and shaped one's idea of what "good teaching" is. The purpose of such reflectivity is for the teacher to become more conscious of these factors—to *surface* them, as it were—in order to celebrate and solidify them, or revisit and refine them, or perhaps even reject them in favor of more fruitful ideas and images of oneself as a teacher. Over the last decade, what I have attempted to add to the theory and technique of teacher reflectivity is the notion of transpersonal reflectivity. Chapters 5 through 7 thus use the terms of psychoanalysis, selfobject psychology and, primarily, Jungian psychology to provide the reader with examples of psychospiritual and archetypal reflectivity. In Chapter 5, I reflect on my own practice as a teacher educator. In Chapter 6 I facilitate the psychospiritual reflectivity of a female Maori professor of social work at a South Pacific university, and in Chapter 7 I facilitate the reflectivity of a female American high school teacher of 30 years.

On a stylistic note, in order to avoid sexist pronominal usage I use the male pronominal forms as standard in approximately the first half of the book and the female pronominal forms as standard in the second half. I believe this is fair and avoids the grammatical and rhetorical awkwardness that often arises with "he/she" constructions.

Inside Education: Depth Psychology in Teaching and Learning is written out of my passionate belief that teachers are heroic people, doing heroic work, often against enormous odds, who need to be supported in their vital mission of nurturing students not only academically but also emotionally and spiritually. This book is one person's attempt to provide some of that support.

CHAPTER ONE

THE PSYCHOANALYTIC FOUNDATIONS OF DEPTH PEDAGOGY

CLASSICAL PSYCHOANALYSIS

Basic Elements of Classical Psychoanalytic Theory and Therapy

Freudian psychology is often seen as revolving entirely around sexual issues. Certainly, there is a heavy emphasis on sexuality in Freud's writings. However, as early as 1914 Freud had entertained the possibility that there were "various points in favor of the hypothesis of a primordial differentiation between sexual instincts and other instincts, ego instincts…" (1957 [1914], p. 106). In other words, sex was important, even central, to psychological functioning, according to Freud; however, the birth and growth of the ego was also important and would come to figure more and more prominently in his picture of the psyche. Thus, as Freud's thinking evolved, he spent an increasing amount of time studying the origin, structure, and evolution of the ego, which he saw as a dynamic, shifting field of memories, perspectives, tendencies, and capacities that we call "conscious awareness." As is shown in this chapter, this germinal interest in the ego would blossom in the second half of the 20th century into what is called "ego psychology," "selfobject psychology," and "self psychology" in the work of later psychoanalytically oriented theorists and practitioners such as Heinz Kohut, D.W. Winnicott, and W.R.D. Fairbairn.

Freud characterized the ego as the individual's means of dealing with the stubborn and omnipresent demands of the natural and social worlds on the individual. It worked in the service of what Freud called *the reality principle*. Neurosis was the failure of the ego to serve as a sort of intermediary in the ongoing battle between one's animalistic drives—comprising what Freud called *the pleasure principle*—and the personal and social roles one must play. Typically, the ego dealt with the essentially anti-social desires of the *id*—the storehouse of the person's forbidden impulses—by banishing them from conscious awareness to the subconscious. However, because psychic energy was, in Freud's 19th century mechanistic worldview, analogous to energy as conceived in physics, it was impossible to eliminate psychic energy by simply pushing it out of awareness. Rather, as was true with any dammed up energy, these banished impulses would constantly clamor for release—for conscious recognition and physical expression—and all the more so as they had been violently held down by the ego because of the demands of the *superego*. The superego was made up of the social and ethical conventions that the individual had internalized in the course of growing up. In his later work *The Ego and the Id* (1957 [1923]), Freud claimed that the superego was, like the id, a mostly subconscious psychic entity.

The overall picture that finally emerged, then, was of a three-layered psyche: the id (which was amoral), the ego (which strove to be "moral" while also gaining as much instinctual gratification as possible), and the superego (which was hyper-moral and hypercritical). Given the fact that both id *and* superego functioned mostly outside of the range of conscious awareness, Freud observed that "the normal man is not only far more immoral than he believes but also far more moral than he has any idea of" (1957 [1923], p. 230). All of these tensions—between the ego and the id, the id and superego, and the ego and the superego—could sometimes be consciously *suppressed* and thereby controlled. But when this was unsuccessful, the result was *repression* or *sublimation*. Repression was the attempt to keep the id-passions of the *libido* entirely out of the circle of conscious awareness so that the ego would not be shocked or paralyzed by having to look directly at its own hidden darkness. This was often unsuccessful, however, because repressed energy would ultimately press to the surface in the painful form of neurotic symptoms—*a reaction formation*. The healthier alternative, and the goal of therapy, was *sublimation,* in which the psyche strategically allowed forbidden energy to express itself in a much reduced,

highly symbolic, and therefore socially acceptable form. The child's desire to handle its own feces, for instance, could be sublimated into the higher artistic desire to work in mud and clay in order to create beautiful pottery and statues.

Freud pessimistically concluded that we are all more or less caught in an ultimately irresolvable tension between biological instincts and social institutions. This will always be the case, said Freud, for we are all animals with passions that must be forcibly cornered and corralled with symbols and sublimations if we are to find ways, as he put it in a now famous phrase, "to love and to work." There is simply no way out of this dilemma. We survive both individually and collectively only through the protection that society offers, but this will always require a large measure of suppression, repression, and sublimation. Freud's despair at our incurably paradoxical condition deepened as he aged. In 1923, he somberly portrayed the ego as "a poor creature owing service to three masters and consequently menaced by three several dangers: from the external world, from the libido of the id, and from the severity of the superego" (1957 [1923], p. 232). The best that therapy could accomplish would be to help the individual attain the normal state of *functional* neurosis in which everyone lives, not the state of *pathological* neurosis in which the patient was a problem for his family, friends, associates, and, above all, society.

Transference and counter-transference

An essential element of the therapeutic process is the *transference*. This is a concept that appears often throughout this study. Greenson has summarized the classical view of the transference as "the experiencing of feelings, drives, attitudes, fantasies, and defenses toward a person in the present which are inappropriate to that person and are a repetition, a displacement of reactions originating in regard to significant persons of early childhood" (1990, p. 151). In other words, the transference is, as Freud put it, "a new edition" of an old problem (1970 [1915– 1917], p. 462)—a *repetition compulsion* in which the patient projects images and issues from his early childhood onto the psychotherapist, usually involving parents or other immediate caregivers.

The goal of therapy—and the tricky task of the therapist—is to work with the patient's transferences in a way that will finally resolve the issue that underlies the transference, thereby eliminating the need for adult repetition of the original problem. The analyst must be able to "contain" the *transference neurosis*—that is, the *projections* of the patient onto him or her—in such a way that the patient can play the old issues out again but this time resolve them satisfactorily in the consulting room. In a sense, therefore, the relationship between the analyst and patient is more important to a cure than any particular theoretical or technical orientations on the part of the therapist. This is why Freud believed that "the outcome in this struggle [to overcome a psychological problem] is not decided by [the patient's] intellectual insight—it is neither strong enough nor free enough to accomplish such a thing—but solely by his relationship with the physician" (Freud, 1970 [1915–1917], p. 453).[1]

Freud spoke of the transference as either *syntonic* or *dystonic*—*that is, either positive or negative.*

> When we examine individual transference resistances occurring during treatment, we find in the end that we cannot understand the employment of transference as resistance so long as we think simply of "transference." We must make up our minds to distinguish a "positive" transference from a "negative" one, the transference of affectionate feelings from that of hostile ones, and to treat the two sorts of transference to the doctor separately. (1990, p. 32)

In either case, the perils and potentials of transference in psychoanalysis are so central to the whole endeavor that Henderson (1967) has called the transference the *pièce de resistance* of psychoanalysis. Indeed, Freud himself is reported to have heartily approved of the characterization of the transference as "the alpha and omega" of therapy (Jung, 1965).

The transference is not a one-way street. Just as the patient projects psychic issues onto the analyst, so the analyst may (and perhaps inevitably does) project his psychic issues back onto the patient. This is known as the *counter-transference*, and it can be especially powerful if the patient is projecting psychic energy onto the analyst that touches one of the analyst's own psychic wounds. "If the analyst is not aware of his or her own shadow response, real harm can be done" as the analyst pro-

---

[1] As with so much else in Freudian psychology, however, it is well to remember that Freud's ideas stem from historical roots and did not simply appear out of nowhere. The early Mesmerists, Magnetists, and other proto-psychiatrists, for instance, had noted the potentially dangerous phenomenon of the patient's growing attraction (often of a sexual nature) to the clinician as well as the patient's identification of the clinician with someone from the past (Ellenberger, 1970).

jects his or her issues back onto the unsuspecting and vulnerable patient (Woodman, 1995, p. 54). For instance, let us say that a female patient projects her need to be protected by a father-figure onto her analyst. Let us further assume that the analyst had a very dependent mother whom he felt it was his duty to protect from the world. If he has not already re-solved this issue, such an analyst, unconsciously driven by the false no-tion that his job in life is to save "damsels in distress," may be especially prone to fall prey to his client's subconscious cries for protection from a father figure. This could undermine the whole purpose of the therapy, which would be to help the woman gain greater independence in life, not to reinforce her patterns of dependency. To make matters even more complex, it sometimes happens that the analyst's counter-trans-ference happens quite apart from anything the patient has done. The analyst in our example may project his need to save females onto his pa-tient even though she has not sent any signals at all that she needs saving by a father-figure.

Although Freud never really stopped viewing the counter-trans-ference in all of its forms as a problem, even he, ultimately, had to admit its potentially curative power. With this recognition, he began to insist on a training analysis for all prospective analysts in which they would themselves be psychoanalyzed. It was not until the late 1940s, however, close to the time of Freud's death, that the psychoanalytic movement began to show a widespread interest in the counter-transference and its therapeutic possibilities.[2]

THE ROOTS OF PSYCHOANALYSIS

It would be a mistake to conclude that Freud somehow spun his model of the psyche in the comfort of his own study and out of the depths of his own imagination. True, Freud conducted a self-analysis and found these things within himself, but one would have to be suspi-cious of *any* theory about the depths of the psyche that did not intu-

---

2 Not many Freudians shared then, however, and not all share even now, this positive view of the possibilities of the counter-transference. For example, Winnicott, an important psychoanalytic theorist and therapist, has tersely restated the classical Freudian position that "the meaning of the word *counter-transference* can only be the [analyst's] neurotic features *that spoil the profes-sional attitude* and disturb the course of the analytic process as determined by the patient" (1988, p. 266). This, however, is rapidly becoming the minority view in the neo-Freudian litera-ture on the counter-transference. Winnicott's disinclination to consider counter-transference a valid part of the therapeutic process may be due to the fact that his work was primarily with children, who, because they are particularly vulnerable, certainly have a special need to be pro-tected against harmful counter-transferences from the analyst.

itively resonate with the theorist's own inner experience. Freud's theory developed incrementally—based upon his own self-analysis and daily clinical practice. Furthermore, in presenting his model of the psyche, Freud was in many ways simply systematizing the considerable body of research into the unconscious and its sexual nature that preceded him by at least a century and with which he was quite familiar. There is no denying either Freud's genius or importance, but we must be careful to avoid the misconception that Freud had somehow single-handedly "discovered" the unconscious. As Ellenberger (1970) has demonstrated, almost all of the elements of Freudian psychiatry had already been postulated and explored by researchers for many decades—and in some instances even a century—before Freud's first works in the late 1890s and early 1900s. Mesmer, Janet, Charcot, and many other less well known psychiatrists, psychologists, philosophers, poets, and even sociologists had argued for the existence of a subconscious whose issues and energies were primarily, even exclusively, sexual.

In the last phase of his writing and practice, Freud would expand the notion of *libido* considerably, calling it *Eros* and depicting it as a sort of generalized life-instinct (still deeply involved with sexuality, of course, but probably not quite completely reducible to it) which was constantly doing battle with a death-instinct that he called *Thanatos*— or the desire of every creature to return to a state of eternal rest in the primal womb of being. In this war, death must inevitably triumph. "The goal of all life is death," declared Freud in *Beyond the Pleasure Principle*, for "the inanimate was there before the animate" (1957 [1923], p. 160).

NEO-FREUDIAN THEORIES

In this section, the focus is on three of the most important psycho-analytic theorists who followed Freud because their thoughts have proven to be especially important in educational theory.[3] Although the three psychoanalytic theorists differ in important ways, they, along with many other neo-Freudians, tend to share certain basic reservations about and revisions to classical psychoanalytic theory.

First, they question Freud's "hydraulic" or "plumbing" model of the psyche, with its vision of the subconscious as unrelenting, blind in-

---

3 The reader who is interested in getting a solid overview of modern developments in psychoanalytic theory might want to begin with Eagle's excellent (1984) study, *Recent Developments in Psychoanalysis: A Critical Evaluation.*

stincts always threatening, like toxic gases in a cramped container, to explode and wound the fragile ego in the form of a neurotic symptom or even shatter the ego in a psychotic break. Even those few recent theorists who still do hold to a model of psyche that relies upon the notion of instinct (most neo-Freudians now see in that model an outdated metaphor of the human organism from 19th century biology) picture those instincts as *including but not limited to sexual ones.* Second, the basic psychological motivation is seen as being the desire to enter into relationship with a significant other or others, and to do so in such a way as to maintain and magnify a sense of personal identity and integration. Sex may figure into this need for relationship but usually it does not—or at least, it is not of primary importance. Third, many neo-Freudians see *psychological health* not simply as the containment of primordial impulses but, more importantly, as the pursuit of ethically and even spiritually significant purposes that provide a person with ethical direction, spiritual meaning, and, in general, personal fulfillment in his or her life (Meissner, 1984; Rizzuto, 1979; Schafer, 1980).

Heinz Kohut

Heinz Kohut is the father of "self-psychology," in which the striving for a stable and holistic sense of self is the overriding psychodynamic objective. Sexual issues will certainly come into play in defining and maintaining a self, as will many other issues, but they will all be oriented to the life-goal of self-definition and self-maintenance (Eagle, 1984, p. 40)—what Kohut called a state of *healthy narcissism.* The person who does not have such a relatively stable and unified sense of self suffers from a *narcissistic wound* (Kohut, 1978). The foundations of a person's sense of self reside in his earliest relationships with primary caregivers—or *selfobjects,* so called because they are the objects of the infant's earliest attention and affection through whom the infant learns about the world and itself (Kohut, 1978). It is important to remember that the selfobject is not, in the final analysis, actually the other person or thing that is helping an individual define himself but is the *image* of that person or thing that the infant (and later the adult) has internalized—or, in psychoanalytic parlance, has *introjected.*

Typically, the infant's central selfobject is its mother. The infant's psyche is so dramatically shaped by its interaction with its mother because it is symbiotically fused with her at this primal stage. Indeed, in the infant's earliest view, the mother is indistinguishable from itself, according to many psychoanalytic theorists.[4] If the mother's interaction with the infant communicates love and acceptance, the infant begins to assume that it is loveable and accepted, and that the world is essentially dependable and beneficent. The infant comes to see itself as essentially a good, stable, and integrated being. In short, the child's *primary narcissism* (Kohut, 1978, p. 430) finds confirmation and gratification in its union with the loving mother, and it does so in two essential ways.

The first is in *the mirroring transference,* which consists in the infant seeing itself through the mirror of its mother's responses to it. The second is in *the idealizing transference,* in which the infant, enshrining the mother as not only the apex of reality but indeed as reality itself, finds its own ideals in its merger with this godly personage. The "idealized parental imago…is gazed at in awe, admired, looked up to, and [is that] which one wants to become…" (Kohut, 1978, p. 430). The idealizing transference is the root of the child's ability to define, have, and maintain values (Eagle, 1984, p. 54). The opposite of this kind of value-instilling mother is the one who communicates to the infant in her interactions with it that she is unhappy that it has come into the world, unduly anxious about it, or repelled by it. This lays the foundation for a variety of psychic disorders in the developing infant and eventually in the adult—especially *the narcissistic personality disorders.* For, what the infant sees in the "mirror" of the mother is its own undesirability, inadequacy, and lack of unity. It thereby learns as well—in a colossal failure of the idealizing transference—that the world is neither welcome nor welcoming but is, rather, rejecting, cold, dangerous, and confusing, and that it is a place that is either valueless or that has values that are unattainable or irrelevant.

The narcissistic personality disorders are pathological attempts to experience the primary mirroring and idealizing that the person never experienced as an infant—or never experienced enough (Kohut, 1978, pp. 440, 478). These pathological manifestations are called *secondary narcissism.* Healthy human development thus originates in primary narcissism and concludes in healthy narcissism. When primary narcissistic needs are not met, the many dysfunctions of secondary narcissism result. In his later work especially, Kohut's focus is on the relationship between healthy narcissism and productivity. He explores "the ways by

---

4 This idea has come under fire recently from some theorists who believe that the child has a sense of its mother as a distinct person, and not just an extension of himself, virtually from the first moments of conscious awareness (Wade, 1996).

which a number of complex and autonomous achievements of the mature personality [are] derived from transformations of narcissism—i.e., created by the ego's capacity to tame narcissistic cathexes and to employ them for its highest aims" (1978, p. 460). Humor, empathy, wisdom, and creativity are fruits of the positive transformation of primary narcissism into mature narcissism.

D.W. Winnicott

From the extraordinarily rich body of work of the British child psychotherapist D.W. Winnicott, we examine three concepts that have had significant educational implications: *holding environments, good-enough mothering,* and *transitional objects.*

Like Kohut, Winnicott sees the roots of psychic health or illness in the infant's relationship with its mother. Ideally, the mother will provide a good *holding environment* for the infant. This may actually involve the physical act of lovingly holding the infant. Yet even when it does not, it does entail the mother providing the child with a physical and emotional context that is appropriate to its needs and beneficial to its growth—an environment, in short, that *holds* the child so that the child can mature in safety:

> A wide extension of "holding" allows this one term to describe all that a mother does in the physical care of her baby, even including putting the baby down when a moment has come for the impersonal experience of being held by suitable non-human materials. In giving consideration to these matters, it is necessary to postulate a state of the mother who is (temporarily) identified with her baby so that she knows without thinking about it more or less what the baby needs. She does this, in health, without losing her own identity. (Winnicott, 1988, p. 259)

Note Winnicott's insistence in the above passage that the mother should provide not only adequate holding for the child but also that she should do so "without losing her own identity." Good mothering does not mean *perfect* mothering in which the mother must always be available to the infant, meeting its every need almost before it arises. A so-called perfect mother would have to forego her own identity, needs, and boundaries. Such *perfect* treatment of the infant, far from actually *being* perfect, is flawed, for it does not allow the infant to experience those moments of opposition that are necessary for it to experience—in healthy and monitored doses, of course—so that it can begin to mature. A mother who psychically fuses with her infant to such an extent that she completely forfeits her own healthy sense of boundaries will present to the infant an unhealthy example of what relationship means. On the other hand, *good-enough mothering* prevents burn-out in the mother by providing for her own identity and even occasional mistakes. "Good-enough mothering gives opportunity for the steady development of personal processes in the baby" (Winnicott, 1988, p. 456)—processes that will feed positively upon the mother's realistic humanity and not her neurotic perfectionism. Needless to say, such mothering is still fundamentally loving, careful, and adequate to the infant's physical and psychic development.

Good-enough mothering provides for the mother's increasing separateness from the child as it begins to mature—a process best embodied and symbolized in weaning. With increasing separation, the infant, and then the older child, comes to sense both physically and emotionally the existentially necessary lesson that there is a grand divide between the world of Me and Not-Me—the Not-Me world first presenting itself to the child's awareness in the form of the withdrawing and sometimes even absent mother. To negotiate the space between the world of Me and Not-Me, the infant will come to rely upon a *transitional object*. To take a prime example: the infant's own thumb, which replaces the mother's breast when the infant wishes to nurse but mother is not available for feeding, is the first transitional object. The thumb, through a basic exercising of the infant's still primitive imagination, comes to replace the absent breast. The thumb is no longer just a thumb to the infant, although the child does not mistake it for a breast either; rather, the thumb becomes a transitional object—a psychologically living symbol whose significance and power lie in the fact that the child's imagination invests it with the power to satisfy at least some of its needs. In the same way, a favorite blanket becomes the child's substitute for the mother when she is away. Through creative fantasy, the child turns the blanket into a transitional object that is now not a blanket or a mother but a "poetic" fusion of both.

> The thumb stands for an external or NOT-ME object, is symbolical of it as we would say. The external object being sufficiently available, it can be used as substitute. This transition is itself allowed to take place slowly and gradually, in the in-

fant's own time. Transitional objects [such as pieces of cloth, dolls, teddy-bears, toys, or what have you] are provided or are adopted which (when the infant is resting from the arduous process of sorting out the world and the self) are cuddled or pushed away without being classified as thumb or breast symbols. (Winnicott, 1988, p. 436)

As the child develops, it chooses more complex transitional objects to symbolically express and deal with the existential gap between its inner and outer realities. In a sense, therefore, all of our philosophical and artistic products, our concepts and images, are highly evolved transitional objects through which we express our fundamental existential need to interpret and interact with external reality. The transitional space is the place and the transitional object is the thing where the interior world of "I" and the exterior world of "Other" can come into fruitful contact. Winnicott even goes so far as to suggest that culture is a collective transitional social object in which a group of people experience and express their shared experience of reality.

W.R.D. Fairbairn

Too often overlooked in discussions of modern psychoanalytic theory, Fairbairn's work amounts to a radical reframing of analytic theory and practice, with particularly important implications for the treatment of the psychoses. Fairbairn's basic idea is that "libido is not pleasure-seeking but object-seeking" (Eagle, 1993, p. 75). It is not primal drives that energize the psyche but the need to enter into human relationship. "It must always be borne in mind...that it is not the libidinal attitude which determines the object-relationship but the object-relationship which determines the libidinal attitude" (Fairbairn, 1992 [1941], p. 34). Instead of primitive drives as the origin of psychic conflict, transformation, and growth, Fairbairn sees the formation of different, and sometimes contending, ego-structures as the central purpose of the psyche. Integrating these ego-structures into a satisfying and productive holistic identity is the basic psychotherapeutic goal and one that, in Fairbairn's view, is a life-long process.

What is most interesting about this important theorist for our purposes as educationists, however, is Fairbairn's insistence that over-intellectualization can represent "a general tendency on the part of individuals with a schizoid component to heap up their values in an inner world" — attempting thereby to avoid and create a substitute for actual relationships with other people in the real world of emotional give-and-take (1992 [1940], p. 8). Fairbairn is here talking about individuals who would almost always rather be buried in a book or sequestered in a lonely lab rather than be with other people. "This high libidinization of the thought process," wrote Fairbairn, is characteristic of people who "are often more inclined to develop intellectual systems of an elaborate kind than to develop emotional relations with others on a human basis"; indeed, such individuals are inclined "to make libidinal objects of the systems which they have created" in lieu of the pleasure of human contact (1992 [1940], p. 21). Intellectualization, "a very characteristic schizoid feature," can thus be misused as an

> extremely powerful defense technique [which often operates] as a very formidable resistance in psychoanalytical therapy. Intellectualization implies an overvaluation of the thought-processes; and this overvaluation of thought is related to the difficulty which the individual with a schizoid tendency experiences has with making emotional contacts with other people. (Fairbairn, 1992 [1940], p. 20)

AN OVERVIEW OF PSYCHOANALYTIC THEORY IN AMERICAN EDUCATION

Psychoanalytic theory has not had nearly the effect on the American curriculum that it seemed destined to have in the opening years of the 20th century, when there were great expectations among such well known Freudians as Anna Freud, Melanie Klein, Susan Isaacs, August Aichhorn, and Oskar Pfister — all of whom had themselves been educators before becoming psychoanalysts. Their hope was that teachers, through adequate psychological training and (ideally) the experience of their *own* psychoanalyses, would be able to teach and interact with students in ways that not only conveyed knowledge but would also be emotionally beneficial, even therapeutic, to the students in their care. Indeed, G. Stanley Hall[5] — one of the most important turn-of-the-

---

5 Despite Hall's apparent approval of "Freudism," as he called it, there are different views on how much Hall really "bought into" the Freudian view. Hall's biographer, Dorothy Ross, argues (1972) that Hall embraced many of Freud's ideas with great enthusiasm. On the other hand, Fuller (1986), a historian of the development of psychology in the United States, believes that Hall's enthusiasm for Freud was mainly political and cosmetic and did not really stem from Hall's core convictions as either a psychologist or educationist.

century American psychologists, author of the immensely influential study *Adolescence* (1904), a founder of the Child Study Movement, and in general a resounding voice in American education—hosted Freud and Jung at Clark University for a series of lectures in 1905. Oskar Pfister, one of the early members of Freud's inner circle, called Hall "the celebrated psychologer [sic] of youth and religion who rallied around psycho-analysis" (1922, p. 173).

The potential for cross-fertilization between psychoanalysis and pedagogy appeared great, and would soon (so it was thought) blossom in the form of new psychologically sensitive practices among teachers in classrooms across the United States at all levels of instruction. The psychotherapeutic wing of American Progressive education in the first half of the 20th century largely arose out of this hope (Zachry, 1929; Cremin, 1964).

The core idea was simple: the teacher, although certainly not a therapist, should nevertheless learn enough about psychoanalysis to know how to guide students in their interactions with each other, with the curriculum, and with the teacher herself so that their unhealthy inhibitions could be overcome and, at the same time, their libido could be harnessed in socially constructive ways. "From this point of view," wrote Caroline Zachry, the chair of the Study of Adolescents Division of the Progressive Education Association, in her 1929 work *Personality Adjustments of School Children*, "it becomes the duty of the school to discover the causal elements in the child's conduct and so to guide him that his personality and emotional adjustments will be constructive, and thus he will be helped properly to face social situations" (p. 3). In her Introduction to *Psychoanalysis: Lectures for child analysts and Teachers* (1930), no less a personage than Anna Freud echoed this sentiment when she noted that the educator, like the parent, needed to bear in mind that "the task of upbringing, based on analytic understanding, is to find a middle road between...extremes—that is to say, to find for each stage in the child's life the right proportion between drive gratification and drive control" (p. 128).

Only a psychologically healthy and therapeutically savvy teacher could truly help the student achieve that balance between the instinctual id and the unforgiving superego. Furthermore, the psychoanalytically wise teacher would know how to draw those students who had fallen into the underworld of juvenile delinquency back into the broad and sunlit fold of socio-cultural normalcy and productivity. This notion of "mental hygiene" in the schools was quite elaborately presented in such superb studies as Oskar Pfister's (1922) *Psycho-analysis in the Service of Education,* August Aichhorn's (1951 [1925] *Wayward Youth,* Susan Isaacs' (1932) *The Children We Teach,* Caroline Zachry's (1940) *Emotion and Conduct in Adolescence,* and most powerfully of all in Redl and Wattenberg's (1951) classic, *Mental Hygiene in Teaching.* Nevertheless, as Hilgard (1987) concluded in his magisterial study of the evolution of academic and clinical psychology in the United States, there was at most only an "indirect influence of psychoanalysis on elementary education[;] the direct influence was meager, at least before World War II" (p. 688). In secondary education, where social expectations, economic demands, and academic stakes were higher, attention to the student's inner life was even scanter. Thus, Zachry lamented in 1929 that although "physical hygiene is avowedly the concern of school authorities, with mental hygiene they have, as yet, shown little concern" (1929, p. 252) — a situation in the public schools that psychoanalysts would continue to criticize in the following decades.

After WWII, as the general public witnessed in the faces of the men and women returning from combat situations undeniable evidence of just how deeply the psyche could be damaged, there was a resurgence of interest in depth psychological theories and therapies (Jansz & van Drunen, 2004). Feeding this renewed interest in depth psychology was the fact that America was now becoming home to a cohort of important psychoanalysts who were immigrating in the late 1940s and 1950s from war-ravaged Europe to write and work in universities and clinics across the United States. Some of these psychoanalysts, such as Bruno Bettelheim and Erik Erikson, even had particular interest in and messages for educational theorists and practitioners (Hilgard, 1987). Despite these powerful influences, however, the effect of depth psychology on education, at least in the public school classroom, remained surprisingly limited even after WW II in elementary classrooms, and even more so in secondary ones. Rather, it was behaviorism (as presented in Skinner's 1956 work, *The Technology of Teaching*) and cognitive developmentalism (as presented in Piaget and Inhelder's 1969 classic *The Psychology of the Child*) that had and continue to have the greatest effect on the public school classroom since the end of World War II (Cremin, 1988).

In 1951, for instance, Redl and Wattenberg expressed surprise that, despite its potential to create more joy in teaching and more excitement in learning, the mental hygiene movement had still not made a noticeable impact on school policies or practices (1951, p. ix). A few years later, Watson (1975 [1956]) pointed to the extremely limited role that psychoanalysis was still playing in education. "Freud's influence has filtered into teacher education by indirection," he wrote. "Teachers are undoubtedly being exhorted to study the causes of emotionally disturbed behavior, but few are yet being given the necessary tools and training" (p. 33). Kubie's observations a decade later were even more dire: "self-knowledge, which requires the mastery of new tools of psychological explanation, is wholly overlooked throughout the entire scheme of 'modern education,' from kindergarten to the highest levels of academic training" (1967, p. 62). Both Laux (1968) and Jones (1968) remarked that, as yet, the findings of psychoanalysis had found expression in the schools only in the case of children with particularly pronounced emotional problems, requiring separate treatment. Louise Tyler picked up the same complaint in the next decade, declaring that "psychoanalytic theory has been in existence for a half-century, yet no attempt has been made to utilize it in any systematic way for curriculum development or for understanding curricular effectiveness" (1975, p. 55). Roberts (1975) saw "bits and pieces" of psychoanalytic theory being employed in the school but nothing systematic or substantial. Kirman (1977) even discerned in this reluctance of the schools to learn from psychoanalysis a form of "unconscious resistance" among policy-makers and principals (p. 160).

Adding to the persistent neglect of psychodynamic approaches in educational theory and teacher education is the fact that in the last two or three decades, social constructivism, which views consciousness more as a product of social dynamics than merely internal ones, has become increasingly visible in scholarly research and writing (Rogoff, 2003). Moreover, neither cognitive nor social constructivism particularly examines (or in some cases, even acknowledges) the workings of the psyche at subconscious or unconscious levels, or how these workings might affect curriculum and instruction.[6] The great curricularist Ralph Tyler thus concluded in 1989 that "even today, this general approval of affective objectives in the school curriculum is not widespread among parents and other community members" (1989, p. 141). And as late as 2002, Barford could still bemoan the fact that in teacher educa-

---

6 Piagetian psychology does examine psychological structures that underlie consciousness and thus bears some resemblance to depth psychological systems (Field, Cohler, & Wool, 1989). However, in its almost exclusively cognitive emphasis, it does not pay enough attention to emotional dynamics to qualify as a depth psychology (Homans, 1989).

tion, it is behaviorism, cognitivism, and humanism that are studied, completely overlooking what psychoanalysis has to offer both the prospective and practicing teacher (2002, p. 42). In fact, the various schools of psychoanalysis have probably had their limited effect on public education over the last 50 years or so mostly through the instrumentality of their philosophical cousin, humanistic psychology, which, as Forbes (2003) has shown, provided much of the foundation for the call for existentially "relevant" curricula in the 1960s and the Open Classroom Movement of the 1970s (Silberman, 1973).

SOME MISCONCEPTIONS ABOUT PSYCHOANALYSIS AND EDUCATION, PAST AND PRESENT

As various cultural critics have pointed out, we are a therapeutically educated culture (Fuller, 1986; Lasch, 1995; Rieff, 1987). Unfortunately, a good deal of that *education* has really been *mis*education, especially when applying psychoanalytic concepts to education. In the following section, we look at four popular but incorrect (or simply incomplete) notions about what psychoanalysis is and does.

Misconception 1: Psychoanalysis is just about sex.

This misconception is probably the easiest one to understand. As we have already seen, however, Freud's understanding of instinct and libido probably broadened considerably in the later phases of his career. What is more, there were members of Freud's inner-circle who, from early on in the history of psychoanalysis, understood that its implications went far beyond mere sexuality. For instance, in speaking to teachers, August Aichhorn, in his book *Wayward Youth* (1951 [1925]) (which contained a foreword by Freud himself), insisted that he would often use the word *sexuality* "in the broad psychoanalytic sense [so that] it must not be confused with genital sexuality" (1951 [1925], p. 216). In his discussion of the Oedipus complex, Aichhorn declared:

> The little boy can no more actually kill his father than he can think of having sexual relations with his mother; his sexual apparatus is too immature. The name "Oedipus situation" only signifies the same tendency translated into the emotions of this stage of development for which the child cannot be held accountable. In psychoanalysis the word "sexual" has come to have a much broader and deeper meaning than was previously the case. (1951 [1925], p. 81)

MISCONCEPTION 1	Psychoanalysis is just about sex.
MISCONCEPTION 2	The educational goal of psychoanalysis is to help the student take an adversarial position regarding socio-cultural norms and institutions.
MISCONCEPTION 3	Psychoanalytic approaches tend to disregard the "non-psychological" factors that affect education.
MISCONCEPTION 4	Psychoanalytic theory, which was embraced by many Progressive educators, in turn embraced the Progressive movement.

Table 1: Misconceptions about psychoanalysis

Oskar Pfister, one of Freud's primary disciples, even understood the term *sublimation* in its literal sense—that is, as a process of making something more and more *sublime*. Much like Plato in *The Symposium*, Pfister (1922) saw in infantile sexual energy and later, in adolescent and adult genital sexuality, the basis for what would finally evolve into a true love of God—just as an oak tree grows out of an acorn but cannot be reduced to an acorn. "A deeply moral conception of life is indispensable to psychoanalysis," Aichhorn proclaimed (1951 [1925], p. 145). Indeed, a belief in God is not only therapeutically viable but also vital, for "the domain of religious ideas offers admirable opportunities of sublimations which do not avoid reality, but on the contrary bring back to it purified energies in rich measure. Religion reveals a world of duty, a field of activity" (p. 146–147).[7]

For the past 80 years, psychoanalytic theory has provided space for those who do not see libido as merely sexual. The literature dealing with the applications of psychoanalysis to educational questions is no exception, using such terms as "mastery," "adequacy," "competency," and so on to highlight the primary psychological importance of the student's need to understand, approach and negotiate a wide variety of cognitive, aesthetic, and ethical challenges. Redl and Wattenberg (1951) captured the essence of this idea by urging teachers to under-

---

7 Few early psychoanalysts would have taken the idea of sublimation quite so far as Pfister, who was also a Protestant pastor, did, although in the last 20 years there have been various studies that have demonstrated the compatibility of psychoanalysis with spiritual worldviews ranging from Zen Buddhism to Christianity (Epstein, 1995; Meissner, 1984; Palmer, 1997; Rizzuto, 1979).

stand that "one of the universal human needs is a feeling of adequacy, of self-respect. As a child proves to himself that he can master his environment by learning how to take care of himself, he satisfies this need. He will start doing this as soon as infancy ends" (Redl & Wattenberg, p. 188). In the same year, Symonds (1951), a psychoanalytically oriented professor of education at Teachers College, Columbia, warned both teachers and parents that "it is easy to forget that even the very young child is striving to attain competence and that his efforts to gain mastery should be respected from the beginning" (p. 184). The great child analyst Lili Peller, whose work attempted to integrate both Freudian psychology with the ideas of the physician and child educator Maria Montessori, demonstrated a way to combine these two approaches to pedagogy in her observation that

> In sublimation ego, id, and superego are on excellent terms. Their actions are synergic, not antagonistic....When a distasteful task is replaced with well-liked work, the change from fatigue to a surplus of vigor may be dramatic....In psychoanalysis we see that the pleasure in functioning is related to specific symbols and fantasies, to specific zonal tensions, to the desire for mastery. (1978 [1956], pp. 92-93)

Certainly, Peller speaks of the developmental unfolding of the child's experience of its erotic zones according to classical Freudian theory. However, her ultimate point is that we must view this development in the *wider context* of the infant's and child's "desire for mastery." Peller's message to teachers, therefore, was two-fold—namely that, as Freud had argued, the child's work and play in the classroom are related to its previous psychosomatic development, but also that, as Montessori held, of at least equal importance are various "component drives": "curiosity, the desire to explore, the wish to acquire and to have as much or more than one's neighbor, the drive to achieve mastery" (Peller, 1978 [1967], p. 116). Indeed, more than 20 years after this statement by Peller, psychoanalytic theorists were still continuing their effort to dispel the popular notion that a Freudian approach to education was solely focused upon the child's "sexuality" and releasing its "repressions." Rather, it was and remains the essential psychoanalytical message to parents and teachers that what is most important to a child is the ability to explore, examine, and master; for, "above all, infants, like older children and adults, get gratification from being a cause, from making things happen, [leading to] *'effectance pleasure'*" (Basch, 1989, p. 779. Emphasis added).

Rudolf Ekstein (1969), co-author of one of the classics in psychoanalytic pedagogy, *From Learning for Love to Love of Learning,* and one of the leading psychoanalytic pedagogues of the 20th century, therefore declared that it was time to update our view of what psychoanalysis had to offer pedagogy. For even though some of the earliest psychoanalytical pedagogues placed great stress upon unleashing the child's libido through educational means and in educational settings, and even though this might have been "a justified reaction to the state of affairs at that time" (given the widespread use of threats and corporal punishment to control the child's "instinctual freedom" at the turn of the century), it was now necessary to "look at both sides of the coin" and affirm the psychoanalytic wisdom in teaching "the requirement of limitation" and "the capacity for delay" that are so vital in a child's ability to achieve mastery—a need that is as psychoanalytically primary as any other, and probably more primary than most (p. 71).

Misconception 2: The educational goal of psychoanalysis is to help the student take an adversarial position regarding socio-cultural norms and institutions.

Ellenberger (1970) sees the origin of modern psychology in late 18th- and early 19th-century Romanticism with its radical individualism. Given this pedigree, it is not surprising that the depth psychologies are often viewed as the means of enabling the individual to shake off the shackles of social norms and—as in the classic movie of youthful defiance, *Rebel Without a Cause*—pit himself against the received gods of culture. It is true that the depth psychologies do encourage the individual to resist blind conformity, especially when such conformity leads to psychic dysfunction. However, it is *not* true that these approaches to the psyche typically *aim* at placing the individual in opposition to society. To the contrary, Freud and Jung stressed the need to heighten the individual's mature appreciation of the boundaries of social and ethical norms. This point emerges quite clearly in the psychoanalytic literature that deals with education, for it has ever been a function of education to transmit to children cultural assumptions about what is normative.

So important was the idea of the child's social adaptation in psychoanalytic theory that some early writers overstated the case, as when Aichhorn declared that "in general, to be social means to have an ego which can subordinate itself to authority without conflict" (1951 [1925], p. 214). In overstressing the therapeutic and educational project of "attempt[ing] to fit the child for his place in society" and rendering him "capable of adaptation to the demands of society," Aichhorn was trying to dispel the notion that psychoanalysis viewed social and ethical norms as merely repressive constraints that needed to be overcome (Aichhorn, 1951 [1925], pp. 7, 187). Yet, even Aichhorn understood well enough that the real goal of psychoanalytic pedagogy was not to make the child's libido a slave of society but, rather, to find ways that libido and ego could jointly function in a way that was individually satisfying and culturally productive. Aichhorn concluded by telling teachers that "although the reality principle acts as a safeguard to the ego, it does not require the ego to renounce all pleasure. The reality principle, too, has pleasure as its goal, but it takes reality into consideration and contents itself with postponed pleasure or with a smaller degree of pleasure" (1951 [1925], p. 192).

Caroline Zachry, a leader of the psychoanalytic wing of the Progressive movement, would echo Aichhorn's theme four years later in her insistence that the school's responsibility was to contribute to "the happiness and social usefulness of the individual," which could only be accomplished if the teacher understood how the child's psyche worked in order to help the child fit into "life as it is" (Zachry, 1929, pp. 61, 78). Anna Freud made a similar point, saying. "The object of the school is above all else instruction—the development of the intellect, the imparting of new knowledge, and the stimulation of mental capacities"—a project requiring teachers increasingly to identify themselves with the child's developing superego (1931, p. 115). "What [teachers] ought to do is to recognize the split within the child [between the superego and id] and act accordingly. If they succeed in aligning themselves with the child's superego, the battle for drive control and social adaptation can be won" (1931, p. 119). And a mere two years later, perhaps the greatest of all child analysts, Melanie Klein—who often openly disagreed with Anna Freud about whether or not the child's libido should be "educated" in quite so stark a fashion as Anna Freud believed—nevertheless admitted that "one of the results of early analysis should be to enable the child to adapt itself to reality. If this has been successfully achieved, one sees in children, among other things, a lessening of educational difficulties as the child has become able to tolerate the frustrations entailed by reality" (1975 [1932], p. 12).

In the years immediately preceding and following WWII, as the need to mobilize a nation was especially pressing, there was an increasing emphasis in psychoanalytic pedagogy on social cohesion and stability. Peter Blos, for instance, a leading psychoanalytic theorist and practitioner in the 1940s, counseled that "it is in the power of education to supply the experiences which can satisfy [libidinal] needs and, at the same time, modify them in terms of social and cultural values" (1940, p. 491). In this way, schools could perform the vital function of helping the student find "values and standards acceptable by society yet distinctly his own" (1940, p. 498)—a theme echoed by the internationally respected analyst Otto Fenichel, who, in 1945 wrote about psychoanalytic pedagogy's mission to teach children to avoid indulging the pleasure principle and to heed the call of the reality principle (1945, p. 583).

Lili Peller sounded this same note when she declared that "this is in our opinion the core of education: *so to direct the child's life and actions that what he does out of innermost joy, out of deepest need, will also be accepted and positively judged in the social world in which he lives*" (1978 [1956], p. 18. Emphasis in original). Pearson (1954), a child psychoanalyst with a special interest in school issues, was quite explicit about the need to dispel the popular misconception that psychoanalysis aimed to give maximum license to the child's desires, insisting that it was the goal of psychoanalytic pedagogy to fit the child into society. "Every educator," Pearson cautioned, must be aware of this fallacy [that psychoanalysis wants to encourage giving free rein to desire] and avoid it by both understanding and making parents aware of "the great importance of helping the child gradually to place himself under the supremacy of the reality principle rather than the pleasure-pain principle" (1954, p. 247).

Even during the tumultuous 1960s in the U.S., many psychoanalytic pedagogues resisted the permissiveness that characterized the decade, continuing to speak about the need for the teacher to represent an "ego-ideal" for the student (Grossman, 1975, p. 67) and to help the student achieve a healthy balance between ego-constraints and libidinal energy so that he would grow up to be neither a "Dull Jack" nor a "Playboy" (Piers, 1969, p. 105). In fact, during a time when, on various college campuses, many teachers were not only condoning but participating in sexual "experimentation" among students, leading psychoanalytic educational theorists like Ekstein were insisting that it is not only probable but even healthy that the student will sometimes "hate the teacher" because of the teacher's important role of insisting upon a balance of desire and socio-ethical constraints (1969, p. 53). If "Freudian" thought was being used by the advocates of sexual "freedom" in the 1960s as the philosophical warrant for their behavior, it was not being similarly construed or used by the Freudian pedagogues themselves. Indeed, the sexual revolution of the 1960s and beyond represents, according to one of Freud's most important sociological interpreters, Philip Rieff (1961), a colossal misreading of Freud, who was, Rieff concludes, "a moralist."

Arguably the most important book in psychoanalytic educational theory to appear in the following decade, *Learning and Education* (Field et al., 1989) carried on exploring the normative goals and visions of psychoanalytic pedagogy, insisting that, more important than sexual needs, were such needs as achieving "self-organization" (Bernstein, 1989, p. 150), engaging in deep interpersonal communication (Wolf, 1989, p. 389), experiencing the *emotional* pleasure of *cognitive* accomplishments (Cohler, 1989, p. 50), and "achieving synchrony between academic and personal development" (Elson, 1989, p. 803). Anthony (1989, p. 102) summed up by saying that, educationally, the governing goal of "the psychoanalytic viewpoint" should be to deal with "significant repressing forces on the epistemophilic drives."

Misconception 3: Psychoanalytic approaches tend to disregard the "non-psychological" factors that affect education.

In the last 40 years or so, there has been an increasing awareness of the socio-economic influences that help to shape a child's experience of and performance in a classroom. However, the prevailing notion that psychoanalytic pedagogies generally do not acknowledge this fact but want to reduce all questions to essentially psychological ones is quite mistaken. As early as 1925, in fact, Aichhorn underlined the importance of not only psychological but also sociological, cultural, and economic factors in understanding and helping the child in the school, especially when that child became "delinquent" and "wayward" (1951 [1925], p. 10).

This theme emerged with renewed vigor in the psychoanalytic literature of the 1940s. Blos (1940) wrote that "we have come to realize that the individual never reacts to an isolated situation, to the learning of history or biology, for example, but is affected by his total life situation in pursuing a specific task" (p. 492). Fenichel (1945) noted that the act of teaching is always socially situated, asserting that "neuroses are an evil originating under the influence of an education dependent not so much upon the opinions and personalities of individual educators but rather upon social conditions which determine educative institutions as well as the opinions and personalities of individual educators" (p. 584). Fenichel took capitalist society particularly to task for creating neurosis in teachers and students (p. 588). Four decades later, Field (1989) would remind her readers that the psychoanalytic approach to education, despite its many virtues, is by no means a panacea, and will be quite ineffective if teachers are not adequately aware of the sociohistorical contexts in which they and their students exist. What is more, to the degree that a student comes from a socio-economically deprived environment, he will be more prone to various psychological impediments to learning (Littner, 1989).

Putting together the various historical, sociological, and psychological factors in a given student's life can tell the teacher a great deal about the student, but it still does not tell everything. For psychoanalysis (like the existential philosophies to which it is related) focuses upon—indeed relies upon—a faith in the individual's ability to transcend all of the *factual* psychosocial determinants of his life in order to define an *ethical* perspective on and response to those facts. As Viktor Frankl (1967), the Jewish psychiatrist who survived the Nazi camps, reminds us, we can choose how to respond to even the most horrific circumstances—even if we cannot change those circumstances, or cannot do so *yet*. We are creatures whose most important characteristic is that we make moral choices. This is a point that Aichhorn, who worked mainly with troubled youth, never tired of emphasizing. As a classical Freudian, he certainly acknowledged the great importance of the first five to six years in a child's personal life as well as social circumstances in shaping his psyche. Still, he made it quite clear that these first years of life are far from completely determining—and that formal education could do a great deal in helping the child gain a new purchase on himself so that he could, to a considerable extent, redefine himself in psychosocially healthier ways (1951 [1925], p. 221). It is the child's essential moral "character," Aichhorn concluded, and not his circumstances, no matter how good or bad they might be, that would have the final say in how well or badly a child did in school, for "the final result...depends on the child's ability to avail himself of the opportunities offered" (1951 [1925], p. 192).

Misconception 4: Psychoanalytic theory, which was embraced by many Progressive educators, in turn embraced the Progressive movement.

Given the praises that certain prominent American educational Progressive theorists like Margaret Naumburg (1927) and Caroline Zachry (1929) sang to psychoanalysis, it may come as something of a surprise to learn that psychoanalysts interested in education did not reciprocate. Here was no mutual admiration society! From at least the mid-1920s until the demise of the Progressive movement around 1957, psychoanalytic theorists and practitioners were fairly unanimous in their vociferous *dis*approval of Progressive education. Contrary to what he saw as Progressivism's tendency to give "free rein" to a child's proclivities and passions, Aichhorn advocated both reward and "punishment" — so long, of course, as the punishment was enlightened, meted out equally in true love and concern for the child, and did not involve either physical or psychological violence. The educator, "must proceed in conformity with life itself and erect dams that curb immediate instinctual gratification or make the gratification impossible" (1951 [1925], pp. 193f, 196f).

Fenichel (1945) carried Aichhorn's critique one step farther, suggesting that what he characterized as the Progressive desire to always make things "nice" in the classroom is wrong because, on one hand, it gives the child *too much* freedom to do almost anything he wants as long as it is "pleasant" (whether or not that thing is educationally useful), and also because, on the other hand, it gives the child *too little* freedom to express appropriate aggression in the healthy form of regulated and stimulating intra-class competition (p. 585). Pearson (1954) was even more unforgiving in his critique — leveled in the sunset years of the Progressive movement — that most Progressive educationists had only a "caricatured" understanding of what psychoanalytic theory was really about — foolishly and simplistically believing that psychoanalysis encouraged free libidinal expression.

Thus, in 1956, the year before the demise of the *Progressive Education Journal* and the effective closure of the Progressive movement as a going concern, Lili Peller prophetically delivered what was perhaps the most withering critique of Progressive education yet, charging it with having created a fantasy-land in many classrooms, where the teacher, striving to be the student's "buddy" (as she disparagingly put it), over-praised and under-disciplined her students (1978 [1956], p. 97). In this way Progressivism created an "artificial child-centered world," which was as emotionally and educationally counterproductive as was an overly strict pedagogical approach (1978 [1956], p. 194). This was educationally calamitous, wrote Peller, because "the pendulum may swing all the way back from overindulgence to strict discipline and still miss the essential" (p. 104), which is to help the child learn to channel his untutored passions into activities that not only foster his *inner* potentials but also enable him to responsibly discharge his civic obligations as a member of a political democracy.

Indeed, it was psychoanalysis, many Freudian theorists believed then and continue to believe now, that, in its ongoing attempts to achieve and maintain a delicate balance between individual desire and social duty, is the psychological approach that is best suited to promote democracy. As Ekstein and Motto (1969) declared, "We believe that the use of psychoanalytic principles and insights in the educational system, including the formal school system, indirectly strengthens the belief in the individual, defines his place in a free and open society and, in return, fortifies this very society" (p. xix)—a *credo* that echoes similar pronouncements throughout the history of psychoanalysis and its traditional commitment to the classically liberal vision of democratic government (Castoriadis, 1991).

Having dealt with some of the more prevalent misinterpretations of psychoanalytic theory and pedagogy, let us now move on to a fuller appreciation of the actual insights that the psychoanalytic pedagogues have given us into teaching and learning.

IMPORTANT THEMES IN PSYCHOANALYSIS AND EDUCATION

Psychoanalytic Theory and the Depths of Learning

In most colleges of education in the United States during the first half of the 20th century, the predominant approach to understanding how students learn was the stimulus–response theory of behaviorism, which saw learning as simply a matter of positive or negative reinforcements for certain behaviors. Little or no attention was paid to what a person was actually thinking or how that thinking was changing in the process of learning. According to behaviorism, the mind was a "black box" into which we could never peer and about which we could, therefore, make no valid "scientific" statements. Thus, there was no qualitative difference between how, say, a rat or dog learned from how a child learned—merely a quantitative one of degree of complexity.

Thankfully, things began to change in the 1960s, as teachers and teacher educators turned increasingly to the developmental psychology of Piaget (Piaget & Inhelder, 1969) and then to Kohlberg (1958) in order to understand the *cognitive and ethical stages* that the child must pass through and the internal *cognitive processes* that the child must master in order to be able to reason scientifically and morally. Then, beginning in the 1980s, the work of the Soviet psychologist Lev Vygotsky (1986) was resurrected in order to understand how the child's cognitive growth was not simply an innately unfolding process, constant for all people at all times and places, but was instead fundamentally influenced by a wide variety of social and historical factors and circumstances (Wertsch, 1985). Together, both Piagetian theory (sometimes called cognitive constructivism) and Vygotskyan theory (sometimes called social constructivism) performed a great service in deepening our understanding of how learning occurs, thereby freeing education from behaviorism's cold, pseudo-scientific grip. However, they did not give enough attention to the emotional, psychodynamic factors involved in learning.

The Inadequacy of a Merely Cognitive Approach to Learning

A constant theme in psychoanalytic pedagogy has been that it is not enough to look merely at the cognitive developmental "stage" that a child is at to understand how he learns. As early as 1922, Oskar Pfister warned that a student's attitude toward school in general or a specific subject—even a specific assignment—may be related to deeper psychological issues (he called them "unconscious educators") that are troubling the child and preventing him from fully engaging with the subject matter at hand. A student who has frequently been beaten by his father may find it very difficult to study, say, a chapter in a history textbook that deals with medieval torture or the treatment of slaves in the American South. The teacher may see only a student who refuses to do a homework assignment. However, the student's resistance is much more painful and complex than that teacher imagines. "When I glance back over my earlier educational activity," mused Pfister,

> I see among my pupils more than one who was in a medical sense healthy, but who has since perished for lack of help, but

whom I could not help because I did not know him and the methods which alone could save him! And is it not most painful to be compelled to say to oneself, "A young soul was entrusted to your care, whom you might have saved if your horizon had not been so narrow, your power so limited." I see about me boundless misery. We should be experts in things educational. We are consulted on many difficult educational points. We should not be merely teachers, but also liberators, enlargers of youthful strength and joy, molders of men in the highest meaning of the term. But, honestly, are we such experts, familiar with instrument [of basic psychoanalytic knowledge] indispensable for this purpose? Many men know more of beetles and mushrooms than...of the child mind. Can he be called a trained educator who cannot distinguish between an obsessional liar and a morally feeble-minded one? (1922, pp. 29-30)

In similar tones, Caroline Zachry (1929) advised teachers that they should teach "the child as a whole, realizing that it is the child that she is teaching and that subject matter is a means toward his growth—not an end in itself." The teacher who takes this more psychologically sophisticated view of her students, trying to understand their "personality problems," will see that those problems are not "something apart from her work, but...essentially part of it." The child's emotional and intellectual development are so intertwined that "success in one is contingent upon success in the other" (p. 272).

In 1940, Blos made the commonsensical but often overlooked point that "no two children in a classroom are having exactly the same experience." This is because "the past and present experiences of the individual," having shaped his psyche, will necessarily determine his emotional response to subject matter—"the meaning it will have for him, his ability to accept it, and the purpose it will serve in his total development" (p. 492). "The child does not react solely with his intellect to mental operations but needs to reinforce them with personal meanings and urgencies which are related to them..." (p. 494), and this can only be accomplished if the child is able to "find in the nature of the subject matter, in the mental processes involved, or in the personality of the teacher some positive contribution to his emotional needs. Failing this he will be ineffective" (p. 496).

Peller (1978 [1945]) not only echoed but amplified Blos's theme five years later, insisting that to understand the way a student internalizes knowledge teachers must consider the student's

> deep and contradicting emotions, his intellectual power, his fears, his ability for keen observation as well as for denying unpleasant facts, his reactions to frustrations, his anticipation of his adult role. Without this complex basis of reaction the child's development would not differ essentially from the results of animal training, and the child would not undergo transmutation into an ethical and social being. (p. 54)

Then, beginning in the 1950s, one sees in the psychoanalytic literature the increasing use of the term "self-esteem" (Symonds, 1951, p. 189). Yet, this was not just to help the child "feel good about himself" but because children with high self-esteem tended to be the most intellectually creative (Pearson, 1954).

Furthermore, intuition and emotion, so essential to creativity, are both grounded in the unconscious. "The processes of insight and illumination appear to be directed by unconscious forces to a higher degree than the process of preparation and verification" (Weisskopf, 1951, p. 53). Ignoring the unconscious can only cripple the student's creativity. Given this extremely subtle interaction of thought and emotion, the behaviorist glorification of instructional technologies—even to the point of advocating the replacement of the teacher by a machine (Skinner, 1956)—was instructionally misguided, psychologically destructive, and ethically wrong. Thus, said Peller in another jab at the behaviorist obsession with technology: "the outstanding book has a better chance to stir the reader than the gesticulating screen teacher" (1978 [1956], p. 98).

In the 1960s, Kubie, a well known learning theorist of that decade, argued that "even when a scientist is studying atomic energy or a biological process or the chemical properties of some isotope," he is still engaged in various levels of emotional activity as well. Consciously, of course, the scientist deals with his subjects "as realities." However, "on the preconscious level [the transitional area between waking and falling asleep], he deals with their allegorical and emotional import, direct and indirect." Then, at the deepest unconscious levels of his psyche, the waking realities of "biological processes, chemical properties, and isotopes" become even more enmeshed in the scientist's own complex emotional dynamics. "On an unconscious level, without realizing it," the scientist's unconscious mind translates his subject matter into its own symbolic language, which will invariably "express the uncon-scious, conflict-laden, and confused level of his own spirit, using the language of his specialty as a vehicle for the projection of his internal struggles" (Kubie, 1967, p. 63).

In his important study, *Fantasy and Feeling in Education,* Jones (1968) critiqued one of the most famous cognitive constructivist theo-ries of learning, that of Jerome Bruner, because he felt that Bruner's model of learning ignored the fact that learning should also be a pas-sionate process of emotional involvement. The *whole* student is in-volved in learning, not just his ability to conceptualize, for his imagina-tion may well be involved in picturing "how to conceive a squared root, a declined verb, a balanced equation, the plural of 'deer'; or the harsh-ness of the Arctic environment, or the nature of myth, or the varieties of human conflict regulation—or the meaning of infinity" (p. 82). "Let us enter it as a fundamental rule," Jones concluded, "that cultivation of emotional issues in classrooms, whether by design or in response to the unpredictable, should be means to the end of instructing the children in the subject matter" (p. 160).

In the following year, Ekstein (1969), in his groundbreaking vol-ume published by the UCLA Center for Learning and Early Childhood Education, *From Learning for Love to Love of Learning,* continued Jones's argument that the cognitivist approach to learning not only did not exclude a psychoanalytic approach but that combining the findings and techniques of both approaches would enrich our understanding of how and why a student does or does not learn. Quoting Kubie, Ekstein pointed out that "our interest in the mind now is not only in terms of trying to clarify the unconscious conflict which holds the child back, but to free the mental forces which make it possible to solve problems, and, particularly to study the nature of those cognitive functions which help us to contribute to the teaching of problem-solving" (1969, p. 111).

In making this seemingly radical suggestion, Ekstein was really proposing no more than Piaget himself had advocated when he said that "the psychology of cognitive functions and psychoanalysis will have to fuse in a general theory which will improve both, through mutual cor-rection" (cited in Anthony, 1989, p. 117). For instance, the highest stage of cognitive development in Piaget's model—the "formal opera-tional stage," in which the person is now able to critically evaluate the ethical and social norms that define his culture—requires a person to take an independent stand with respect to that culture, and this in turn requires a fairly high degree of emotional stability and ethical courage. "[C]apacities to think abstractly, independently, and relativistically ...demand not only new cognitive structures, but finally a shift in locus of authority and responsibility [onto the student] in learning" (Henderson & Kegan, 1989, p. 286).

This accent on the interactive possibilities of psychoanalytic and cognitive approaches in the classroom has become more pronounced in the last several decades. Kirman (1977), for instance, argued that it was simply common sense to realize that the child's emotional state would affect his learning, and that, in turn, the child's ability to learn and do well in the classroom would affect his emotional state. To illustrate this point, Kirman noted that in the best child-rearing practices in the home, "there is no artificial separation of the emotional and the intellectual. Neither should there be in the classroom" (p. vi). "From prenatal life and the early postnatal period, emotional, social, and 'cognitive' learning must be viewed as occurring together." Consequently, any educational program should "begin at the 'beginning' to support all domains of 'intelligence'" (Greenspan, 1989, p. 239).

In other words, just as there is an "official curriculum" with essentially cognitive goals that teachers then personally "operationalize" in their own unique ways, so *there is also an unofficial, "subjective curriculum"* (Cohler, 1989, p. 52; Eisner & Vallance, 1985). This refers to how the student *experiences* the official and operational curricula. The student's experience will include "such factors as the child's relationship with both teachers and fellow classmates, the personal significance of the curriculum, and the importance of a sense of self as a requisite for taking on the challenge of new learning" (Cohler, 1989, p. 57). The subjective curriculum need not be limited just to the student's experiences but may include the teacher's experiences as well. By this view, the subjective curriculum is, "in part, the invention of both teacher and students. Each one projects distillates of his own inner perceptions and experiences, past and present, onto the subject under study, be it mathematics, reading, history, or literature" (Field, 1989, p. 853).

Educational Problems with Emotional Roots: General Statements

Although it is undoubtedly true that "psychoanalytic inquiry regarding education should focus both on factors interfering with learning [as well as] those contributing to enhanced learning" (Cohler, 1989, p. 66), the fact is that the focus of the psychoanalytic educational theorists over the last eight decades has been mostly on educational problems. That this was the case from the very beginning of the interaction of psychoanalysis and education should not be surprising, perhaps, since Freudian psychology was born of an attempt to understand and treat psychological illnesses, especially neuroses.[8]

Thus, although Melanie Klein addressed the complete range of problems in children's psychic functioning in the course of her career, her first cases, and many of her subsequent cases, were of children whose presenting issues in her consulting room related to learning problems (Hall, 2002, p. 24). Klein was of the opinion that Oedipal neuroses in children "show themselves, among other things, in excessive educational difficulties and it would be more correct to call them neurotic symptoms or characterological difficulties [than educational ones]" (1975 [1932], p. 100). Fenichel observed that it was generally true that "in carrying out a 'work of learning' or 'work of adjustment,' [a person] must acknowledge the new and less comfortable reality and fight tendencies toward regression, toward the misinterpretation of reality, toward the longing for passivity and dependence, toward wish-fulfilling fantasies" (1945, p. 554).

Six years later, Redl and Wattenberg (1951) developed this theme considerably with their outline of various neurotic "mechanisms" that "inhibit learning" in children, listing many specific dysfunctions under the general diagnostic headings of "mechanisms of denial," "mechanisms of escape," and "mechanisms of shift and substitution" (1951, pp. 51–70). It is beyond the scope of this chapter to delve into all of these psychic "mechanisms" of learning-inhibition; however, mention should be made of just a few of them: specific emotional blocks relating to a particular subject (i.e., a child who has trouble studying about a famous person's mother because of a troubled relationship with his own mother), free-floating anxiety (which can attach itself to a specific topic or activity in the classroom for no apparent reason), and sibling rivalry

---

8 The fact that Freud focused on the neuroses and Jung on the psychoses helps to explain the very different models of the psyche that each one ultimately formulated. Freud focused on those facts and factors of one's ego development that engender neurosis while Jung looked at the pre-egoic and trans-egoic factors that underlie the psychoses. These two different foci—which have recently been coming increasingly together in the work of certain neo-Freudian and neo-Jungian theorists and clinicians—undoubtedly played a role in the unfortunate break between the two men in 1913 (Mayes, 2005a; Mayes, in press).

at home (which can result, for instance, in a child constantly clamoring for the teacher's attention in a classroom or bullying).

Pearson (1954) concluded that learning problems arise as the result of some sort of conflict between the ego and superego, on one hand, or between the ego and id, on the other hand. An example of the former would be a child whose perfectionist parents expect so much of him academically that he develops severe performance-anxiety and cannot perform well, or even perform at all. An example of the latter would be a child who, having been psychosexually enmeshed with his mother in an Oedipal situation, has such conflicting attitudes about his female teacher, on whom he has projected his mother-image, that his attitude and behavior toward the teacher are unpredictable, overly emotional, and thus prevent him from participating appropriately in classroom activities. Indeed, such a child, harboring sadistic fantasies about its mother, may not only act them out in classroom misbehavior but may also find ways to incite the class to take part in this destructive flight of unconscious collective fantasy (Kirman, 1977). Pearson also discussed how students of any age who suffer from a heavy burden of guilt and a consequent need to be punished may invite castigation from the teacher by acting up and acting out in class in a wide variety of ways.

According to Ekstein (1969), the origins of these and similar problems sometimes lie in the child's earliest experience of its mother and breast-feeding. After all, do we not often speak of learning in terms of ingesting food? One *devours* a book, *consumes* information, *chews on* new ideas, tries to get the *flavor* of an argument that somebody has *cooked up,* takes time to *digest* facts or concepts, and sometimes is even required to *regurgitate* knowledge on tests. Surely these colloquial parallelisms are not gratuitous but reflect a fundamental tie between taking in abstract pieces of knowledge cognitively and taking in nutrients physically. Considering how much a baby learns of its world in its first feeding encounters with its mother—whether the world is safe, full, and soothing or whether it is unpredictable, unsatisfying, and meager—helps one appreciate Ekstein's surprising suggestion that "the first curriculum struggle ever developed does not take place in school but rather ensues between mother and infant as she is nursing her baby. The full breast is the first curriculum the baby must empty and dig*est in order to meet the goal and requirement of sati*ation" (1969, p. 49). Focusing on another developmental issue, Kirman (1977) noted that if toilet-training is not handled well—if, for instance, the parent is impatient with the child, severe in handling him, openly disgusted with the whole process in general—the child "learns" that he is also disgusting and that his products— "what comes out of him" (at first physically and then conceptually)—are bad, inadequate, and a cause for shame. The classroom consequences of this may include underperformance and blocked creativity despite innate talents.

Moreover, developmental damage to the child at any stage may impede the "courage to try" and "courage to learn," which are vital to intellectual growth (Cohler, 1989, pp. 49, 53). For, "no matter how great the opportunity, motivation, or innate capacity, no learning will occur unless the individual finds within himself the courage to try" (Bernstein, 1989, p. 143). The child who has trouble putting together a project for a science fair may be scientifically gifted but developmentally wounded. This theme, so prominent in psychoanalytic pedagogical literature from its earliest days on into the 1970s, continued to be stressed and explored later on, perhaps in the greatest detail in Field et al.'s *Learning and Education* (1989). There, the crucial point was made that not only did a child's development affect his experience of schooling but that his experience of schooling would, in turn, affect his subsequent development. A person's experience of school—his triumphs and tragedies there, his loves and alienations, hopes and disappointments—form a significant part of his "life narrative" (p. 36). A rich, vibrant, and humane store of experiences regarding one's school years goes a long way in promoting mental health, whereas an opposite set of experiences may continue to peal like a dire bell throughout the student's life. In short, psychic dysfunction can damage the student's "learning ego" (Anthony, 1989, p. 108) to such an extent that "the many drive-determined aspects of learning—for example, conflict, anxiety, defense, repetition, regression, specific and nonspecific transferences and counter-transferences, and the like"—may undermine the teacher's best efforts if that teacher does not have at least a basic understanding of these phenomena and how they may manifest themselves in students from infants to adults (Salzberger–Wittenberg, 1989).

Hall was therefore not overstating the point when he recently claimed, in looking back over nearly a century of psychoanalytic theorists who concerned themselves with schooling, that one of the most significant contributions of psychoanalysis "has been its theories on intellectual and creative inhibition" (2002, p. 14). This is so because psychoanalysis, "more than any other discipline...is well-placed to remind us that willingness and ability to learn are shaped by influences far-removed from conscious and rational motives" (Barford, 2002, p. 12).

Educational Problems with Emotional Roots: Specific Issues

We now turn to a brief look at just a few representative examples of the myriad psychodynamic educational problems that have been discussed by the psychoanalytic pedagogues over the last eight decades.

Oskar Pfister gave various examples of student behaviors that should have alerted him to psychodynamic problems during his teaching years but didn't at the time. Some of them, he felt, would have been relatively obvious if he had had even rudimentary psychoanalytic knowledge: the presence of dark and troubling themes in a student's compositions, a student developing tics during a certain kind of activity or discussion, an emotionless façade in the presence of some teachers but not others, and so on. Even subtler problems would become obvious to the psychoanalytically educated teacher. Imagine a boy, wrote Pfister, whose problem related not to a cognitive *inability* but rather to his *ability*. This boy is "an excellent calculator who devours figures with absolute intellectual hunger and attacks geometrical lines with an affectionate regard. Is not this the solitary," Pfisters asks, who,

> during recess and on the way to school, avoids all comrades; and did there not a short time ago fall from his portfolio a leaf which he grabbed up quickly and frightened to death, concealed as rapidly as possible; so rapidly, indeed, that we could only catch the superscription: "Death, the Reliever." Might not there be some connection between the mathematical super-performance, the social deficiency, and the title of the poem? (1922, pp. 19–20)

Caroline Zachry (1929) also dealt with the problem of neurotic over-performance in students. Zachry tells of a Jewish girl named Esther who lost herself in her school work because she was shunned by her gentile peers. In this instance, it was not academic under-performance that was the problem but over-performance, concluding for Esther in a complete nervous breakdown. Like Pfister and Zachry before her, Melanie Klein reported many cases of students whose problem was that they were too "perfect" — a fact, she believed, that would probably alert most psychoanalytically attuned teachers to the possible presence of some form of concealment, compensation, or obsession in the child: Klein mentioned as evidence the young patient who was an obsessively good student but showed virtually no emotions, or the girl whose academic excellence arose from a neurotic mother-fixation (Klein, 1975 [1932], pp. 67, 90).

More prevalent in Klein's clinical practice, however, was the problem of *poor* classroom performance. She pointed to the case of a boy who was reluctant to take part in any crafts activities that involved taking something out of a box, which Klein and the boy finally understood to stem from his guilt about unconscious aggressive fantasies of attacking his mother's body. Inhibitions in classroom play as well as in learning can "possess every degree of strength and every variety of form," and the teacher should at least entertain the possibility that the inhibition has a psychic source. This is all the more pressing in terms of the child's future since "such inhibitions in learning are often the basis of later vocational inhibitions..." (Klein, 1975 [1932], p. 98).

Other examples include the case of a girl who had trouble working out a puzzle containing the words "sick," "heart," and "well" because of her anxiety about her mother's illness (Redl & Wattenberg, 1951); a boy whose number phobia stemmed from his association of that number with a traumatic event; a girl whose problems with long division were ultimately traceable to a separation anxiety; and a boy whose refusal to take part in sports grew out of his fear of homosexual-sadistic behaviors directed against him by his classmates in the locker room and on the playing field (Pearson, 1954). Another example, this time of "performance anxiety," illustrated how excessive praise of a little boy's paintings when he was two years old had so stressed the child that, by the time he began school he was unable to paint at all despite (or rather, because of) his innate talent (Peller, 1978 [1958]). This is why psychoanalytic knowledge is so vital in teaching, for the psychoanalytically sensitive teacher can help a student's psychodynamic issues be resolved as productive sublimations, not neurotic dysfunctions. For instance, poetry, as "an oral-erotic play of chewing and sucking nice words and phrases," is sometimes able to creatively embody the unconscious energy of students whose experiences during the oral phase of development were problematic (Pearson, 1954, p. 214). Or it may be that in some cases a student's interest in drama is the productive symbolic expression of what would otherwise result in morbid exhibitionism (Pearson, 1954, p. 216).

In the 1960s the tone shifted noticeably among the psychoanalytic pedagogues with a pronounced emphasis on how the psychoanalytically informed teacher can stimulate and tap her students' fantasies and feelings for normative educational purposes, drawing the student's unconscious into the study of subjects ranging from art to geography, civics to history, and physical education to creative writing. Such psychoanalytic knowledge is quite useful for the humanities or social science teacher, too, since "any lesson in the humanities or social studies which confronts children with the truth of its subject matter—be it family life among the Eskimos, the invention of the steam engine, the Boston Tea Party, the death of Abraham Lincoln, or what have you—will naturally provide effective stimulation of their emotions and fantasies" (Jones, 1968, p. 244). The crucial point for the teacher to bear in mind is that

> The accommodative aspect of intelligence is interfered with when what can be learned or what one is supposed to and consciously intends to learn is associated with a repressed fantasy, memory, or idea. On the other side of the coin, displacements can be the cause of intense affective interest in anything which unconsciously represents that which is repressed. Fascination, curiosity, and a particular absorption may be manifestations of such displacements. (Schwartz, 1989, p. 561)

Barford's elegant phrase, "the imaginal domain," captures much of what psychoanalytic educationists have been writing about for the last 80 years: it refers to that "unique domain of learning where objectives ideas and subjective emotions are joined together" (2002, p. 57)—the landscape on which many classroom dramas are played out, dramas that the psychoanalytically wise teacher can help bring to a successful conclusion in order to promote psychosocially healthy purposes.

The model, neurotic student

Certain teachers may find it difficult to see scholastic excellence as a problem—especially at a time when both neo-liberal and neo-conservative federal agendas for educational reform stress "excellence" on standardized tests as the only legitimate educational goal. Especially recently but throughout its history, psychoanalytic pedagogy has warned that prizing only academic excellence in a child not only *reinforces* existing neuroses in children but can actually *create* them.

Again, some of the earliest and best statements regarding this issue in the psychoanalytic literature are to be found in Melanie Klein's writings. Speaking of what she called a healthy "instinct for knowledge," she proclaimed that the fundamental educational question from a psychoanalytic point of view is how to promote "a relatively undisturbed development" of that instinct, which will ideally "turn freely in a number of different directions, yet without having that character of compulsion which is typical of an obsessional neurosis" (1975 [1932], p. 103). About 20 years later, Redl and Wattenberg (1951) cautioned that a certain kind of compulsive conformism, which slavishly submits to every teacher and school rule, is not evidence of a child's adaptation to the culture of the school but is, instead, a red flag signaling that the child's behavior, at school and at home, is probably the result of fear. Hence, "when a boy or girl shows signs of being unusually anxious to please, we should realize we have a delicate problem on our hands, instead of feeling flattered" (p. 204). For, this child, seeing himself as an object, learns only in order to confirm his servitude, not to gain intellectual and moral freedom. This confounds the whole purpose of the educational enterprise. "In a sense, each bit of good work [such students] do is a gift, or more accurately a bribe. Their actions carry this meaning, 'See, I've done what you wanted; I've proved that your wish is my command. Now, reward me by taking me under your wing. Lift me to joy by saying you like me'." (Redl & Watternberg, 1951, p. 203). The teacher would be well advised to remember that there are children "whose defensive specialty is that of excessive intellectualization" (Jones, 1968, p. 230)—children whose neurotic strategy consists in "the frequently defensive use of the purely intellectual act" (Piers & Piers, 1989, p. 202).

Such pronouncements clearly echo Kohut's (1978) idea that over-intellectualization (and perfectionism in general) is often symptomatic of a narcissistic personality disorder. It also relies upon the idea of what Winnicott (1988) calls "the false self." Fairbairn's (1992 [1940]) assertion that many people construct elaborate intellectual structures as a psychotic defense mechanism against authentic engagement with life is also relevant here. Indeed, Fairbairn's work is particularly insistent and poignant in calling attention to the fact that "overvaluation of mental contents" is ultimately a desperate attempt "to heap up values in the inner world" to the exclusion of external reality, and therefore is symptomatic of an unhealthy "libidinizing" of thoughts and theories, typically concluding in some form of "fanaticism" (Fairbairn, 1992 [1940], pp. 15–20). And what is true for students in the schools is even truer for scholars in the university, where "'intensive inquiry' may in fact be pathological, and may lead us to consider carefully the degree of psychopathology incorporated in all research or intellectual work" (A. Hall, 2002, p. 39). When this is the case, then "knowledge itself may be a defense against learning" (Britzman, 1999, p. 10).

Transference and counter-transference

The psychoanalytic pedagogues have made much of transferential dynamics in terms of the student–teacher relationship, even claiming that a transferential understanding of the teacher–student relationship was the most important insight that psychoanalysis had to offer education (Pearson, 1954. See also Mayes, 2002, 2004, 2005a). Thus, it is to that crucial topic that we now turn.

TRANSFERENCE. The best early statements regarding the transference in education came from Aichhorn (1951 [1925]), who wrote that when a student's response to a teacher is puzzling to the teacher because of its inappropriateness, it may be that the student is transferring a parental issue onto him. "In such cases, what you see being enacted before your eyes," the analyst advised teachers, "are really only repetitions and new editions of very old conflicts of which you are the target but not the cause" (p. 88). This is so, said Anna Freud (1930) because "there is in the individual a compulsion to repeat in later life the pattern of his earlier love and hate, rebellion and submission, disloyalty and loyalty"—a compulsion that the student almost instinctively aims at the teacher (p. 109). Yet, this need not be a bad thing, noted Blos (1940), if the teacher is psychoanalytically sensitive, because the teacher, who in some senses is a "safer" person than a parent, "may be in a better position than the parent to help the adolescent deal with new emotions, and may receive the transferred feelings of the student as a parental figure" (p. 494). Redl and Wattenberg (1951) seconded this sentiment in their assertion that, next to the parent, the teacher is the most likely target of the student's projections regarding his earliest caregivers (p. 235), which is why it is crucial for the teacher to understand the transference (Pearson, 1954).

In the 1960s, various scholars, noting the increasingly close connection between homes and schools, predicted that this would increase the propensity of the child to transfer family-of-origin issues onto schools and teachers (Grossman, 1975). They even felt that, in the later grades, the psychotherapeutically sensitive teacher could occasionally help the student understand his classroom transferences so that that student could gain insight into the deeper issues involved. "The goal is first to help the child identify the feelings expressed in his attitude toward the teacher and then to help him assess the degree to which these feelings are appropriate to their relationship and how they affect it" (Grossman, 1975, p. 65). True, one or two lone dissenting voices warned that although it was important for teachers to understand the transference, it was not wise for them to try to *work with it* in the classroom because they did not have adequate training to do so (Fox, 1975). But the overwhelming majority opinion among the psychoanalytic pedagogues was that "if there is little transference, then little will be emotionally meaningful in the classroom and little can generalize to the outside. It is important to note that once the transference is recognized, the teacher has the most powerful tool ever discovered to influence the lives of the students" (Kirman (1977, p. 49).

Salzberger–Wittenberg (1989), acknowledging the professional and situational constraints on how and when the teacher can cultivate the transference, have voiced the general feeling of psychoanalytic pedagogues that it is appropriate to do so if the teacher is psychoanalytically adroit. The teacher is not a therapist, she admitted, who needs overly intimate knowledge about the student. However, it is only common sense to recognize that teaching may have a healthily therapeutic dimension.

> [W]e do not need to unravel a person's past history in order to understand him. If we are observant, we can gain insight into his assumptions and beliefs from his behavior and reactions to ourselves and others in the here and now. Awareness of the transference elements enables us to have some space to think about the nature of the relationship, to take a more objective view of it. (Salzberger–Wittenberg, 1989, p. 36)

Cozzarelli and Silin (1989), drawing on the work of Kohut, asserted that it is vital that the teacher understand the transference because she will inevitably receive the idealizing and mirroring projections of the student. The teacher can use such transferences in order to model behavior that will make her a good "ego ideal" for the student. Indeed, Cozzarelli and Silin warned that the teacher who does not understand the transference may unconsciously misuse its energy in order to inappropriately satisfy her own ego at the expense of the student's legitimate need to find and emulate an ideal. Similarly, Wolf (1989) averred that the teacher is almost always some kind of "selfobject" for a student, for "teaching…is at least in part a selfobject function" in which the student discovers much of himself—his potentials and limitations—in his mirroring and idealizing transferences onto the teacher (p. 381).

The thinking of the important neo-Freudian theorist D.W. Winnicott has also been used to portray the classroom as a "holding environment" wherein the teacher can provide a safe space for the child to grow, just as the mother does for the developing infant. "Since our earliest learning arises in the intimate relationship of parent and child, each new course reawakens in students the need to have a target of idealization and to have their efforts admired" (Elson, 1989, p. 789).

> Whether the course is biology, mathematics, sociology, or child care, the teacher provides a holding environment.... This holding environment is one in which the empathic understanding of the teacher creates the conditions which allow the student to reveal what he does not know. Seeing the student at his least effectual, and yet not breaking off contact or shaming him because of his limitations, becomes in itself a novel, healing experience for the student. (Elson, 1989, p. 801)

As we saw above, it is, in Winnicott's view, not so much the "perfect" mother as the "good-enough" mother who is most likely to create a realistic, sustainable holding environment for the child. This idea has evolved in some psychoanalytic literature about teaching into the notion of "the good-enough teacher" who can help the student define a transitional space where he can experiment in ways that offer both safety and a limited degree of risk (Wool, 1989, p. 750). That the teacher should have this capability should not be surprising since some of Freud's earliest work dealt with the tendency of the child to transfer issues onto the teacher. What is new, however, and what has been explored with increasing depth and detail over the last eight decades, has been the perils which the teacher can avoid and the possibilities she can cultivate if she has even a rudimentary understanding of the dynamics of the transference.

COUNTER-TRANSFERENCE. Just as the analyst who is not aware of his own unresolved psychic issues can project them onto the patient and harm him, so the teacher can damagingly project his issues onto the unsuspecting student. It is not exactly the latest breaking news that some teachers exert unfair types and degrees of power over their students in the classroom because of a sense of personal inadequacy outside of the classroom. Probably everyone has had at least one teacher who is on a "power trip." Such things would be much less common and lethal, the psychoanalytic pedagogues have declared, if the teacher, understanding his counter-transferences, learned either *not* to counter-transfer or to do so in a way that was ethically and pedagogically fruitful. Such psychoanalytic knowledge would help the teacher understand how and why he responds to students, especially certain students, as he does, thereby allowing him to respond to them better.

> Teachers, more than members of any other professional groups except psychoanalysts, are exposed to the instinctual temptations arising from the unconscious of those with whom their work is concerned, in this instance pupils. Children are freer than adults in their direct expressions of hatred, envy, destructiveness, jealousy—particularly sibling rivalry—ridicule, cruelty, anger, uncleanliness, sexual curiosity, exhibitionism, oral eroticism, masochism, and the rest, and this relative freedom offers a great unconscious temptation to the teacher to do likewise. (Pearson, 1954, p. 256)

Various scholars have offered some rules-of-thumb for teachers to help them avoid negative counter-transferences and cultivate positive counter-transferences. For instance, a teacher who might negatively project his desire to "save" female students because of psychological enmeshment with his mother (a negative counter-transference) could learn to tame and productively use his "savior" counter-transferences so as to be of greatest service to all of his students, male and female, without becoming psychologically enmeshed with them (a positive counter-transference). We will deal with this issue in much greater depth in upcoming chapters. Additionally, teachers can understand and control their counter-transferences more effectively if they: (1) develop self-awareness, (2) seek satisfactions outside of the classroom, (3) evaluate possible dissatisfactions in their personal and professional lives and then seek help on specific questions, (4) talk things over with friends individually and in groups, (5) develop new avocations, and (6) recognize new possibilities in teaching so as not to try to get psychic gratification inappropriately from students (Redl & Wattenberg, 1951).

So adamant have the psychoanalytic pedagogues been about the need for the teacher to intelligently and sensitively manage his counter-transferences that in the literature during the 1920s through the 1950s, there were many serious calls for the teacher to undergo some form of analysis during the student-teaching years, just as an analyst-in-training must do. The last serious call along these lines came from Jersild and Lazar (1962) in their study of hundreds of teachers who had actually undergone therapy and then reported its generally quite positive effects on their teaching.[9] Furthermore, because the student's issues will frequently revive similar issues that are unresolved in the teacher from when he was the student's age, "the teacher must understand two children: the children he confronts in the classroom and the vestigial child within himself" (Fox, 1975, p. 164).

THE THERAPEUTIC CLASSROOM

In this concluding section, we look briefly at how the psychoanalytic theorists have addressed the quite crucial issue of how a teacher may *fulfill a therapeutic function* without engaging in the dangerous illusion that he *is a therapist.*

Pfister (1922) pointed out that since teaching and learning are inevitably emotional processes, knowledge of emotional dynamics is an essential arrow in the teacher's professional quiver. William Heard Kilpatrick (1925), the well known Progressive theorist and practitioner, said teachers should understand psychoanalysis, not because they wish to be therapists, but simply to be of most help to students in their emotional growth (p. xii). Blos (1940) argued that psychoanalytic knowledge should be a part of teacher education curricula in order to help teachers understand their students' general developmental issues and at least some of their present behaviors that might otherwise threaten, seduce, or confuse the teacher (p. 505). In gaining and using this knowledge, the teacher is by no means performing some sort of "medical function" (Redl & Wattenberg, 1951); however, it *is* part of the teacher's duty to help "relieve the child of some emotional pressure. At the minimum, it may keep him from getting worse. On the positive side, it may increase the probability of success in treatment being undertaken by outside agencies" (p. 347)—a point that is even more apposite today than when it was made in 1951, owing to the much larger number of young people currently in therapy.

Reflecting the liberatory pedagogical aims of many educationists in the 1960s, Kubie (1967) declared that, because "the next goal of education is nothing less than the progressive freeing of man," the teacher could best reach this political goal "through psychoanalytically rich ed-

---

9 It is not entirely clear why the call from psychoanalysts for teachers to undergo analysis seems to have ended in the early 1960s. It may relate to Americans' increasing disenchantment with psychoanalysis in general throughout the second half of the 20th century (Eagle, 1984) and their disinclination to have it imposed on teachers in such a personal way. This is a subject that requires further study.

ucation" (p. 70). This decade also saw increased calls for the teacher to know "how to cultivate and deploy aroused imaginations, and their attendant emotions" in order to help free the child both intellectually and politically—but to do so as a teacher, not a therapist (Jones, 1968, p. 85). The psychoanalytic pedagogues over the last several decades have not lessened but increased their insistence that there is a therapeutic component to the teacher's role—if, indeed, the teacher wishes to address and shape the total character of the student. For, "the teacher, if he or she is to be successful, must function as a psychotherapist, not in the formal sense of conducting therapy sessions with the students, but in the practical sense of being alert and responsive to the psychological needs that students evince both by what they do and what they do not do" (Basch, 1989 p. 772). Indeed, according to Field (1989), it is precisely the psychoanalytically savvy teacher who will know his limits and thus be less, not more, likely to try to perform functions that should belong to the therapist alone. Discussing a program at the Chicago Institute for Psychoanalysis which provided teachers with psychoanalytic knowledge relevant to teaching, Field, a director of the program, pointed out that it did not endeavor to

> [turn] teaching into therapy nor [did] the faculty [conceive] its function as therapists rather than teachers. On the contrary, this dawning recognition of the commonalities in the two functions [of teaching and therapy] has furthered our understanding of the differentials, and, at the same time, helped promote more integration in of cognitive and affective modes in learning and teaching. (p. 944)

Elson (1989), another analyst participating in the Chicago Institute Program, stressed that "our purpose was not to make therapists of teachers. Rather we worked together toward understanding the barriers to learning, the unexpected hostility, so difficult to withstand, by which students covered over the shame of not knowing and the fear of failure" (p. 805). The recent distinction between a "mastery conception" of teaching and a "therapeutic conception" of teaching nicely captures what it means for a teacher to teach in a therapeutic mode without trying to be a therapist.

> According to the mastery conception, someone who continues to hold conflicting beliefs, even after it has been "brought out" to her attention, is considered peculiar. This is not the case with the teacher-therapist: she is inclined to read the situ-

ation from a perspective that recognizes that there are cases of ambivalence that actually reflect a state of internal conflict. In these cases, being caught midway is seen as a condition in which the learner signals that she is undergoing a process of change....Unlike the teacher-master, the teacher-therapist interprets the dissonance as a symptom of a dilemma and often as an indication that the learner is in the process of confronting herself. (Shalem & Bensusan, 1999, p. 30)

PSYCHOANALYSIS AND EDUCATION: THEMES, PROBLEMS, AND PROSPECTS

In this chapter, we have laid a groundwork for further explorations into depth psychology and education by examining some of the major themes that have emerged in the psychoanalytic literature regarding education. We have seen that later Freudians such as Kohut, Winnicott, and Fairbairn continued where Freud left off, ultimately turning from his idea of sexual instincts as the driving force of the psyche and focusing upon the definition and maintenance of a cohesive self as the primary psychic imperative. These theorists added a variety of new terms to the psychoanalytic lexicon—terms which would later become important in the vision of teaching and learning in psychoanalytic theory: narcissism, the narcissistic wound, selfobjects, and the mirroring and idealizing transferences (Kohut); holding environments, good-enough mothering, and transitional objects (Winnicott); and hyper-intellectualism as a psychotic defense mechanism (Fairbairn).

Two of the great themes running throughout the writings of the psychoanalytic pedagogues are, on one hand, the enormous potential of psychoanalysis to humanize education and, on the other hand, its general failure to penetrate the official structure of public schooling. The psychoanalytic pedagogues have attributed this failure to everything from unconscious resistance on the part of teachers and policy-makers to the depersonalizing educational agendas of capitalism. Indeed, even in the one instance where there was a broad acceptance of psychoanalytic principals in education—namely, in the psychoanalytic wing of Progressivism—psychoanalytic theorists critiqued the way that these principles were put into practice, asserting that the Progressive classroom coddled students in its permissiveness while simultaneously foreclosing legitimate expressions of aggression and competitiveness. The relationship between psychoanalytic theorists and public education has been both patchy and stormy.

Not surprisingly, psychoanalytic pedagogy has been highly critical of the depersonalizing consequences of behaviorist pedagogy. While taking a more amiable view of Piagetian constructivism, the psychoanalytic pedagogues have also been critical here, insisting that learning is more than just cognitive accommodation and assimilation but involves the person's deeper hopes and fears, loves and hates, all of which make up "the subjective curriculum."

Even a glance at the last 80 years of the prestigious psychoanalytic journal, *The Psychoanalytic Study of the Child*, reveals at least one article in each of its combined 300-plus issues that discusses a particular learning disorder, and only a few could be mentioned in this chapter. Yet, of all of these issues, many psychoanalytic pedagogues believe that the idea of transference in teacher–student relationships is the single most important issue that psychoanalysis addresses for the educationist. For this reason, we examine this topic in greater depth in the final section of this book. The psychoanalytic pedagogues have vociferously claimed that the teacher, although not a therapist, can, if armed with a basic knowledge of the fundamental principles and practices of psychoanalysis, teach in ways that are psychologically wise and sometimes even therapeutically efficacious.

The psychoanalytic pedagogues have been quite concerned — especially since the 1930s — to dispel false ideas about psychoanalysis and its applicability to education. They have spilled a great deal of ink rooting out the most popular misconceptions about psychoanalysis: that it is just about sex, that it minimizes the impact of non-political factors on education, and that it aims at pitting the individual and his desires against society and its necessary constraints. To the contrary, the psychoanalytic pedagogues highlighted the educationist's responsibility to socialize the child along fairly conventional lines psychosexually and socially, and to do so in a way that paid full attention to the historical, cultural, and economic factors involved in education. This was even true in the radical 1960s. Although admitting the importance of sexuality in the individual's psychic functioning, the major psychoanalytic writers on education have identified the development of an integral self in fruitful existential encounter with others as the primary psychological motivation and goal from infancy to death.

Now, with these basic ideas and elements of psychoanalytic pedagogy in hand, we turn to a related, but new, topic—namely, how Carl Jung's archetypal psychology allows us to greatly expand upon these concepts in order to picture and put into practice a pedagogy that is both psychologically and spiritually satisfying to teachers and students. But this will require a solid basic knowledge of Jungian thought and practice, which is the subject of the next two chapters.

CHAPTER TWO

FROM THE PERSONAL TO THE TRANSPERSONAL

Jung and the Realms of Psyche

Between about 1905 and 1913, Carl Gustav Jung was considered Freud's most gifted and important disciple. Freud's hope was that Jung would oversee the growth of psychoanalytic theory until it became the dominant approach. This was not destined to be.

What makes Freud and Jung's falling out so sad is that it was unnecessary and impeded the progress of depth psychology in the 20th century. It is now becoming ever clearer to a new generation of depth psychologists that Freudian theory and Jungian theory, far from being contradictory, are often compatible and even mutually enriching in many ways. There is now a growing attempt to unify Freudian and Jungian theory, in both their classical and contemporary forms, not only in psychological studies but in educational (Mayes, 2005a), cultural (Adams, 1996), sociological (Gray, 1996), theological (Ulanov, 1999), and literary (Polette, 2004) studies.

BEYOND THE SEXUAL HYPOTHESIS

Although the reasons for Jung's departure from the Freudian camp are many, it is clear to most scholars of the subject that one of the fundamental reasons for the break between the two men was Freud's insistence that at the heart of every neurosis—indeed, at the heart of psychological functioning in general—was the sex drive. Jung "was too much the empiricist to close his eyes to the great influence of sexuality in human life" (Frey-Rohn, 1974, p. 137). Yet, as he asserted in his essay "On Psychic Energy," the first draft of which was written during his break with Freud, "sexual dynamics is only one particular instance in the total field of the psyche. This is not to deny its existence, but merely to put it in its proper place" (1960, p. 30). Indeed, even at the height of his association with Freud, Jung had shown signs of doubt (which Freud sensed and resented) that sex was the all-in-all of psychodynamics. Tracing Jung's writings during his psychoanalytic phase with Freud, one sees him coming increasingly to the damning criticism that "before Freud nothing was allowed to be sexual, now everything is nothing but sexual" (Jung, 1954b, p. 105).

It simply flew in the face of common sense, Jung believed, that every distinctly human impulse and aspiration—from love for one's parents to the creation of great art, from a sense of civic duty to the perennial longing for communion with the holy, from fighting for a toy on the playground to the conflagration of world wars—was merely the symbolic expression of sexual needs. Human beings are multifaceted. No single impulse or instinct could possibly explain everything about them. For this reason, Jung also criticized Alfred Adler—another of Freud's erstwhile disciples who, like Jung, had broken ranks and formed a new school of psychology—because of Adler's insistence that "the will to power" was the nuclear core that alone powered the operations of the psyche. Again, Jung admitted the importance of the drive for power, but he denied its adequacy as a complete answer to every mystery of human thought, feeling, and behavior. Such reductionism, "the leitmotif of all one-sidedness," did ethical and emotional violence to humans by portraying them as one-dimensional caricatures. "The protean life of the psyche is a greater, if more inconvenient, truth than the rigid certainty of the one-eyed point of view" (Jung, 1954b, p. 83)

We are beings who are motivated by sex and power. However, we are also social beings who find fulfillment in relationship. We are cultural beings whose self-identity is rooted in our sense of connection to both our near and distant ancestors. We are political beings who see the good life as inseparable from the good society, for which we are often willing to die to create and support. We are historical beings who understand ourselves in terms of collective triumphs and failures that span centuries, even millennia. We are intellectual beings who seek knowledge for its own sake because we love it. And we are spiritual beings—creatures of eternity—who find no ultimate rest until we establish a heart-connection with what we believe to be final, great, and immortal.

THE ARCHETYPES
AND THE COLLECTIVE UNCONSCIOUS

In Freud's model of mind, subconscious phenomena were essentially the result of either: (1) the *repression* of painful memories and impulses that were incompatible with successful ego functioning or (2) the *suppression* of primitive sexual and power drives that posed such a threat to the ego that they were never allowed to surface in the first place. Especially in the case of repression, the nature of the individual's unique subconscious was thus a function of his personal experiences which varied from individual to individual.[1] Jung's objection to the Freudian view of the exclusively personal nature of the contents of the subconscious was not that it was wrong, but simply that it was too limited.

Certainly, each person's unique history would produce a unique set of conscious and subconscious issues in that person. Jung never denied the biographical specificity of each person's psyche. In fact, he insisted upon it. However, he observed that each human being—like any living organism—innately possessed certain fundamental ways of experiencing, understanding, and acting *in* the world and *on* it. These inborn perspectives and predispositions, which preceded individual experience, were more deeply embedded in the individual's psyche than his merely personal subconscious. Indeed, they were the primal bedrock upon which both the conscious and subconscious mind would subsequently develop from birth to death. These specie-specific ways of seeing and being resided, Jung claimed, not in a personal subconscious but in a *collective unconscious*—"collective" because it was innate and similar in all human beings, "unconscious" because it existed in a much more ancient and much less accessible realm of psyche than the person's transitory and experientially conditioned *sub*conscious. The collective unconscious consisted of *archetypes*. The notion of archetypes is the most important—and difficult—of all Jung's contributions to the study of the psyche.

---

1 Yet it is also true that, as early as 1924, Freud began to discuss certain archaic elements of the psyche that were innate in all people yet influential in the individual's psychological functioning (Frey–Rohn, 1974).

Archetypes are the primary structures and categories through which we experience and act upon both our inner and outer worlds. Archetypes both *enable* and *constrain* human knowledge. They are *enabling* because they are the filters of human experience that allow us to understand and act on our world. They are *constraining* because we understand and act on our world *only* through these filters. What we experience is not necessarily reality as such, and certainly not reality in its totality, but simply the version of it that filters through the archetypes.

Since his college days, Jung frequently admitted his indebtedness to Immanuel Kant and his assertion in *The Critique of Pure Reason* that we could never see a "thing in itself" but could only register our *interpretation* of it through *a priori* epistemological lenses.[2] Even time and space, said Kant, might not exist as such in the universe but only appear to do so because "time" and "space" are primary categories through which we see, and in terms of which we act, upon the world. Whether "time" and "space" exist as we perceive them—indeed, whether they exist *at all*—we can never say with certainty. What we *can* say with certainty is that they are *archetypes of human experience*. And, as we shall see, they are only two of the many archetypes that shape our experience *of* the world at the same time as they will set the general outlines of what we will be, do and make, both individually and collectively, *in* the world.

The frustrating thing about archetypes is that, since they *precede* everything that we know, then, by definition, it is impossible to know them as such. According to Jung, archetypes are "the inherited possibility of human imagination" (1953, p. 65), "typical modes of apprehension" (1960, p. 137). As inborn determinants of our higher psychological operations, they are the "spiritual" correlates of those physical instincts that determine our biological functions (1960, p. 138) and thus could be poetically pictured as the "image of instinct in man" (1968b, p. 179). Looked at in broader historical terms, archetypes constitute "the *functional disposition* [of people throughout different times, places, and cultures] to produce the same, or very similar, ideas" (1956, p. 102. Emphasis added). Note here that the archetypes are *not* those historically recurring ideas themselves (which we *do* experience directly) but rather the inborn *disposition* (which we *do not* experience

---

2 The reader who is interested in examining the philosophical background and ramifications of Jung's work should consult the following sources: Kelsey, 1984; Nagy, 1991; Pauson, 1988; Samuels, 1997; Stein, 1982; Wehr, 2002.

directly) to produce such recurring ideas. Hence, archetypes could also be characterized as "the stock of inherited *possibilities of representation* that are born anew in every individual" (1968a, p. 156).

All archetypes have both a light and a dark side, a conventionally "good" and conventionally "bad" side—although, is shown below, what seems to be "good" is not always (or not *only*) good, and what seems "bad" is not always or only bad. At any rate, the nature of one's experience of the archetype will depend on which side has been activated and set in motion—or as Jungians say, "constellated"—by a particular event, thing, person, or situation in the inner or outer world. This light/dark duality characterizes every archetype. The light side of the "savior archetype," for instance, manifests itself in Jesus; its dark side in Hitler, who, claiming to be the savior of a nation and a race, constellated this archetypal energy in an entire people.

In one of his best known examples, Jung compares an archetype to the invisible force that governs the formation of a crystal.

> A comparison with the crystal is illuminating inasmuch as the axial system determines only the stereometric structure but not the concrete form of the individual crystal. This [individual crystal] may be either large or small, and it may vary endlessly by reason of the different size of its planes or by the growing together of two crystals. The only thing that remains constant is the axial system, or rather, the invariable geometric proportions underlying [the actual crystal]. The same is true of the archetype. In principle it can be named and has an invariable nucleus of meaning—but always only in principle, never in its concrete manifestations. (1968a, p. 80)

Frey-Rohn's (1974) excellent definition of archetypes characterizes them as "preconscious categories which [channel] thought and action into definite shapes" (p. 92). Other Jungians have pictured archetypes as "a kind of mold for the accumulation and discharge of psychic energy" (Odajnyk, 1976, p. 25) and speculated that they might actually *be* patterns of energy at the deepest and most formative levels of the psyche (p. 143). As such, they are "irreducible and primary," "the structural nature of the psyche itself" (Palmer, 1995, pp. 8, 114). Using a computer metaphor, Samuels has said that archetypes "constellate experience in accordance with innate schemata and act as an imprimatur of subsequent experience" (1997, p. 27).

I would like to offer the following definition of the archetypes and the collective unconscious. The collective unconscious is the dynamic psychic matrix from which all our other psychic functioning—conscious and subconscious—emerges. It is composed of archetypes, which can be pictured as constantly interacting, occasionally overlapping, and subtly morphing "patterns of energy." Through the archetypes, we interpret and shape our subjective and objective worlds in a distinctly human manner that has, in the most essential ways, remained fairly constant throughout history and across cultures. Because the archetypes are the irreducible *basis* of how we experience our inner and outer worlds, they can never be the direct *object* of that experience. How an individual experiences and uses archetypal energy is variable, depending largely upon his native health, character, and personal experiences as well as upon the many cultural factors, past and present, that have shaped him—cultural factors that are themselves, in large measure, the products of collective archetypal processes.

Archetypes and Archetypal Images

Although it is impossible to experience an archetype directly, it *is* possible to access, experience, work with, and to a certain extent "understand" archetypes in an indirect but still enormously compelling manner because archetypal energy manifests itself in the form of archetypal images and symbols. The archetype in its primordial state can never be immediately apprehended, but its symbolic manifestations can. The situation is analogous to that of wind creating patterns in the sand. We cannot see the wind that creates various figures in the sand but, since we do see the figures, we can infer various things about the basic structure and dynamics of the shaping wind by analyzing its varied sandy traces.

The primacy of symbols and images in Jungian psychology

Jungian psychology focuses primarily on the archetypal symbols produced in dreams, art, literature, cultural narratives, and religion, for it is felt that these offer particularly rich and accessible means of most directly and compellingly experiencing and "understanding" the archetypes.

Some people have misinterpreted Jung as saying that archetypal *symbols* are somehow passed down biologically from generation to generation. In other words, they have accused Jung of maintaining that if, for example, a person in ancient Egypt believed in the reality and saving power of the death and resurrection of the god Osiris, then that person's child would somehow be born with an image of Osiris planted in his mind and that this image would gradually emerge and claim the child's loyalty as he matured. But Jung abandoned very early in his career this naïve but then popular Lamarckian notion that actual images could be transmitted down the generations—unlike Freud, who clung to it in such works as *Totem and Taboo* (1910) and *Moses and Monotheism* (1939).

The child is *not*, Jung asserted, born with an image in its mind of Osiris or Dionysius or Christ or any other god whose death and resurrection promise salvation to all believers. What the child *is* born with—and indeed what we are *all* born with, said Jung—is "the archetype of the savior," which has embodied itself from culture to culture in various historical and mythical figures—different *archetypal savior images* of the same *savior archetype*.

The many different savior figures enshrined in the wide variety of world religions as well as in artists' creations and even individual's dreams, constitutes one strand of that "empirical evidence" mentioned above that allowed Jung to hypothesize the existence of many different archetypes in the collective unconscious. Indeed, Jung asked, how else could we explain the otherwise puzzling anthropological fact that various cultures which could not have possibly had any direct or even indirect contact with each other have so often produced so many stories and practices that, despite the surface differences from culture to culture, are strikingly similar in their essential structures and psychosocial importance? (Campbell, 1949; Frazer, 1935; Neumann, 1954)

Although he was well read in the discipline, Jung was not an anthropologist—and, while it was not through anthropological evidence that he initially came to the idea of archetypes and the collective unconscious, he did draw on such evidence more and more in developing his understanding of the nature and dynamics of archetypes. Rather, it was as a novice psychiatrist at a clinic in Switzerland that the idea really hit him with full force, and it happened one day when he was making his usual rounds. In his autobiography, *Memories, Dreams, Reflections* (1965), Jung recounts the story. There was a young man in his thirties whom Jung had been treating at the Burghölzli Clinic in Switzerland. A schizophrenic and megalomaniac, the patient thought that he was Christ. Jung did not just dismiss the stories and experiences as simply "psychotic," for he had a hunch that they contained something more than could just handily be "diagnosed" as an "illness." This hunch was confirmed four years later when he saw that they resembled an ancient, obscure Mithraic creation myth (1960, pp. 150–151).

> One day I came across [the young patient], blinking through the window up at the sun, and moving his head from side to side in a curious manner. He took me by the arm and said he wanted to show me something. He said that I must look at the sun with eyes half shut, and then I could see the sun's phallus. If I moved my head from side to side the sun-phallus would move too, and that was the origin of the wind. I made this observation about 1906. In the course of the year 1910, when I was engrossed in mythological studies, a book of Dietrich's came into my hands. It was part of the so-called Paris magic papyrus and was thought to be a liturgy of the Mithraic cult. It consisted of a series of instructions, invocations, and visions. One of these visions is described in the following words: "And likewise the so-called tube, the origin of the ministering wind. For you will see hanging down from the disc of the sun something that looks like a tube. And towards the regions westward it is as though there were an infinite east wind. But if the other wind should prevail towards the regions of the east, you will in like manner see the vision veering in that direction." (1960, pp. 150–151)

Could this correspondence between a schizophrenic's fantasies and an ancient creation myth be due to the fact that this uneducated young man had somehow read or even just heard of this obscure Mithraic fable somewhere and was now producing it from the depths of his subconscious? Although unlikely, this was possible. And it was easy enough to reduce the dream to merely Freudian sexual terms. After all, its central image was a phallus! Still, Jung was not inclined to dismiss this young man's experience as mere sexuality or as just something the youth had picked up and forgotten in some book.

Indeed, from that point on, Jung, who was adept at various ancient languages and a competent scholar of ancient mythologies, started to notice in his practice and studies many other correspondences between individual psychological contents and mythic patterns that simply could not be reduced or dismissed. The parallelisms between the dreams and hallucinations reported by his patients in his bustling clinic, on one hand, and the myths he read in old volumes spread out over his sequestered study, on the other hand, grew in their number and convincingness. In the images and behaviors produced by his patients, many of whom were humble Swiss villagers with little formal education and no access to texts in ancient history and comparative mythology, Jung began to record and analyze what would ultimately amount to thousands of instances of such parallels. Jung concluded that the almost endless varieties of archetypal images were *not* heritable—but that archetypal structures *were*. Archetypal images *changed* according to a wide array of personal and cultural circumstances, yet archetypal structures were *invariable* according to human nature. Archetypal images were *personal and cultural*; the archetypes, *transpersonal and trans-cultural*.

The gallery of archetypal images

Archetypal psychology has proven quite fertile in literary studies. Frazer (1935), in his classic literary-anthropological study *The Golden Bough,* noted the importance of the dying and resurrected god in many religions throughout history. Neumann (1954) studied the literary and religious significance of the archetype of the Great Mother. And in what is perhaps the best known of such studies, *The Hero with a Thousand Faces,* Joseph Campbell (1949) identified what he called the "monomyth." Since the monomyth has many educational applications that figure prominently throughout this book, let us study it a bit more closely.

In examining a vast body of literature from early Assyrian creation myths to modern novels, Campbell found that many of them portrayed an archetypal Hero who went through the following stages, either literally or symbolically, in his journey from innocence to wisdom: the call to adventure, his acceptance or refusal of the call, the experience of some sort of emotional rebirth just after crossing a threshold into a forest or desert, confrontation with an Ogre or Seducer who arises to challenge the newly empowered Hero, the proffering of supernatural aid by a teacher (often a Wise Old Man or Woman), the Hero's discovery and winning of his mate, the slaying of the Ogre or Seducer, and finally the Hero's return to society as a transfigured person who is able to restore his failing community with his new-found wisdom and energy. This heroic pattern—leaving home, entering a spooky region of unknown dangers, confronting life-threatening challenges, receiving supernatural assistance in order to meet the challenge, finding one's beloved, and returning to society in order to restore it with the new knowledge and powers one has gained—occurs with such frequency and regularity that we may reasonably conclude that its various elements say something universal about the human condition.

It is a matter of considerable debate among Jungians whether there are just a handful of basic archetypes, many of them, or whether (if they are constantly morphing and intermeshing fields of energy) they can even be numbered at all. Archetypal *images*, on the other hand, which can take on any form depending upon an individual's inherent creativity as well as the pool of cultural symbols at his disposal, are, for all practical purposes, innumerable. Nevertheless, there are certain archetypes and archetypal images that surface in both the life of the psyche as well as the life of a culture with particular frequency and force.

Examples of *archetypal narrative patterns* include: the hero's/heroine's journey through a forest or desert of trials; the dethroning of an old king and enthroning of a new, young one—often accompanied by the restoration of the kingdom; the sacrificial death and resurrection of a savior-god—also accompanied by the restoration of the kingdom; the struggle of a young man and woman to marry against some great odds—often the result of certain social sanctions.[3]

Some of the most important *archetypes of persons or animals* include: king, queen, trickster, lover, bride and groom, wise one/teacher, disciple, divine child, eternal child, shadow, magical/helpful animal, dragon/leviathan, nurturing mother, witch, harlot/temptress, Amazon, psychic medium, law-giving father, evil king, rogue, warrior, *senex*, devil, and savior.

Archetypal events include: birth, baptism, initiation, education, vocation, courtship, matrimony, ritual sacrifice, death, and final judgment.

Some of the most prominent *archetypal landscapes and structures* are the wilderness, city, home, place of instruction, temple, battlefield, heaven, and hell.

Certain *geometrical shapes* are also prominent not only cross-culturally in art and religion but in dreams: circles, squares (especially crosses), and triangles (especially in three-person godheads). Certain numbers also seem to have particularly profound psychological and spiritual significance and are therefore probably of archetypal import: one, signifying unity; two, duality; three, the reconciliation of tension in

---

3 Northrop Frye's (1957) *Anatomy of Criticism* remains the best study of archetypal patterns in world literature.

a new (i.e., third) perspective which unites but transcends the opposing polarities; and four, the creation of a new foundation upon which the new perspective can become established. The prime numbers also seem to have particular psychospiritual significance.[4] Indeed, Jung felt that numbers were only secondarily significant as the means of counting. Their primary function is psychological in that they are "an archetype of order which has become conscious" (Jung, in von Franz, 1984, p. 268).

JUNG AND THE PERSONAL REALM

Despite his primary focus on the transpersonal domains of the psyche, there are many elements in Jungian psychology that can easily and usefully be interpreted in personalistic terms with which most Freudians would feel quite comfortable (Fordham, 1994, 1996).

The Persona

One of the best known terms from Jungian ego psychology is persona. The origin of the term is in ancient Greek drama. The *persona* was the mask that actors wore or held up before their faces while they were on stage in order to portray a certain character or emotion. Jung's use of the term refers to the assortment of protective façades that we all construct and wear throughout our lives. They vary from situation to situation. During a job interview, we generally don a façade that radiates confidence, competence, and teachability. During a date, our façade exudes charm, interest in the other, and perhaps a trace of seductiveness. Our façade as teachers in front of a class is often one of deep wisdom and broad knowledge, even when we are struggling to answer a student's question that taxes our competency (Craig, 1994). A façade functions to assure others, and ourselves, that we are "one of the group," that we "know the rules" and are willing and able to play by them—and, in general, that we are "doing just great, thanks!"

It is usually important in therapy for the client to take off his personas (or at least lower them) in the safe haven of the consulting room. This is indeed one of the great purposes of depth therapy. However, it is often neither desirable nor possible to shed personas—or to do so to the same degree—in the rough-and-tumble of daily interpersonal relation-

---

4 For more on the archetypal significance of numbers, especially numbers one through four, see Jung, 1960, 1968a; see also see von Franz, 1984, for a discussion of the relationship between numerical archetypes and different conceptions of time.

ships. To be absolutely straightforward, fully disclosing, and completely honest in every interpersonal situation would be naïve in most circumstances, dangerous in many, and fatal in some. Personas are thus not inherently false, merely protective. No sooner could a person function without a persona than a crab could without a shell. It is important to bear in mind that although the persona is a vital component of healthy ego functioning, it is not the same thing as the ego. The ego, according to Jung, is "a complex of ideas which constitutes the center of my field of consciousness and appears to possess a high degree of continuity and identity." As such, the ego is (or should be) greater than the persona, and there is clearly something wrong if our consciousness of ourselves as individuals goes no deeper than the face we put on for others to see (Jung, 1921, p. 425).

Personas only begin to be a problem when a persona no longer works obediently as the ego's servant but becomes its master—when it begins to overshadow the ego's awareness of itself. The person diminishes or even disappears as a unique "subject." He becomes merely the "object" of others' perceptions of him—or what he fancies those perceptions are or what he would like them to be. In other words, an individual becomes so preoccupied with how he appears to others that this concern dominates his conscious awareness—and, indeed, becomes his consciousness. In Jungian terms, such a person is persona–possessed.

The Shadow

A radio program of the 1930s began each week with the chilling question that echoed in living rooms across America, "Who knows what evil lurks in the heart of man?" The chilling answer was: "The Shadow knows!" In Freudian terms, this shadow-character is a symbol of the id, the repository of all of the individual's dammed impulses and banned memories which, conflicting with the purist demands of the superego, are subconsciously felt by the ego to pose a dire threat to its ability to function in a socially and ethically acceptable manner. The ego is Dr. Jekyll. The Shadow is Mr. Hyde.

Jung's coining of the term *shadow* certainly includes the Freudian idea of repressed and suppressed psychic contents that are seen as evil— but it also goes far beyond it. Jung defined the shadow as "the 'negative' side of the personality, the sum of all the unpleasant qualities we like to hide, together with the insufficiently developed functions and the contents of the personal unconscious" (1953, p. 66, n. 5). With the phrase "the sum of all the unpleasant qualities we like to hide," we are on solid

Freudian ground. What is new is the additional phrase: "together with the insufficiently developed functions...." Not only does the shadow include that which the Freudian ego and superego deem unseemly; it also includes tendencies and abilities—some of them possibly good—which the individual has not sufficiently cultivated but are "insufficiently developed." Many people who read Jung miss this crucial point. They equate the Jungian shadow with the individual's "evil side," completely identifying the shadow as the devil within us.

To be sure, part of the shadow is evil. There are activities or roles that are deemed inappropriate and put in the shadow because they are inappropriate, even morally wrong. However, with the phrase "insufficiently developed functions" Jung is alluding to another part of the shadow—an undiscovered component of the personality that is not necessarily bad or even dangerous. Indeed, it is potentially creative and good. An example of this—one that was more common several decades ago than today—would be a young woman who wanted to be a professional athlete but whose parents were vehemently against it because they did not consider it "feminine" for a female to be seen on the battleground of seriously competitive sports—and even less feminine for her to make her living doing it. Anxious to please her parents, such a young woman might stifle, even repress, her healthy desire to be an athlete, even going so far as to repress any interest at all in sports. She might even come to "agree" with her parents that sports are "bad" for women. This woman's hopes and gifts as an athlete would be relegated to her shadow, and she would wonder throughout her life why she always got so depressed whenever one of her daughters joined an athletic team at school.

Conversely, a young girl who loves to play with her Barbie, dress up in lacey and frilly clothing, invite her friends and dolls to tea-parties that she hosts, and who dreams of growing up to be a nurturing wife and mother, might relegate that laudable vision of herself to her shadow if her parents and schools insisted (as was often the case in the 1970s and is not infrequently the case today) that such things are philosophically and politically backward for a young woman. This girl might banish her nurturing side to the shadow—and wind up years later as a frustrated and lonely woman in a dead-end middle-management position, wondering late at night in her empty office what went wrong along the line, why she goes from one man to another, and why she drinks too much. In these examples, the authentic self has been exiled to shadowy realms because the child's most significant selfobjects judged them "gender inappropriate." In the terms provided by Winnicott and Kohut, they were forced to relinquish the transitional objects and activities that were most deeply meaningful to them and thus suffer from a narcissistic wound.

Overly restrictive gender-roles are not the only factors in shadow formation. A host of other activities or roles may be consigned to the shadow because the child learns that they are unacceptable to "our" socio-economic class, "our" political party, "our" ethnic group, or "our" religion. The point is that some of these shadow-elements not only can but should be brought to consciousness and realized in action. Also residing in the shadow are other "insufficiently developed functions" that we ignore and banish to the realm of shadows — but not because our ability with them poses a threat to others. We deny and dismiss them because we are not good at them. Jung called the domain of a person's limited competencies that person's *inferior function*.

Maturely examining one's shadow also demands that a person frankly come to terms with his emotional and moral limitations. Jung correctly claimed that one of the great benefits of looking at one's psychic and ethical shortcomings is that it makes a person more tolerant, less prone to point the withering finger of reproof at other individuals as well as at "other groups and other forms and levels of culture" (Neumann, 1973, p. 97). Jung often noted that there is no surer cure for a "holier-than-thou" attitude than looking long and hard at one's own shadow, for one will find almost every evil and absurdity that disfigures the world in one's own heart. Indeed, from Buddhism to Judaism, from Islam to Christianity, the world's major religions have always preached the bitter but unavoidable truth that the source of evil lies in the individual and must therefore be found and expunged individually. To be sure, there are social evils that we must energetically address. However, unless we face our own evil, all of our social-reforming fury will probably generate more darkness than it dispels. "Physician, heal thyself!" is advice that really applies to us all. Shadow-work permits one to become more real, less perfectionist — a good thing since, as we saw in Winnicott's notion of "good-enough mothering," perfectionism is generally neurotic. We saw in Chapter 1 how perfectionism in the classroom can lead to teacher burnout and student anxiety. We continue to examine the idea of the "good-enough teacher" in later chapters as well.

The good news in doing one's own shadow-work is that one becomes ever better at harnessing shadow energy in productive ways. This should not be surprising since one cannot control what one does not know. With the energy of the shadow understood and bridled, like a wild stallion brought under the wise control of a firm but gentle master, the individual is not only more empowered but (and here is the paradox!) more empowered to do good.

Another reason for engaging in the hard work of examining one's shadow has to do with *projection*, another Jungian term which, like persona, has become well known. The idea of projection is quite simple, and its recognition certainly predates Jung: we condemn most harshly in others what we refuse to see in ourselves. Of course, Jung is not claiming that whenever we judge something or someone to be morally wrong in some respect we are simply projecting shadows. Jung, a conservative Swiss who had witnessed the grotesqueries of two world wars, was a very firm believer in the reality of evil and wrote a great deal on the subject. What Rieff (1961) has said about Freud is equally true of his disciple: he was, in the last analysis, a "moralist." There is real evil in the world and there are times when it must be exposed as such.[5] Jung's point was simply that until we face our own shadow, we will never know if the evil we are "observing" is truly an external fact or a projected mirage. This is why the shadow comprises "the true moral problem of the individual" (Frey-Rohn, 1974, p. 61) and why shadow-work is "a suffering and a passion that implicate the whole man" (Jung, 1960, p. 208).

In dreams, the shadow is usually the same gender as the dreamer and often has something dark associated with it. The dream character might have a dark complexion and/or dark hair (a fact which generally seems to be as true for patients of color as for white patients); the figure may be wearing dark clothes; sometimes he or she is literally standing in or peeking out of a shadow. The fact that the shadow has been "despised" by consciousness can also be symbolized in the dream by the shadow being an alien, a citizen of an opposing country, a member of a minority group, a criminal, or a beggar; or by being somehow unethical, sick, or menacing (Adams, 1996). Whatever specific form it takes, when such an "outcast" figure does make an appearance in a dream, it

---

5 One reason that Jung rejected traditional Christian dogma was its Augustinian insistence that evil is not real in itself (for God created everything, and it is unthinkable that he could create anything evil) but is, rather, the "absence of good" — *a privatio boni*. Especially in light of the concentration camps of the Second World War, Jung felt it was not only philosophically incorrect but morally grotesque to say that evil does not really exist.

is important to consider the possibility that it is representing the shadow and thus comes bearing important information about what needs to be acknowledged and, in some instances, used by the ego.

Personality Types ·

In his study of ancient literature, science, and medicine, Jung had often noted the importance of four-pointed symmetrical forms— quaternities—to many great thinkers, who saw in it the structural core of everything from the human body to the cosmos. Jung thus concluded that the quaternity was an archetypal form. Jung pointed out that quaternities often were comprised of two paired opposites within a whole—a cross within a circle, a "unification of a double dyad" (1968c).

Jung's interest in the phenomenon was primarily clinical, for many of his patients reported dreams that had quaternities—both imagistically in the form of four-chambered mandalas and thematically in the form of characters who "squared off" as paired opposites. Observing that his patients seemed to divide into four basic personality types, which he called the thinking, feeling, sensate, and intuitive types (1954a), Jung further categorized these types into two sets of paired opposites: thinking/feeling and sensate/intuitive. Wishing to avoid simplistic interpretations of his theory, Jung was quick to add that everyone had elements of all four of these ways of interacting with the world within himself. Furthermore, he insisted that no personality type was intrinsically better than the other three. Each was simply a different way of engaging with the world, and each had its own peculiar strengths and weaknesses. Although no one should be schematically reduced to just one psychological function, most people tend to use one particular function more than the others, which, Jung said, can be identified as that person's *superior function*—the opposite of his inferior function, which is typically banished to the shadow. Knowing what a patient's superior function is can be therapeutically useful. It can also be educationally useful as we shall see later on.

---

6 Although I am subsuming Jungian typology under Jung's ego psychology, it must be borne in mind that there are certainly archetypal aspects of the issue of one's personality type. However, since the superior function is one's primary way of dealing with the world, and furthermore since one's inferior function usually is primarily a shadow issue, it seems sensible to discuss personality as primarily an ego function.

The four functions: Thinking and feeling, sensation and intuition

"Thinking is the psychological function which, following its own laws, brings the contents of ideation into conceptual connection with each other" (Jung, 1921, pp. 481–482). The thinking type is analytical. He utilizes paradigms and systems to negotiate his world. Feeling, which is at the opposite pole from thinking, "is entirely a subjective process between the ego and a given content, a process, moreover, that imparts to the content a definite value in the sense of acceptance or rejection ('like' or 'dislike'). The process can also appear isolated, as it were, in the form of a mood..." (1921, pp. 434ff). Feeling types see the world in terms of emotional preferences that stem from deeply held values.

The other paired opposites are the sensate and intuitive types. The sensate negotiates his world in terms of how it presents itself to him in immediate perceptions and sensations. The sensate type relies upon "the psychological function that mediates the perception of a physical stimulus. It is, therefore, identical with perception.... Sensation is related not only to external stimuli but to inner ones, i.e., to changes in the internal organic processes" (1921, p. 461). Athletes are often sensate types. Intuition, by contrast, "is the function that mediates perceptions in an unconscious way.... In intuition a content presents itself whole and complete, without our being able to explain or discover how this content came into existence" (1921, pp. 453–454). The intuitive person always seems to sense how or why a situation came into being and what direction it will probably take. Many psychotherapists are intuitive types (Mattoon, 1985).

As previously mentioned, Jung called a person's basic type his superior function. The opposite pole is the person's inferior function. Thus, thinking types tend to have the most problems with having, sorting out, and managing their feelings, whereas feeling types struggle most with thinking analytically about their emotions and judgments. Sensate types, whose inferior function is intuition, struggle with grasping the deeper causes and broader possibilities of a given concrete fact or situation, whereas intuitive types often inhabit a world of imagination and thus are not adequately tuned in to their immediate physical realities. Additionally, each person has an auxiliary function—or the thing at which he is "second best." Thus, a sensate type might also be inclined to have strong emotions about immediate situations, which would make feeling his auxiliary function.

The two attitudes: Introversion and extraversion

To complete his typological system, Jung added one final dimension — that of the *attitudes*. There are two fundamental attitudes: *introversion* and *extraversion* — popular terms which originated with Jung. The four functions times the two attitudes yields eight basic personality types.

> Introversion is an inward turning of libido, in the sense of a negative relation to the object. Interest does not move toward the object but withdraws from it into the subject. Everyone whose attitude is introverted thinks, feels, and acts in a way that clearly demonstrates that the subject is the prime motivating factor and that the object is of secondary importance. (1921, pp. 452–453)

> Conversely, extraversion is an outward turning of libido. I use this concept to denote a manifest relation of subject to object, a positive movement of subjective interest toward the object [an "object" in this case being not only a thing but also a situation, event, or person]. Everyone in the extraverted state thinks, feels, and acts in relation to the object, and moreover in a direct and clearly observable fashion, so that no doubt can remain about his positive dependence on the object. In a sense, therefore, extraversion is a transfer of interest from subject to object. (1921, pp. 481–482)

Just as each of the four major types must be thought of only as a tendency, introversion and extraversion must be seen as ways of relating to the external world that are "habitual" but by no means not exclusive.

The popular Myers-Briggs Type Indicator was devised on Jungian principles. Gardner's (1983) theory of multiple intelligences also contains elements of Jungian typology. Indeed, many currently popular devices for categorizing personality can be traced back to Jung's seminal work in typology. Jungian typology has been quite influential in educational research and practice, especially in identifying and improving teachers' and students' styles of relating to each other and the curriculum.

ARCHETYPAL TRANSFERENCE AND COUNTER-TRANSFERENCE

Transference

The reader may recall from Chapter 1 Greenson's definition of the transference as "the experiencing of feelings, drives, attitudes, fantasies, and defenses toward a person in the present which are inappropriate to that person and are a repetition, a displacement of reactions originating in regard to significant persons of early childhood" (1990, p. 151). This is a definition of transference that would be acceptable to both classical psychoanalysts and current selfobject psychologists.

But Jung went even farther in his view of the transference by claiming that in the transference clients also made transpersonal, archetypal projections onto the analyst. Not only might transferences not be merely sexual; they might not even be merely personal. Indeed, most Jungians insist that at the center of every personal complex[7] (and the transference is essentially a complex that a client is projecting onto his analyst) is a transpersonal, archetypal core. Its power radiates from the depths of the collective unconscious and permeates the individual's unique identity and issues.

However, an important warning is in order here. A person should not be allowed to use the archetypal realm as merely a way of fleeing from his personal problems. This is what Jung called inflation. The personal side of one's problems cannot just be wished away by the individual trying to simply lose himself in an inflated fairyland of archetypes. Personal issues must be addressed head-on or they will reappear in ever more serious forms. As Jung wrote, "The overpowering of the ego by unconscious contents...possesses a prodigious psychic virulence...and is capable of the most disastrous results" (1960, p. 223–225). Inflation can lead to intolerance and fanaticism, as when a person tries to "transcend" his personal problems by embracing some grand cosmic ideology or religion that he hopes will, in a hurricane of divine grace and ultimate salvation, wash away his personal existential responsibility for his life in the here and now.

This interaction of the personal and archetypal in the transference can occur in any emotionally charged venue — from the consulting room to the classroom. Consider the rather common example of the male cli-

---

7 Although "having a complex" about something has come to mean something entirely negative in popular parlance, this was not how Jung saw complexes. As he wrote, having a complex "only means that something discordant, unassimilated, and antagonistic exists, perhaps as an obstacle, but also as an incentive to greater effort, and so, perhaps, to new possibilities of achievement. In this sense, then, complexes are nodal points of psychological life which we would not wish to do without; indeed, they should not be missing, for otherwise psychic life should come to a standstill" (1921, p. 529). See Ellenberger (1970) for the historical precedents of the idea of a "complex" in pre-Freudian psychiatry.

ent or student who craves unconditional moral, psychological, and sometimes even physical nurturance from a female therapist or teacher. She may well suspect that the client or student is projecting onto her his personal Oedipal needs which his mother was never able to satisfy, not having been a good-enough mother who offered safe transitional spaces and transitional objects, all of which he (the client) is now attempting to find in the therapist and her consulting room. Psychoanalytically based theories have a great deal to say of value about this kind of situation.

What they do not allow for is the possibility that the client may also be sensing in the therapist the universal attraction exerted by the archetypal Great Mother back into the cosmic womb (Neumann, 1954).[8] Only a transpersonal analysis can bring this information to the level of ego awareness and provide ways of using it to clarify and liberate, rather than confuse and cripple, consciousness. Having a vocabulary and techniques for understanding and working with such interplays of ego and archetype is the special forte of Jungian psychology (Edinger, 1973).

Counter-transference

The therapist's counter-transferences—or her projections back on to her client or student—also have personal and archetypal components. For instance, it is easy to see how a male therapist or teacher, the object of "God-the-Father" projections onto him, might let it go to his head! He might get inflated by the archetype. It certainly seems to happen often enough with male surgeons!

However, it is true that, to some degree, the therapist really does embody the archetype of "The Healer" just as a teacher may embody the archetype of the Wise Old Man or Woman. It is not only legitimate for a doctor or teacher to draw on the power of these archetypes; it is psychologically and morally vitalizing to do so. Indeed, not doing so can lead to alienation from oneself and one's work. What de Castillejo has written about general practitioners in medicine, for instance, could, mutatis mutandi, apply to many different people in various walks of life—especially, as we shall see, to teachers.

---

8 However, Freud's nirvana principle and death instinct, which resemble the all-consuming aspect of the archetypal Great Mother, address this issue in some measure and in rather archetypal terms—additional evidence of the unnecessary breach between psychoanalysis and analytical psychology, which can inform each other in both theoretical and practical ways (see Samuels, 1997).

[General Practitioners] have been vociferous about their un-
just remuneration and inferior status in the medical hierarchy,
but I have never heard them mention what is much more likely
to be the fundamental nature of their unhappiness: that the archetype of a healer which has sustained and nourished them
throughout the centuries has fallen from their shoulders leaving them as little cogs in the great machine of modern medical
practice. It is not a greater share of the world's wealth they
lack, but "mana." (de Castillejo,1973, p. 22. Emphasis in
original.)

(Counter)transference and Temenos

Because of their extreme psychological importance, the archetypes
generate strong emotions in a person when they emerge in the form of
archetypal images, and "it is this emotionality of archetypal images that
endows them with dynamic effect" (Adams, 1996, p. 102). Jung used
the word *numinous* (from the Greek word for "spirit") to describe the
spiritual intensity of that experience. He often spoke of encountering
the archetypal realm as a *mysterium tremendum et fascinans*, a tremen-
dous and fascinating mystery. Although spirituality should not be reduced merely to an exciting inner experience of the archetypal realm
without any moral responsibilities or consequences (as some neo-
Jungians all too glibly and dangerously do), there is no doubt that the
experience of the archetypal realm generally produces the conviction of
spiritual reality.

Therapy is an emotional experience. When archetypal energy is
fully operative in the transferential dynamics in a consulting room, the
atmosphere can become even more affectively electric, supercharging
the therapeutic setting, and turning it into what Jung called a *temenos*
or "sacred precinct." Consulting rooms are not unique in this respect.
Wherever people are passionately engaged with each other in a potentially transformative experience—the battlefield, the classroom, the
bedroom, the meditation hall, a football field, a boxing ring, or even the
dinner table—that location can suddenly change into a temenos. Some
neo-Jungians even make the intriguing claim that the idea of the temenos is more than merely symbolic, and may involve the actual generation of psycho-physical energies that form a transpersonal, quantum
field in which very subtle energies of the analyst and patient come into
contact (Schwartz-Salant, 1995; Spiegelman & Mansfield, 1996). This
quantum field may also be fertile ground for certain paranormal phe-

nomena, especially what Jung called *synchronicity* (Spiegelman & Mansfeld, 1996). Most people have experienced synchronicity at some time in their lives. For instance, you dream of a person whom you have not seen or heard from in twenty years and the next morning there is a call from that person on your answering machine; or you and a friend are talking about a poem by your favorite poet over lunch, and later that afternoon in the library you pick up a book that has fallen off the shelf and notice that it is opened to that very poem.

I have often experienced synchronicity in both my consulting room and classroom. For instance, I was recently giving a lecture in a graduate seminar on curriculum theory regarding the oppressive effects of linear, mechanical views of "time" on teaching and learning. Since this is a point that I feel quite strongly about, I found myself critiquing the impersonal, subjectively impoverished view of time —which dominates not only assembly lines but also public schools —with passion and perhaps even a touch of eloquence. "The mechanical view of time," I declaimed, "forces students and teachers into a mental straightjacket and crucifies creativity. This is both educationally and ethically wrong!" Just as I said this, the clock on the classroom wall let out a loud "grumble" and then, quite suddenly, stopped dead in its tracks. The class let out a collective gasp. There had never been any previous malfunction with the clock throughout the entire 14 weeks of our class—nor, for that matter, in the decade that I had taught in that classroom. Seizing the drama of the moment, I continued with my point about time and then brought my lecture to a dramatic conclusion. Precisely as I said my last word on the subject, the clock grumbled again and started up.

Whenever there is a strong archetypal energy at play in an interpersonal situation such as the consulting room or classroom, intriguing archetypal dynamics are set in motion that are pregnant with extraordinary possibilities in the sacred precinct where that relationship is taking place.[9]

9 The reader interested in Jung's idea of synchronicity might want to consult the following works: Progoff, 1975; Peat, 1988; von Franz, 1984; Main, 2004; Charet, 1993; and of course Jung himself, especially his essay "Synchronicity: An Acausal Connecting Principle" (1960), which, however, is considerably less clear than the work of those who have written about Jung's conception of synchronicity.

CHAPTER THREE

JUNG'S LIFESPAN PSYCHOLOGY

Part 1: The Construction of the Ego— From Infancy to Young Adulthood

INFANCY AND CHILDHOOD

Jung's picture of the lifespan consists of infancy and childhood, adolescence and young adulthood, midlife, and old age and death (Mattoon, 1985).[1] Jung's most important contributions in developmental psychology undoubtedly have to do with the last two stages, and it is these that we spend the most time examining. However, just as Jung offered important insights into the dynamics of the ego, he also contributed to our understanding of the development of the ego in its most critical phases, from infancy to young adulthood. This especially merits our attention as educationists since this is the developmental span of children and youth in the schools.

Jung mostly agreed with Freud's mapping of the major shifts that characterized growth from infancy to young adulthood. Jung felt Freud's portrayal of the child's psychosexual growth from the earliest oral phases to the concluding genital ones was essentially correct.[2]

---

1 Stevens (1999) offers a slightly different rendering of the Jungian model that includes transitional sub-stages.

2 However, the Jungian theorist Erich Neumann has reworked these earlier developmental stages in archetypal terms by talking of the child's evolution from the uroboric stage (intrauterine and neo-natal fusion with the mother), to the matriarchal stage (increasing perception of the mother as "other"), to the patriarchal stage (the first stages in the development of the ego).

JUNG'S LIFESPAN STAGES
INFANCY AND CHILDHOOD
ADOLESCENCE AND YOUNG ADULTHOOD
MIDLIFE
OLD AGE AND DEATH

Jung's only major point of disagreement regarded the Oedipus complex. Jung agreed that this complex existed but felt that it signified much more than Freud suspected. Jung admitted that the male child might wish to merge with its mother during a brief period, but Freud had not addressed the fact that the female child apparently wished to do so, too. This desire might sometimes be sexual, but this was only an outgrowth of another, more basic psychological fact, namely, the child's natural but regressive longing to return to the blissful comfort of the womb—and not only the physical womb of its biological mother but the cosmic womb of the archetypal Great Mother. Jung felt that Freud was so possessed by this archetype and its sexual manifestations that he was blind to all the other archetypes (Jung, 1967).

Researchers in both psychoanalytic and archetypal camps agree that the child's ego-consciousness starts to assume a recognizable form around three years of age—although there is considerably less agreement regarding how this happens. Melanie Klein's (1975 [1932]) view of the process of the child's ego-formation is still the base upon which many researchers of various orientations build their models. According to Klein, the primordial wholeness of the infant's natal consciousness soon "de-integrates" into various foci of awareness in the child—pockets of consciousness—that are keyed to different situations. In this necessary and healthy "de-integration" (which should not be confused with the negative phenomenon of *dis*-integration) the child starts to "defuse" from the mother as its sole focus. Instead of mother being the all-in-all of reality, she now becomes an object—although still the most important one—among various objects.

Whenever mother is providing whatever the infant wants (usually nursing) upon demand, the infant perceives her as a "good breast." However, when mother fails to do so, or chooses not to do so, she is demoted in the infant's mind to the status of a "bad breast" (Winnicott, 1988). Experiencing the mother as a "bad breast" is traumatic for the infant, but it is vital that it have this experience, for it must learn that there is often a difference between what it wants and what the world provides. The experience of the "bad breast" is teaching the infant in the most palpably organic ways that the world is not just an extension of its desires from moment to moment. It is something "else." This sets the stage for the infant to begin to see other people *as* others, not merely extensions of itself.

Let us return to Klein's notion of the first de-integrations of consciousness into foci of awareness. She went on to observe that the child's ego is the product of the ability to *reintegrate* these foci into a functional complex when either reality demands it or the child simply desires it. This explains why the child now (generally around three years of age) begins to refer to itself with some regularity as "I" and not as "he," "she," "Jake," "Maria," or "Baby." This confirms Jung's very early mention in the ego-psychology literature that the ego is a complex, not just a unitary thing-in-itself that somehow magically springs into being at a certain point in the course of development. Rather, the ego is an accretion of experiences and potentials. Still, how all this comes to be, Jung felt, is largely mysterious, rooted in deeper archetypal dynamics. "The ego, ostensibly the thing we know most about, is in fact a highly complex affair full of unfathomable uncertainties" (Jung, 1963, p. 107).

Jung saw neurosis as a low-level disturbance of this sense of ego-continuity but not so severe as to eliminate that feeling of unity. In psychosis, however, the psychic "membranes" that hold the ego together are so compromised that they rupture, resulting in a torrential invasion of collective unconscious contents into an storm-tossed ego that is now torn up and washed away like a small boat reduced to floating shards and splinters in a hurricane (Jung, 1954b p. 207). In archetypal terms, this psychic catastrophe amounts to being devoured by the Terrible Mother of the primordial ground of reality, embodied, for instance, in the character of Medea from Greek drama, who ate her children. She is also the archetypal mother of psychosis, which is literally true of the mother who fails to be a stable and supportive selfobject for the child by providing a holding environment that allows the child's personality to form coherently. The proper nurturance of the child's growing ego at home, at school, and on the playground is thus crucial to its later psychosocial competency; for, without a firm ego-foundation laid in these first three years, the child will later be prone to a grim assortment of neuroses and psychoses.

ADOLESCENCE AND YOUNG ADULTHOOD

From the moment of conception onward, intrauterine development is geared toward one great goal: the physical birth of the child as a biologically viable being. In a parallel fashion, adolescence is the time of "psychic birth" for the young person because she is "forming" within the womb of family, school, and society in order to emerge as a viable psychosocial being. This requires that the young person begin to separate from her parents during this period and learn to deal responsibly with her budding sexuality; for, without doing so, she cannot form a family of her own or carve out a creative role for herself in society.

In indigenous, first-world cultures, time-honored and clearly defined initiation rites—their origins in the mists of ancestral memory—typically guide a youth in the transition from adolescence to young adulthood. These rites take many forms, of course, depending on the culture and whether or not the initiate is a male or female. Initiation rites generally seem to be more complex and perilous for males than for females, and this is probably due to the fact that a male, in order to establish his psychosexual identity, needs to break the Oedipal bond to the mother. The female, on the other hand, continues to discover important aspects of her psychosexual identity through deepening identification *with* the mother. Thus, the need for a shattering initiatory break is, generally speaking, either not present in the female or less than for the male (Chodorow, 1978). There is doubtless significant cultural variation in this pattern (Rogoff, 1984) but as a rule-of-thumb it seems to hold good (Conger & Galambos, 1997). "Hence," wrote Jung, "nobody is in a position to deny the enormous historical importance of initiations" (1953, p. 231).

In contemporary society, we have lost touch with these psychosocially critical rites of passage. Public education, increasingly forced to regiment itself around the demand for obedient and efficient "worker-citizens" (Spring, 1976) in a transnational corporate economy, offers very little by way of honoring the perennial need of youth to undergo archetypally rich initiatory trials. Nevertheless, the *need* for initiation persists in the human psyche, for it is an archetype. "The whole symbolism of initiation rises up, clear and unmistakable, in the unconscious contents" of the modern mind no less than the "primitive" one (Jung,

1953, p. 231). If ways cannot be found to provide youth with spiritually rooted and socially stable forms of initiation, then they will search out or invent initiations in the form of dangerous drugs, perilous sports, promiscuous sex, and violent behavior. Mattoon (1985) is certainly right that "the 'unbearable age'—adolescence—might be more bearable …if the culture provided an adequate initiation, comparable to the rituals of many preliterate societies" (p. 171).

May I offer as one possible example of "an adequate initiation" in modern society, an important tradition of my religious community? In Mormon culture, it is expected that, barring any limiting physical or psychological debilities, a young man and his family will save money throughout his youth in order to pay for his two-year mission for our church when he reaches 19. He is expected to live throughout his youth in a manner that will allow him to take on this responsibility at the designated time. A young woman may certainly do so as well at the age of 21, and is sometimes even encouraged to do so. However, it is much more of an expectation for boys than girls.

Male missionaries serve only with other males, and females only with females. Throughout the mission (two years for a male, 18 months for a female), the young person has extremely limited contact with his or her family, and only in the form of letters and rare phone calls. The missionaries must adhere to an austere schedule and standard of behavior in group-living situations with fellow missionaries in order to learn more about the Gospel and how to preach it effectively. Not infrequently, these young people find themselves in uncomfortable, even quite dangerous situations in inner cities or other countries, which they must rely upon their leaders as well as prayer to negotiate. Indeed, many missions are situated in the most perilous inner cities around the world, and the missionaries walk up and down those streets everyday in order to share their message and also to look for opportunities to be of whatever practical service they can in those communities. Most adult Mormons look back on their missionary years as the most difficult and also the most meaningful in their entire lives.

Here are all the essential components of an authentic, sane, and fruitful initiation: separation from family, particularly mother; separation from members of the opposite sex; bonding with other initiates in tasks that are rich in spiritual significance yet often enough accompanied by a degree of danger; guidance by initiating elders through a complex, rule-governed process; and ultimately a return to society as a transfigured being, a young adult, who is now ready to take his or her place as a family leader and a contributor to the larger social good—a person, in short, whose "natural aims" have, as Jung said, been allowed to develop in a way that puts them in the service of larger "cultural aims."

Part 2: The Process of Individuation— From Midlife Until Death

Beginning with the publication of G. Stanley Hall's massive study, *Adolescence,* published in 1904, the 20th century witnessed the emergence of variegated models of "normative" psychosocial development. But whether the model dealt with sex like Freud's, cognition like Piaget's (Piaget & Inhelder, 1969), or moral reasoning like Kohlberg's (1958), they all shared one assumption: sometime around 13 years of age, the individual's psychological development was thought to have more or less peaked—Freud's developmental scenario culminating in *genital sexuality,* Piaget's in *formal operational reasoning,* and Kohlberg's in *post-conventional moral reasoning.* Any further psychological development in the individual was seen as merely a refinement of what she had already accomplished by the tender years of her early to mid-teens.

Jung did not quarrel with such models of psychosexual development as far as they went. His only objection—and one which should not surprise the reader by this point—is that they did not go far enough. Why should human development be seen as more or less finished so very early on in life? "It is a great mistake," Jung warned,

> to think that the meaning of life is exhausted with the period of youth and expansion, that, for example, a woman who has passed the menopause is "finished." The afternoon of life is just as full of meaning as the morning; only, its meaning and purpose are different. Man has two aims; the first is the natural aim, the begetting of children and the business of protecting the brood; to this belongs the acquisition of money and social position. When this aim has been reached a new phase begins: the cultural aim. (1953, p. 74)

The Freudian model offered a plausible analysis of the "natural aims" of pairing, procreation, and profession. This is not surprising given Freud's belief that the purpose of therapy was to show the individual how to "love and work"—*natural* aims *par excellence*. But were procreation and profession all there was to life? Apparently, Freud thought so (Rieff, 1961), which is why, even when he did speak of the cultural aims of forming and maintaining a society through religion, ethics, and art, he reduced them to symbolic displacements of primitive sexual and aggressive instincts. Jung, on the other hand, saw in cultural aims the individual and collective impulse to *evolve and transcend*—socially, aesthetically, ethically, and spiritually—and to do so, moreover, in ways that would both drawn upon and add to the best wisdom of humanity. What we call "culture" is the accumulation of that "best wisdom of the race" (Jung, 1964).

Indeed, Jung's and Freud's differences in this respect reflect an even deeper interpretive divide between them. Freud's approach to understanding a psychosocial phenomenon was "historical"; he looked at its *causes*, hoping thereby to discover how to cure its *pathology*. Jung's approach was "teleological"; he wanted to know a psychosocial phenomenon's *purposes*, hoping to promote its natural (even if temporarily misdirected) *trajectory toward health*. Freud asked: "How did this dysfunction come to be and how can it be eliminated?" Jung asked: "What is the wisdom in this illness that can be tapped to promote health?" Jung wrote:

> The reductive standpoint...always leads back to the primitive and elementary. The constructive standpoint, on the other hand, tries to synthesize, to build up, to direct one's gaze forwards. (Jung, 1954b, p. 105)

In like manner, old age was not to be seen as simply a wasting away of former potencies. Rather, the process of aging must, like all of nature's phenomena, have a forward-looking aim, a salutary purpose—one that was uniquely within the domain of the elders of a community to explore and express. As the elder moved closer to death and what lay beyond it, she was uniquely positioned to share her wisdom with her family, ethnic group, nation, and, even, species. And, cautioned Jung, woe to the society that worshipped youth and discarded the elderly! It would very soon fall into disarray, running amuck in the seductive but poisoned fields of unbridled sensuality and moral relativism—if, indeed, there were any morality left at all. Without the orienting power of higher cultural aims, without due respect accorded the stabilizing spiritual wisdom that accrues in the second half of life, a culture could not survive.[3]

THE MIDLIFE CRISIS: PRELUDE TO INDIVIDUATION

The psychosocial tasks of life's first half are formidable. According to Jung, these include: the formation and maintenance of a viable ego structure, the fruition of sexual love in marriage and the creation of a family, and the discovery and extension of one's social potency in various realms of collective endeavor.

Yet, although difficult, these tasks undeniably have a matching degree of charm: they are vital and attractive. They require enormous effort, to be sure, but it is effort that the young body and psyche—if reasonably healthy—not only *can* but *long* to expend in the up-and-coming young adult's hunger for the gratification of her "natural aims." The ego, finding itself increasingly empowered, plants its proud flag in family and society and claims a certain sphere of it as its own.

Then come what I like to call the "exasperating victories" of midlife. Having achieved at least some degree of what it set out to accomplish, the ego finds itself the victim of its own successes. In shaping her personal identity, forming a family, discovering her lifework, and coming to some terms with the social constraints within which she must operate, the person has created a psychosocial safety net, to be sure, and feels protected—but this net of security may soon begin to feel more like a psychosocial straightjacket of restrictions in which she now finds herself immobilized. In the family created, the circles of friends developed, the profession cultivated, and the whole range of life-promises made and accepted, the individual finds herself tied up in a nexus of commitments which both duty and expediency make it difficult, even impossible, to turn her back on. Nor is the existential fear of limitation merely psychological. Youth's mounting energy begins to give way to age's creeping fatigue, the supple body gets drier and stiffer, memory no longer serves, and the portion of time that remains in one's life grows smaller than the portion that has passed—and continues to pass ever faster.

---

3 See Michael Gellert's (2001) excellent study, *The Fate of America: An Inquiry into National Character*, for a Jungian analysis of this problem in postmodern American culture.

The reader will almost certainly recognize these as symptoms of the "midlife crisis." Faced with these dreary prospects, some people will do whatever they can to avoid looking at them straight on. They quit their jobs, leave their families (especially males), take on younger lovers, and spend too much money on clothes, cars, face-lifts, and exotic vacations. Or they numb themselves in deadening routines, excessive drinking, smoking, and the stupor of endless hours in front of the television or computer screen. Jung was the first among all modern psychologists to not only confront these facts in his model of psyche but to build something good, wise, and practical out of them. He accomplished this by demonstrating how in the second half of life the individual need neither degenerate nor stagnate. Instead, she can *individuate.*

Individuation: Life's Second Heroic Quest

In the psychology of individuation, "we are no longer concerned with how to remove the obstacles to a man's profession, or to his marriage, or to anything that means a widening of his life, but are confronted with the task of finding a meaning that will enable him to continue living at all—a meaning more than blank resignation and mournful retrospect" (Jung, 1953, p. 74). Whereas the archetype of the heroic quest manifested itself as a push for social establishment in the first half of life, the quest-archetype in the second half of life takes on the meaning of a search for connection with the universal and divine. The first half of life revolves around empowering the *ego* as a personal and social entity; the second half of life revolves around the emergence of the higher *Self* as a transpersonal and moral possibility.[4] Thus, Jungians often capitalize the word "Self" (although Jung did not) in order to stress that the individual is not relinquishing her identity but is, in fact, expanding and enriching it through a deepening connection with a higher source of power and love—a transpersonal, archetypal source, a greater Self.

By no means, however, does the emergence of the Self in the individuation process mean the *destruction* of the ego as it is sometimes mistakenly interpreted as doing. Jung made it very clear that the destruction of the ego is always catastrophic and can only mean disorientation and even psychosis. The ego becomes the adversary of the Self

---

4 Jung started using the term "self" (with a lower-case "s," however) around 1928 to indicate a state of consciousness and form of identity that is higher than the "I" of ego (Wehr, 2002, p. 203).

only if it stubbornly insists that its limited empirical perspective accounts for all of reality. Like a wise horse that learns to be controlled by the gentle promptings of its master, the *enlightened* ego is open to constant influxes of energy and direction from the Self.

The Self needs the ego. It is only when the ego is secure that a human being has a firm enough foothold on life's basic emotional and social realities to find the desire and strength to climb up life's mountain to the next moral and spiritual level—individuation. Individuation is a ripening vision about life, not a psychedelic escape from it! Individuation is also the synthesis of the universal and particular—and in that sense the solution of the great Western philosophical question of whether the universal category is really real (as in Plato) or whether the particular entity is really real (as in Aristotle). Nature's answer, according to Jung, is that *both* are really real in the form of the individuated creature—and that the individuated human being is the most morally real of all.

Again, we must bear in mind Jung's fundamental assumption that a phenomenon's importance does not basically lie in its past history but in its future possibility. Jung's psychology is teleologically oriented through and through, *prospective* at every turn. Thus, Jung agreed with the Jesuit paleontologist Teillhard de Chardin that the human being, although evolved from primal dust, was being shaped into a being of eternal consequence, stature, and durability. What began as an amoeba would end up as an angel. *Per aspera ad astram!* This makes individuation a moral and spiritual imperative for every human being. Indeed, Jung even speculated that it is God himself who lays the imperative to individuate upon every creature, but most particularly and dramatically upon man (Jung, 1968b). It is in this sense that, as Jaffé has put it, "individuation has to be understood as the realization of the 'divine' in man" (1975, p. 9). The idea of individuation reflects Jung's essentially optimistic, spiritual view of humanity and the cosmos, which is why Homans (1979) has said that Jung's work is a "hermeneutics of affirmation" as opposed to Freud's "hermeneutics of suspicion" (Ricoeur, 1976).

Yet, in another sense—and one that is peculiar to man—individuation is *not* a natural process at all. It is, in fact, an *opus contra naturam*, a "work against nature," as Jung was fond of saying. By this, Jung did not mean to imply that human individuation can in any sense ever be seen as perverse. He simply wanted to stress that human individuation requires such heroic moral effort, unwavering commitment to inner exploration, and such hard-won psychospiritual clarity that the natural man with his "natural aims" resists it, much preferring the easier paths of dullness or decadence, the safer road of spiritless "normalcy." Individuation should not conjure up in us the image of some sort of blessed finality, of the autumnal serenity of the quiet old one as she drowsily sits by a dying fire, taking long soporific draughts off of her cup of accumulated wisdom. "Individuation is not, in Jung's view, an elimination of conflict, more an increased consciousness of it, and of its potential" (Samuels, 1997, p. 103).

Jung believed in a natural aristocracy—one that has nothing to do with cultural privilege, socio-economic station, or even "intelligence" as our schools are forced to narrowly define that term.

> The possibility of psychic development...is not reserved for specially gifted individuals. In other words, in order to undergo a far-reaching psychological development, neither outstanding intelligence nor any other talent is necessary, since in this development moral qualities can make up for intellectual shortcomings. It must not on any account be imagined that the treatment consists in grafting upon people's minds general formulas and complicated doctrines. There is no question of that. Each can take what he needs, in his own way and in his own language. (Jung, 1953, pp. 116–117)

Of course, the educational implications of this notion are immense, as is shown in the succeeding chapters.

Individuation: Towards a psychology of the spirit

In one sense, individuation is similar to Maslow's (1968) idea of "self-actualization," Sartre's (1956) notion of creating oneself in freedom and good faith, and Kohut's (1978) idea that each individual has embedded in her a unique "nuclear program" which she must discover and live out in order to enjoy optimal creativity and psychological health. On the other hand, Jung's idea of individuation reached for more than just this. A comparison with the growth of Maslow's theory of the psyche is instructive here.

Maslow's researches ultimately went beyond the realm of personal "self-actualization" into the transpersonal. He concluded near the end of his career that a person never could fully actualize if she did not find something greater than herself to love, something that would provide her with a principled basis from which to serve others, a transpersonal reality that gave her life ultimate meaning. Above and beyond the personalistic needs of self-actualization (which he had previously seen as the highest stage of psychic development), Maslow began to insist upon a fundamental, inborn human need to go beyond oneself; to make psychological contact with "the naturalistically transcendent, spiritual, and axiological" (1968, p. vi).

He called this religion with a little "r" since it does not require commitment to a specific religious doctrine. This form of "religion" — which Maslow felt could and should figure prominently in both the consulting room and the classroom — is

> transpersonal, transhuman, centered in the cosmos rather than in human needs and interest, going beyond humanness, identity, self-actualization, and the like.... Without the transpersonal, we get sick, violent, and nihilistic, or else hopeless and apathetic. (1968, pp. iii–iv).

Jungian individuation is precisely what Maslow meant by religion with a little "r." As such, individuation is a personal, even sacred, process that in some senses defies discussion or description. Yet, if Jungian psychology is to be of any practical use and theoretical interest, it cannot stand mute in the face of this mystery. It must say something about it, and it must do so in terms that are as valid, precise, and systematic as possible.

Jung wrote that a fundamental "aim of individuation is nothing less than to divest the self of the false wrappings of the persona..." (1953, p. 174). As we have seen, this does not mean the obliteration of the entire persona, just the false part, for even the individuated person remains a social being who must operate in varying social situations, and this will always entail some degree of persona functioning. What it does mean, however, is that the individual's personas are purified of the dross of self-serving falseness. What remains are personas that more accurately reflect the essential moral nature of the person who is wearing them.

This greater congruence between the person's essence and her social presence heightens the energy and authenticity of any social interaction in which an individuated person is present. What is more, a charismatic character often finds herself put into leadership positions in groups, sometimes even against her will, because others sense the psychospiritual wisdom that informs her persona. She becomes what Jung called "a mana personality" (1953, p. 151).[5] In many First Nation cultures, the primal energy of mana or its equivalent is thought to invest certain persons with special spiritual power that makes them most suitable as leaders (Eliade, 1954). Hence, "the mana-personality...will be... the Self of the group, its creative center, and it will be from him in his capacity as a leader and creator that the collective will receive its values" (Neumann, 1973, p. 61). A leader with charisma is the same thing as one with mana. In the following chapters both the perils and possibilities of being a mana-teacher are explored.

We already looked at the shadow in considerable depth in Chapter 2. Here it will suffice to touch lightly upon the concept as it relates to the process of individuation. Individuation means maturation, and it is impossible to be mature if a person has not looked honestly at her own shadow. Not doing so, she will live in a series of antiseptic illusions about herself. Until a person has frankly examined those parts of herself which she had formerly discarded—acknowledging the bad elements for what they are and resurrecting the potentially good elements for what they may become—she will never be complete. Indeed, she will project those parts onto other people in ways that are both psychologically and morally toxic. Doing one's shadow-work in therapy is an essential step in the individuation process. It also has multifarious educational implications, as shown in the succeeding chapters.

Individuation also entails understanding and interacting with one's *anima*. With the idea of the anima we come across a new and centrally important concept in Jungian psychology. The term is Latin, the feminine form of the word for soul. The masculine form of the word is *animus*. In Jungian psychology, it is the feminine anima that is most important for men, whereas for women it is the masculine animus that plays an important role in psychological functioning. If we choose to imagine the psyche as a landscape, the misty land of the anima lies just beyond the valley of the shadow (Jung, 1963, pp. 125–126). She stands on the threshold of the collective unconscious, beckoning the individual

---

5 We are speaking of mana personalities in a positive sense here. However, Jung (as did Freud before him in his own inquiries into group psychology) was quick to add that some mana personalities, not having healthily integrated archetypal energy but merely being possessed by it, can exert fanatical sway over a group. Hitler, of course, is a prime example of someone who psychotically embodied an archetype (the Germanic warrior-god of the forest, Wotan) in a way that both reflected and contributed to the mass psychosis of an entire people. (See Jung's essay "Wotan," 1964, pp. 179–193.)

into the deeper mysteries of psyche in particular and life in general. Perhaps that is why the anima-function is symbolized in the psyche by a figure from the opposite sex. Woman will always be the great enigma for man—primally attractive, promising both delight and dilemma, and man will always serve the same function for woman. Little wonder, then, that in the economy of psychological symbolism, it is a contrasexual figure who stands for the multivalent, enchanting pull of the collective unconscious upon the galvanized consciousness. When the anima and animus appear in dreams, it is as a woman to the male and a man to the female. Of course, contrasexual figures in dreams may have erotic significance. However, we must always be open to the possibility that such figures simultaneously have a more transcendent significance, that they are pointing the dreamer the way to the profound psychological and moral truths that live, move and have their being in the realm of the collective unconscious.

As the archetypes draw the individual into his or her psychic and moral depths, the anima (for the man) and animus (for the woman) can—and indeed must—be recognized and honored by their "effects," which "can be made conscious" although the anima and animus, being archetypes, "[exceed] the limits of consciousness and [are] therefore... never...the object[s] of direct cognition" (Jung, 1963, pp. 125–126). These "effects" are the appearance in our dreams, fantasies, and waking experiences of anima/animus characters who greatly attract us and seem to be pulling us into the centrifugal influence of an ever widening mystery. Attending to those figures, attempting to understand as clearly as possible what they are symbolizing about how to grasp and live our lives with deepest significance, and then acting upon that knowledge in freedom, responsibility, and courage—all of this is what it means to make the anima/animus "conscious" so that it can be one's personal guide on the road to individuation. Whereas youth will almost inevitably project anima/animus images upon influential others (as shown in the following chapters, teachers are often the targets of such projections!) it is crucial that the individuating adult withdraw those projections and find his or her own inner spouse to accompany him or her on the road through the dense forest of aging to the Holy Grail of individuation.

Learning how to integrate one's contrasexual elements without forfeiting one's primary gender identity is a major requirement of individuation in Jung's conservative view. The man must find and honor his inner female, the woman her inner male. There must be an inner marriage (Dourley, 1987). Called the *mysterium coniunctionis,* or "mystical union," it symbolized the internal joining of the male and female principles. Jung called this psychic synthesis of the male and female principles a *syzygy,* borrowing a term from the medieval theologian St. Abelard. Jung saw the syzygy symbolized in religious texts, doctrines, and practices throughout history—the incestuous marriage of the brother-prince and sister-princess in ancient Egypt; the synthesis of the masculine principle of yang and the female principle of yin in Taoism; the spiritual seeker's quest for the Divine Beloved in Yoga and Sufism; and the mystical marriage of Christ and his bride, the Church, in Christianity (Jung, 1944).

Learning how to reconcile opposites in general is an indispensable part of individuation. This process requires seeing what is of value in seemingly conflicting points of view—and then uniting those points of view in a higher perspective. Youthful folly would bifurcate life into a series of black and white choices, but wisdom consists in discovering a higher middle-ground that not only balances extreme positions but forges a more mature synthesis out of them—a "third," as Jung often called it, which, because it goes beyond the entrenched terms of the two opposing positions, often takes on the form of a reconciling symbol. Jung named this ability to generate a higher third out of paired opposites the transcendent function (Jung, 1953, p. 80). In Trinitarian religions (both Eastern and Western), in the proliferation of triangular shapes in various cultural and artistic products, and in the appearance of narrative "triangles" in dreams, Jung saw symbolic evidence of the universality of the transcendent function.

Jung was drawn to Eastern thought because he felt it grasped—in ways that Western philosophy had never really done—how both psyche and cosmos rested on the peaceful reconciliation of opposites. Nor, felt Jung, had Western philosophy—with its passion for binary logic—sufficiently honored the fact that, given enough time, all things ultimately turn into their opposites. Jung was fascinated with this principle, *enantiodromia,* by which all things revert into their opposites in order to find a higher synthesis. The "union of opposites through the middle path" has great therapeutic and educational possibilities, Jung felt, for "wisdom never forgets that all things have two sides..." (1963, p. 334). The realization that every question has two sides, that each side (given enough time) will turn into its opposite, and that both sides must ultimately be reconciled in a higher vision and union, is the basis of tolerance and humility—and the heart of individuation. It is also the basis of a truly humane education.

The centrality of symbols in the individuation process

Since Jung saw symbols as the essential tools of the transcendent function, we must ask, "What is a symbol, according to Jung?" It is "the best possible expression for something that cannot be expressed otherwise than by a more or less close analogy" (Jung, 1921, p. 63, n. 44). Referring to a reality beyond the grasp of mere conscious logic, a symbol is an intuitive window into the transrational essence of the personal subconscious and collective unconscious.[6] As such,

> the symbol is the primitive exponent of the unconscious, but at the same time an idea that corresponds to the highest intuition of the conscious mind. (Jung, 1978, p. 44)

It is not enough merely to analyze our symbols (as in Freudian psychology). We must engage in a living interaction and dialogue with them in dreams, art, myth, religion, and education. Doing so is indispensable in the individuation process, which, as a transpersonal and transrational process (although never an impersonal or irrational one), must rely on symbols to access and express those deeper and higher realities than the merely propositional language of syllogistic discourse could ever understand or articulate (Jung, 1968a, pp. 157–158). St. Paul's description of the word of God also describes the power of the symbol, for both the divine word and the symbol are

> quick and powerful, and sharper than any two-edged sword, piercing even to the dividing asunder of soul and spirit, and of the joints and marrow..., a discerner of the thoughts and intents of the heart. (Hebrews 4: 12)

Indeed, some theologians see in the Jungian project of individuation some similarities to the religious one of the individual's unique unifica-

---

6 The prefixes sub- and un- in "personal subconscious" and "collective unconscious" do not mean that these psychic realities are less than ego consciousness but rather that they lie beyond the limits of ego consciousness. Rudolf Steiner, the founder of anthroposophy, indicated this in naming these two domains the personal subconscious and the transpersonal supraconscious, respectively (Wehr, 2002). I feel that this is a more accurate way of characterizing these two domains. Nevertheless, I retain Jung's terminology.

tion with the Spirit of Christ or Buddha Nature (Clift, 1982; Ulanov, 1999).[7]

Due to its complexity and transcendental potential, a symbol should never be confused with a mere sign—a difference that Jung was often at pains to clarify. A sign is just an arbitrary token that mechanically stands for something else in a one-to-one correspondence.

Through a symbol, however, we experience a complex spiritual reality not only in the best way possible but, indeed, in the only way possible. That is why symbols are not just an epistemological "fall-back" position when the language of logic fails. Rather, symbols are the highest epistemological road we can take to truly touch the mystery of life in its archetypal richness.

Given the central role of symbols in Jungian therapy, it should not be surprising that art often plays a role that is every bit as important as conversation and dream analysis. Jung put such a premium upon both the production and appreciation of art in the individuation process be-

---

7 The question "Was Jung religious?" is a complex one in Jungian scholarship. Some argue that Jung was essentially religious, that the archetype of the Self is an imago Dei (as Jung himself often called it)—that is, the "image of God" in the human psyche owing to its completeness, robustness, profundity, and moral grandeur. By this view, the Self is that part of man that God made "in his own image."

There are many other scholars, however, who, while agreeing that Jung was trying to define a "religious psychology," maintain that he actually did both religion and psychology harm by trying to make psychology too "mystical" and religion too "psychological," thus compromising the fundamental identity and power of each. And yet others see the whole question of Jung's possible religiosity as either irrelevant or unanswerable since Jung straddled religion and psychology in so many different and idiosyncratic ways throughout his career, defining a very unique space that fuses religion and psychology, that what he ultimately came up with is not "reducible" to either.

This latter position is probably the dominant one in the Jungian literature—and the one that tends to be held by most of the first-generation Jungians who personally studied under Jung. Each of these positions undoubtedly contains some truth, since the way in which Jung speaks and writes about the relationship of the Self to God understandably varies. Much depends on the audience he is addressing and the context in which he is addressing them (Is he writing a letter to a clergyman, addressing a scholarly audience in an academic piece, or speaking to a group of psychiatrists at a medical conference?), the particular question that he is trying to answer (Does it have to do with a personal, clinical, historical, or philosophical issue?), and the phase of his career from which the characterization is taken (his earlier phase being more strictly medical, his middle phase more "existential," and his last phase more "religious"). The reader who is interested in pursuing the complex topic of Jung's "religiosity" should begin with the following sources: Chapman, 1988; Clift, 1982; Dourley, 1984; Edinger, 1985; Homans, 1985; Kelsey, 1984; Mayes, 2005a; Neumann, 1973; Odajnyk, 1993; Palmer, 1997; Stein, 1982; Ulanov, 1999; Wehr, 2002; White, 1982 [1952].

cause "the great secret of art...and the creative process consists in the unconscious activation of an archetypal image, and in elaborating and shaping this image into the finished work. By giving it shape, the artist translates it into the language of the present, and so makes it possible for us to find the way back to the deepest springs of life..." (1966, p. 82). This does not mean that the individuating person needs to be an artist. It does mean, however, that she needs to find ways to grasp and enact the archetypal wisdom that is embedded in the symbols produced in her dreams, fantasies, and her own creations. Jung's view of the crucial psychospiritual importance of the symbol forms a principled basis for a critique of the present marginalization of art and intuition in public education—a point examined herein.

The great problem of "modern man in search of a soul," Jung often declared, was that we live in a personal and cultural drought of meaningful symbols to energize and organize our spiritually adrift lives. "Now, we have no symbolic life," said Jung, in a conversation with a group of British psychiatrists,

> and we are all badly in need of the symbolic life. Only the symbolic life can express the soul—the daily need of the soul, mind you! And because people have no such thing, they can never step out of this mill—this awful, grinding, banal life in which they are "nothing but."... [T]here is no symbolic existence in which I am something else, in which I am fulfilling my role, my role as one of the actors in the divine drama of life.... That gives the only meaning to human life. That gives peace, when people feel that they are living the symbolic life, that they are actors in the divine drama.... [E]verything else is banal and you can dismiss it. (1954c, pp. 274–275)

The Jungian view of symbols has interested many of those scholars, artists, and theologians over the last century who believe that (post)modern culture has become spiritually arid—"desacralized" (Berger, 1967). Looking for ways to "resacralize" it, many of these thinkers and cultural workers have concluded that this can best be done by promoting personal and collective discovery of the archetypal realm.

The politics of individuation

Jung is sometimes accused of having been apolitical. But this charge is untrue. Jung had little patience with any approach, either philosophical or psychological, that was "too personal," that "exclude[s] [a person] from human society," for such an attitude is "obviously wrong" (1954a, p. 46). A person cannot know herself—and what is individuation but knowing oneself?—without knowing herself through others, in their responses to her and her responses to them. In fact, she must not only know others, she must know herself as others in her shared humanity with them, and for others in ever deepening compassion and service toward them.

Furthermore, Jung insisted that one cannot really know a person without knowing her culture and the archetypal wisdom upon which it rests. Thus, Jung's studies throughout his career focused on the psychospiritual wisdom of a very wide range of cultures—many of which he personally visited—from the Elgonyi of Africa to the Pueblo Indians of New Mexico.

The perennial wisdom of First Nations became integral to his evolving understanding of the psyche. More than any other psychologist in the first half of the 20th century, Jung set the stage for the emergence of a truly "multicultural psychology" (Adams, 1996) through an archetypal approach to social issues in general.[8] The implications of this approach for multiculturalism in education have not even begun to be explored and could form the basis for many scholarly articles, dissertations, and books (Mayes et al., 2007).

Indeed, Jung's vision was very political. However, in his insistence that the individual and her psychological integrity should be the ultimate standard in judging the validity of a political movement or theory, Jung clearly was bucking the tide of collectivism that characterized the politics of the 20th century, whether that collectivism manifested itself most clearly and despicably in the form of Soviet communism or in the

---

8 However, see Lasch (1995) and Rieff (1987) for the argument that the movements toward a therapeutic culture ultimately stem from and further the disintegration of traditional values and institutions. According to Lasch and Rieff, therapy represents a narcissistic preoccupation with the individual's subjectivity. In short, by this view, the widespread movement towards therapy signals the decline of Western culture, the abdication of personal ethical responsibility, the "psychologization" of what are essentially moral problems, and the rise of a ubiquitous "Me-ism." See Giddens (1990, 1991) for a counter-argument with which I personally agree.

form of a corporate capitalism that produced the soulless "organization man." Having witnessed the world torn asunder by two world wars, Jung had no illusions about merely political solutions, whether touted by the Right or Left. By themselves, he did not believe that they would ever lead to a good society filled with psychologically and morally healthy citizens.

For all that, Jung was a revolutionary—but not the sort that was ever bound to win the approval of ideologues of any political stripe. "Every individual needs revolution," Jung wrote,

> inner division, overthrow of the existing order, and renewal, but not by forcing them upon his neighbors under the hypocritical cloak of Christian love or the sense of social responsibility or any of the other beautiful euphemisms for unconscious urges to personal power. Individual self-reflection, return of the individual to the ground of human nature, to his own deepest being with its individual and social destiny—here is the beginning of a cure for that blindness which reigns at the present hour. (1953, p. 5)

Jung's political message was very much the same as that delivered by every major religion: true reform of society begins with reform of oneself. Jung never said that we should not always be in search of ways to make a better society. Indeed, he and Freud were the first 20th-century psychologists to recognize the political dimensions of many neuroses and the neurotic characteristics of many governments (Freud, 1939; Jung, 1953). Jung understood the need for social engagement in the holistic psychological and moral economy of the human spirit. Jung's vision of individuation entailed "a clarification of one's roles and responsibilities as a citizen, not a flight from them" (Chapman, 1988, p. 80). However, he condemned the collectivist person who neglected her own inner development. And he also had harsh words for the self-absorbed rich, who suffered from an underdeveloped sense of social responsibility—what he called "atrophied collective adaptation" (1954a, p. 7).

Jung's constant theme was simply that our starting point must be the recognition that "all culture begin[s] with the individual..." (1953, p. 205). Society exists for the individual, not vice versa. Indeed, "it is...ludicrous to say that the individual lives for society. 'Society' is nothing more than a term, a concept for the symbiosis of a group of human beings. A concept is not a carrier of life. The sole and natural carrier of life is the individual, and that is so throughout nature" (1954a, p. 106).[9] Let us by all means strive to create a moral society, said Jung, but let us always remember first that "morality...rests entirely on the moral sense of the individual and the freedom necessary for this" (1953, p. 153). This requires that any program for political and educational improvement must, above all, grant privileged status and "special attention...to this delicate plant 'individuality' if it is not to be completely smothered" (1953, p. 155). Hence, Jung's was ever a voice of warning against losing ourselves, individually and collectively, in any sort of "-ism." Every educational or political reform must be weighed against the danger of turning the student or citizen into a "mass man" or "mass woman" (1954b, p. 48).

It is wrong to accuse Jung of apoliticism in light of his firm belief that each person is by definition a world-historical being, a socio-cultural creature, who bears "his whole history with him. In [each person's] very structure is written the history of mankind. This historical element in man represents a vital need to which a wise psychic economy must respond. Somehow the past must come alive and participate in the present" (Jung, 1921, p. 338). As we saw earlier in examining Campbell's Hero's myth, the enlightened hero—if he is to fully realize his heroic fate—must return to society to share his saving wisdom with his family and society. "Individuation and initiation each have a social component.... Self realization must become fruitful in the social realm" (Wehr, 2002, p. 259).

Another political aspect of Jungian psychology has to do with his insistence that individuation requires the withdrawal of projections. Jung came to believe in the existence of national, cultural, and racial psyches—all of which naturally have their shadow sides. "We are white and industrious, but they are dark and lazy"; "we are dedicated to science and human betterment, but they are superstitious, sensual, and greedy"; "we represent cultural evolution, they want to return to the darkness of the jungle." In this dynamic of exteriorization, a cultural or national shadow is "transferred to the outside world and experienced as an outside object. It is combated, punished, and exterminated as 'the alien out there' instead of being dealt with as one's own 'inner problem'" (Neumann, 1973, p. 50). Until such collective shadow projec-

---

9 See also Berger (1967) and Greeley (1974) on the modern movement towards individualistic spirituality in contemporary Western culture.

tions are extracted from the individual breast one by one, they will be projected upon other nations, cultures, and races—with terrible consequences (Jung, 1964). The projection of such collective shadows is the major cause of intolerance, racism, and war—more important than merely economic or political factors, Jung said. The alien or enemy is first dehumanized and then physically obliterated, which is why "no war can be waged unless the enemy can be converted into the carrier of a shadow projection" (Neumann, 1973, pp. 57–58). Helping students learn to recognize and withdraw such projections is a fundamental goal for any Jungian-oriented pedagogy that wishes to promote peace.

Individuation across the lifespan

Jung said that the individuation process should not start any earlier than around 35 years of age. Only at mid-life, said Jung, does a person have enough control over her ego functions and enough experience of life to discover and practice its archetypal truths. Only then is one able to control and reconcile the opposing poles of ego and archetype and not be consumed by either one of them. Naturally, a person with some substantial experience of life—the kind one has usually garnered by midlife—can engage in the individuation process with a maximum degree of maturity. However, is it necessarily true that midlife is a kind of magical threshold and that before reaching it, it is simply impossible to individuate in any way or to any degree? Various neo-Jungians have begun to doubt this.

After all, individuation is the search to be all that one can be, to realize one's unique identity in the context of one's shared humanity. Although this search will usually yield its best fruits in the second half of life, it seems to me undeniable that it can, and does, occur in the first half of life as well.

Indeed, even something as basic as the child's ongoing separation from her mother in the first years of its life can itself be seen as the first necessary step on the journey to the discovery of oneself as a unique being—and could therefore be construed as a sort of proto-individuation. This is the view of the noted pediatrician and Jungian child psychotherapist Michael Fordham (1994). For instance, in the famous good-breast/bad-breast dichotomy, Fordham sees the infant starting to confront the fact that every archetypal reality has a light and dark side. Later on, as the child's fantasies become more organized and she develops the language to speak about them, it is possible to see in her fantasies a variety of archetypal themes and images that are struggling to find individuated form and expression (Fordham, 1994, p. 73). "The need to construct (or discover) the self is widespread and need not be confined to the second half of life," for "individuation is a continuous process throughout life" (Fordham, 1994, pp. 15, 50). Consider, for example, the adolescent's hero/heroine journey. Where an individual is passing through an archetypal pattern of experience in order to achieve greater self awareness and social usefulness, do we not have, by definition, an instance of individuation?

Samuels (1997) offers a handy solution to this controversy in Jungian psychology. He notes that there are really three senses in which we can use the term individuation: (1) as an ongoing process that occurs with increasing degrees of self-awareness over the entire lifespan but that occurs in a more limited fashion in the first half of life; (2) a process that for some people naturally seems to emerge with a special type of clarity, urgency, and potency in the second half of life, usually after an initiating crisis; and (3) a process that a person can volitionally initiate and strategically pursue in the course of formal therapy at various points in her life. Fordham and his associates are clearly talking about individuation in the first sense, whereas Jungian traditionalists are referring to the second and third meanings of the term. In the educational applications of Jungian theory that follow, I draw upon all three senses of the term.

CHAPTER FOUR

NEW HORIZONS IN ARCHETYPAL PEDAGOGY

INTRODUCTION

In this chapter, some of the major pedagogical implications of Jungian psychology are examined.

The first set of implications in Part 1 of this chapter, "Archetypal Reflectivity," revolves around the idea that the teacher–student relationship is fundamentally an archetypal one. I look at several archetypes of the teacher—with special reference to archetypal transference and counter-transference—to lay the groundwork for the more intensive exercises in "archetypal reflectivity" about oneself as a teacher in Chapters 5, 6, and 7.

The issues discussed in Part 2, "Eve, *Eros,* and Education," stem from the assumption that archetypally feminine modes of seeing, being, and acting in the world are not adequately honored (and sometimes not even considered) in American educational theory and practice—at least from the middle-school years on. Here, I speculate about what it would mean if we allowed the archetypally feminine perspective of *Eros* to have equal sway in our theory and practice with the archetypally masculine perspective of *Logos* that presently prevails.

Finally, in Part 3, "Teaching in the Spirit," I suggest ways in which an archetypally sensitive pedagogy may provide important clues about how the public school classroom in a pluralistic society may become a site of lively conversation and mutual respect regarding cultural and spiritual commitments and questions.

Part 1: Archetypal Reflectivity

In the last several decades, there has been a small but growing movement in teacher education programs in colleges of education to encourage students to reflect deeply upon the psychological and political factors that have figured into their decision to become educators. Those factors underlie their sense of calling. Special focus is usually placed on how psychological, cultural, and political factors affect one's internal images of "good teaching" and classroom practices (Bullough & Gitlin, 1995; Mayes & Blackwell-Mayes, 2002; McLaren, 1998; Pajak, 2003). The goal of such reflectivity is to help teachers achieve greater self-awareness, leading to greater emotional fulfillment and political efficacy in their work. The prospective teacher who is reflecting biographically or politically on her sense of calling as a teacher is really posing to herself various questions regarding the internal and external forces that have led her to want to be a school person—and how those forces shape the way she teaches.

For instance, in what I (Mayes, 2001) have called "biographical reflectivity," a prospective teacher reflects on issues that revolve around such topics as the following: What personal needs, wounds, hopes, abilities, and fears played into my decision to become a teacher? How are these dynamics and needs getting addressed and expressed in my classroom? Are they changing as I develop as a teacher? Is my development as a teacher affecting them? Are they benefiting me and my students—or are they ever destructive or inappropriate? Looking at the period of my life when I decided to become a teacher, how did the developmental challenges and potentials of that period figure into that decision as well as into my idea of what a good teacher is? How do my current life-stage issues figure into my sense of calling and classroom practice?

Biographical reflectivity often centers on people who have played a role in one's decision to become a teacher. Such people might be called "pedagogical selfobjects" in Kohutian terms, for it is in relationship with them that one has learned to define oneself as a teacher. The questions to spur reflectivity along these lines would include the following: Was there a person or set of persons who were particularly influential in my decision to teach? What was the nature of my relationship with those individuals? Were the relationships open-ended and empowering or were they filled with guilt or fear? For instance, did I have a teacher whose positive example stimulated me to be a teacher? Why does that example resonate so deeply with me—that is, what does it tell me about who I fundamentally am, what I fundamentally value, and how I plan to bring all of that to my own students? Do I need to revisit any of those values in light of my greater maturity at this stage in life—either further cultivating them, modifying them in light of some other insight I have gained, or even rejecting them now in favor of a higher wisdom that I have gained?

On the other hand, did I have a teacher whose negative example prompted me to want to become a teacher in order to "get right" what she had gotten so wrong? Why was her way of teaching so offensive to me? Did it relate to other psychodynamic issues in my life at the time? Was I perhaps projecting part of my own shadow onto her so as not to have to confront a problem of my own? Do I still find her approach to teaching as wrong now as I did then, or do I see it in a somewhat or even very different light now—one that might make me more sympathetic to her and that might even allow me to incorporate elements of her example that are, in fact, healthy and useful but that I have not allowed to be part of my self-image and practice as a teacher because of my resistance to her?

Biographical reflectivity—typically in the form of journal work, group processing, and contemplative techniques—provides a way to approach these questions (Mayes, 1998, 1999, 2001, 2004) and thus answers the call issued by the psychoanalysts whom we studied in Chapter 1 for teachers to examine the psychodynamic determinants of why they became teachers and how they teach.

Biographical reflectivity is very useful in encouraging the teacher to deepen her sense of calling and refine her practice. However, by itself biographical reflectivity, built upon psychoanalytic foundations, does not typically go very far beyond the merely personal domains of the psyche. There also needs to be "archetypal reflectivity" in which teachers consider their calling and practice in the psychospiritual terms provided by Jungian psychology. Chapters 5, 6, and 7, in which I reflect upon my own practice and also help other teachers reflect upon theirs, offer concrete examples of archetypal reflectivity that the reader can use to spur on her own reflectivity either individually or with other teachers. In this chapter, I lay a foundation for those specific exercises in archetypal reflectivity with a general discussion of the archetypal nature of the teacher–student relationship.

THE ARCHETYPAL NATURE OF THE STUDENT–TEACHER RELATIONSHIP

It is impossible to picture the life of an individual or a culture without those innumerable acts of teaching and learning that shape our lives at virtually every point. From the cradle to the grave, our lives are one learning situation after another. Some of it happens in schools, although far from all of it does.

For instance, Winnicott speaks of "the nursing couple," referring not only to the mother teaching the infant the primal facts of feeding and, thereby, the elemental dynamics of relationship, but also the infant, through acceptance or rejection of mother's ways of relating to him, teaching *her* how to be a mother. At the other end of the spectrum, when we die, we do so with more or less grace, depending on how well we have learned about dying from the deaths of others, whose courage and humor or hopelessness and fear have taught us about the mechanics of mortality. From our first to last breaths, we are teachers and learners. Something that is so deeply woven into who we are, how we grow, and what we may become is, in its very essence, archetypal. Whenever someone teaches and someone else learns, an archetypal situation is constellated.

This is surely why Jung was against any educational practice that did not honor the inherent sanctity of the teacher–pupil relationship. This is not to say that education may never be technical and instrumental. Of course it may be—and sometimes must be. But when an individual or a society has so lost touch with the archetypal roots of the educational act that it can frame it *only* or even just *primarily* in technical and instrumental terms, then teaching and learning cease to be moral endeavors—and degenerate into the mindless motions of automata outputting or inputting information at the will of some invisible governing elite or other. Education, to be real, must constantly aim at confirming and deepening the individual in her unique identity and perspectives, not serve as a tool for objectifying the many in the service of the socio-economically privileged few.

One senses just this danger in such widely influential documents as *A Nation at Risk,* which, with an Orwellian touch of poetic justice, came out on the eve of 1984. It set the tone for other federal educational "reform" documents in its stingy insistence that "the basic purposes of schooling" must be the reestablishment of America's "once unchallenged preeminence in commerce, industry, science, and technological innovation" (*A Nation at Risk,* 1983, p. 5). By this military–industrial view, education ceases to be an ethical exploration in psychospiritual growth and democratic empowerment—and becomes instead an instrument of empire-building in crude pedagogical disguise. We might well fear at such a juncture that Lawrence Cremin's (1988) grim prophecy had already come true—namely, that the military-industrial complex would become a military–industrial–*educational* complex. Or as Jung observed, "it cannot be the aim of education to turn out rationalists, materialists, specialists, technicians, and others of the kind who, unconscious of their origins, are precipitated abruptly into the present and contribute to the disorientation and fragmentation of society" (in Frey-Rohn, 1974, p. 182). "Man is not a machine that can be remodeled...as occasion demands, in the hope that it will go on functioning as regularly as before but in a quite different way. Man carries his whole history with him; in his very structure is written the history of mankind" (Jung, 1921, p. 338).

ARCHETYPAL TRANSFERENCE
AND COUNTER-TRANSFERENCE IN THE CLASSROOM

Reflecting upon one's practice in terms of selfobject as well as archetypal psychology inevitably involves considering both the positive and negative elements of students' transferences onto oneself as a teacher and one's own counter-transferences back onto them. Some of my own experiences as a teacher might help to illustrate this point.

I teach at a conservative religious university where I share my students' faith but often do not share their politics, mine having been shaped in the 1960s, well before I was a member of our church. My left-of-center approach to the history and purposes of United States public education almost invariably elicits shadow projections from many students, particularly my undergraduate students, who, confusing political conservatism with moral virtue, see in my cultural liberalism not only as an ideological threat but potentially a spiritual one. Understanding the archetypal transferences at play in these cases in my classroom makes it easier for me to process and manage them more effectively and sensitively—and to do so in a manner that is of greatest benefit to my students while also protecting my own emotional space. What is going on in such cases is not really a personal issue between me and my students (although they may initially think it is) and not even primarily a political one. It is fundamentally a psychospiritual one. What is essentially at stake is not *my* politics but *their* archetypal hero's or heroine's journey.

In the archetypal hero's journey, the first person whom the hero or heroine often meets after he or she enters the archetypal forest-of-trials—i.e., passes the "threshold of initiation"—is the sorcerer or trickster. These are seductive characters. Their blandishments and entreaties are fraught with danger. They are masters of mischief, archetypal shadow figures who elicit the students' own shadows, and for that reason are often perceived as negative. However, they are also positive, even indispensable, characters in the hero or heroine's journey because they serve the function of luring the young novitiates into the road of psychospiritual experience—and thus down the path of psychospiritual growth. It is not surprising, then, that my younger students (and sometimes even my older ones), entering the path of a heroic confrontation with new, strange, and even unsettling ideas every time they step through the door of my classroom, sometimes see me as a sorcerer or trickster. I am a projection of their shadows.

Probably very few teachers have ever thought of themselves as projections of their students' shadowy fears about unexplored possibilities in themselves and in the world. However, every teacher who has ever forwarded a fact or proposed a theory in class that forces a student out of some comfortable but wrong preconceptions knows how it feels to be the sudden object of some student's suspicion or even rage. Whereas previously the teacher may have experienced only sunshine and smiles from that student, now sultry rain clouds seem to swirl ominously around the student's head and then shoot toward the teacher's desk like a dark missile. Knowing how all of this operates at both the personal and archetypal levels—indeed, simply knowing *that* it is happening—can help the teacher understand (and, in understanding, healthily endure) the student's otherwise hurtful projections. It can provide the teacher with a wise equanimity that will allow her to move her student, and indeed her whole class, onto higher intellectual, emotional, and moral ground.

A student will sometimes also project onto a teacher the archetypal figure of the Wise Old Man or Woman—other important characters whom the Hero and Heroine meet in their journey. Jung felt that these Wise Old Ones who appear so often in dreams, myths, and fantasies "personify meaning" (1963, p. 233)—meaning that goes beyond the little lessons of the workaday world. The meanings that the Wise Elders bear are of a higher intellectual and moral order. The Wise Ones are the harbingers of archetypal truths. Jung thus characterizes them as "an archetype of the 'spirit'" (1956, p. 437). Their amulets, tokens, and incantations are instruments and symbols of the spiritual messages that they are bestowing upon the young Hero and Heroine in search of the right path. "The old man knows what roads lead to the goal and points them out to the hero. He warns of dangers to come and supplies the means of meeting them effectively" (1968a, p. 221). The Wise Old Man and Woman typically assume the role of a "guru..., magician, doctor, priest [or priestess], teacher, professor." The Wise Old Man and Woman are essentially pedagogical archetypes (1968a, pp. 215–217).

However, most teachers would have to admit (as I certainly do!) that students sometimes admire, even revere us more than our all-too-human limitations really merit—especially when we come impressively bedecked with advanced degrees, tenure, and publications that dazzle our young novitiates. Understanding that a student's Wise Elder projections onto oneself as a teacher are often archetypal and may have little to do with oneself personally can help a teacher not overestimate her actual degree of competence and knowledge in her field of expertise. In classical Jungian terms, realizing that one is the object of an archetypal projection can prevent psychic inflation and help one realistically assess what her abilities and limits as a teacher and scholar truly are. In this way, the teacher can be of the greatest service to her students emotionally, ethically, and academically. Failing this, the teacher may too easily become puffed up with a false sense of competence. She will create an unreal bubble of self-importance around herself that, sooner or later in the course of the term, must be burst by a question to which she does not know the answer, a situation that she cannot handle, or a student's cunning challenge to her shaky sense of superiority.

THE ARCHETYPE OF THE GREAT MOTHER: THE USES AND MISUSES OF THE COUNTER-TRANSFERENCE

As mentioned in Chapter 1, transferences can be either positive or negative—that is, either *syntonic* or *dystonic*. A syntonic transference, according to Freud, is "the transference of affectionate feelings" from patient to doctor, whereas a dystonic transference is the transference of "hostile" feelings (1990, p. 32). A student's transferences onto a teacher may also be syntonic or dystonic. Similarly, a teacher's counter-transference onto a student can be either syntonic or dystonic. Let us look in a bit more depth at syntonic and dystonic transference and counter-transference at the archetypal level in the classroom by focusing on an archetype that operates with particular frequency and intensity in many classrooms. This is the archetype of the Great Mother. It is an archetype which a teacher can consciously cultivate in herself and productively use with her students in a syntonic counter-transference onto those students. However, if the teacher becomes possessed by the archetype, it can cause a dystonic inflation in her, leading to serious problems for both her and her students (Edinger, 1973).

The Great Nurturing Mother and the Great Devouring Mother

Many people choose to become teachers not for extrinsic rewards such as status and money but for intrinsic ones (Lortie, 1975) which include a sense of social mission, gratification at increased emotional intimacy with their students, and delight in seeing students spiritually blossom under their care. One thinks of Noddings' (1992) belief that great teaching can only occur when the teacher has profound "care" for her students intellectually, emotionally, and ethically. The "care" that the teacher feels and the growth and gratitude that she sees in her students are the teacher's "psychic rewards." I would like to suggest that Noddings' commendable view of teaching is a beautiful pedagogical fruit whose roots lie deep in the rich archetypal soil of what Neumann (1954) called *The Great Mother as Nurturer*.

The archetype of the Great Nurturing Mother points to that which is fertile, loving, and receptive in the cosmos. It is from her universal womb that all creatures emerge, and it is to her womb that they long to return. She is the great feminine principle of Taoism, Yin, which Lao Tzu characterized in the Tao Te Ching as "the gate to all mystery." She is the "eternally feminine drawing us upward" about which Goethe wrote in Faust. She is the archetypal core of Freud's Nirvana Principle. The Great Nurturing Mother is probably also the archetypal core of the Oedipus complex, which, seen in this broader and brighter archetypal light, represents more than just the child's desire for psychophysical merger with its biological mother but also (and more importantly) its longing to transcend the limitations of mortality and return to the timelessness of eternal succor and security in the arms of the Great Heavenly Mother. Although one suspects that this archetypal energy is more common among female teachers than male teachers, it is undoubtedly present in the classroom practice of nurturing male teachers, too.

Every archetype has its shadow—with a corresponding potential for psychological and moral misuse, especially by someone who is inflated with the heady energy of that archetype. The shadow of the Nurturing Great Mother is the Devouring Great Mother (Jacoby, 1984, p. 77). Inflated in her role as a matriarch, the Devouring Great Mother, recoiling in anxiety at the prospect of her children abandoning her and her queenly realm, does everything within her power to keep her children dependent upon her, psychically latched onto her, and is thus unable to ever fully emotionally commit to anyone else, especially a spouse. In my own counseling practice, I have found that many divorces occur because the husband, never having psychologically "divorced" himself from his mother, can never really be completely psychologically "wedded" to his wife. Indeed, he generally wants his wife to be a mother to him and at the same time wants her to be content with the role of playing second fiddle to his mother. Nor is the Great Devouring Mother's hold limited only to her sons. She may also enslave her daughters. Some females with eating disorders also stand in the shadow of this (appropriately named) devouring matriarch (Woodman, 1995).

If the therapist or teacher—especially women—are aware that they are tapping into archetypal Great Mother energy and learn how to not only use it, but contain it within appropriate bounds, the results can be fruitful for them and those who are entrusted to their care. If they do not, however, therapists and teachers can begin to psychically prey on their clients or students with perfectionist demands, subtle jabs, and guilt-trips that disempower their clients or students by keeping them "children." The Great Devouring Mother-Queen infantilizes her children so that they will remain her pawns in the consulting room or classroom.

Another potential problem arising from the teacher's inflated identification with this archetype is that it can lead to emotional and physical exhaustion. Take, for instance, the teacher who burns out after several years of working at a lower socio-economic status school where she has made it her personal business to try to "save" every disadvantaged student in her classroom, giving all of her energy, both in the classroom and out, to be a "mother" to her students. Without discounting the genuine goodness in her actions, there might also be in her family a pattern of inordinate sacrifice on the mother's part that is due to a lack of appropriate personal boundaries. What is more, this same teacher—who, let us say for the sake of example, is a devout Roman Catholic who reveres Mary—might also be inappropriately identifying with this archetypal embodiment of the Great Nurturing Mother to such an extent that she is, without being consciously aware of it, inflated with—and ultimately undone by—the archetype's call for super-human sacrifice.

In Chapter 6, we look at a teacher, Christy Ann, who gracefully embodies the archetype of the teacher as Great Nurturing Mother and wisely avoids stepping into any of the shadows of the Great Devouring Mother. A poem that she wrote at the end of the term to her students at a secondary school for boys in Hawaii poignantly expresses the care of the teacher as the Great Nurturing Mother, whose love, psychically and ethically clear and clean, sets her students free. Christy Ann's counter-transference of the archetypal energy of the Great Mother onto her students is syntonic.

PARTING IS SUCH SWEET SORROW

We have, of necessity, built a wall,
a formal wall between us,
but today I call down that wall
to let you see a me whose heart
is bursting with love
and with sorrow at this parting.

You are the sons I never had—
the warriors and poets,
statesmen and clowns.
And because we play these roles,
I never say I love you,
but I do.

Today I'm losing
a hundred brown-eyed sons.
Most I'll never see 'til resurrection time.
But the strains of your soulful laughter
will always echo through
this trembling heart....Godspeed.

THE MULTIFACETED ARCHETYPE OF THE TEACHER AS PROPHET

Many of the best teachers fulfill a sort of prophetic function in that they proclaim through what they teach, and embody in how they teach it, truths that are deeper and more durable than what the technical language of the workaday world provides (Bullough et al., 2002). The words of such prophet-teachers vibrate at archetypal frequencies that instinctively attract not only the minds but also the hearts of their students. Jung wrote of these prophet-teachers that

> whoever speaks in primordial images speaks with a thousand voices; he enthralls and overpowers, while at the same time he lifts the idea he is seeking to express out of the occasional and transitory into the realm of the ever-enduring. He transmutes our personal destiny into the destiny of mankind, and evokes in us all those beneficent forces that ever and anon have enabled humanity to find a refuge from every peril and to outlive the longest night. (1966, p. 82)

Let us look at just a few forms that this archetype of the "teacher as prophet" may assume.

The Teacher as a Prophet of Science

It is easy to see how a teacher can reach great archetypal heights in the classroom when the subject-matter is, say, philosophy, literature, or art. But isn't this less likely to happen in a physics, chemistry, or algebra class? The answer to this is a resounding "No!" as any inspired math or science teacher knows. Indeed, various Jungians have suggested that nothing is more archetypal than science and its mathematical languages. As historians of science have convincingly shown over the last several decades, any scientific model or method of interpretation rests upon ultimately unprovable assumptions about the nature of things (Kuhn, 1970). What the Jungian students of the history of science have gone on to argue is that those assumptions stem from various archetypal structures and predispositions.

In physics, the Nobel-laureate physicist Wolfgang Pauli (Pauli & Jung, 2001) speculated in a book that was tellingly entitled *Atom and Archetype* about the archetypal bases of Kepler's theory of celestial mechanics. Extrapolating from that example, Pauli suggests how any microphysical or cosmological model must rest, in the last analysis, upon a set of fundamental archetypal patterns, images, and procedures that, being a priori, could never be demonstrated propositionally. Indeed, propositional logic itself rests upon intuitions that are ultimately as archetypal as any others.

In underscoring this point, Robertson (1995) has illuminated the archetypal bases and mathematical implications of *Gödel's Proof,* which, to Bertrand Russell's dismay, thoroughly confounded his project in his most famous work, the *Principia Mathematica,* of devising a math that was internally consistent at all points and self-contained in its lack of reference to any non-mathematical (i.e., purely intuitional, archetypal) assumptions. As Russell himself was ultimately forced to admit, Gödel's Proof successfully challenged this absolutist position, showing that even the most rigorously "logical" math ultimately rests upon intuition, "poetic" imagery, and epistemological filters that, in the last analysis, are hardly distinguishable from what Jung meant by an archetype. Von Franz (1974, 1978), following another line of mathematical inquiry, has examined at length the archetypal nature of the numbers one through five, thus lending psychological support to the great mathematician Poincaré's insistence that the ultimate reality of a number—its "significance" at the deepest spiritual and ontological levels—can only be fully grasped intuitively and imagistically, and that a number is only secondarily a token that is used to describe physical reality. Of course, the Pythagoreans and other ancient mathematicians took a similarly archetypal and spiritual view of the nature of numbers.

In the field of biology, Rupert Sheldrake (1981) has suggested the existence of "morphic fields," which really are quite similar to the Jungian notion of archetypal fields of energy. These fields govern the emergence and evolution of species. Sheldrake's theory unites biology, psychology, and ontology in ways that Jung often hinted would be necessary if archetypal psychology were to develop (Jung, 1964; Conforti, 1999).

Regarding the study among physicists and philosophers of the nature of time, the contemporary astrophysicist David Peat (1987) has argued that time, being first and foremost a subjective experience and therefore relative to the frame of reference in which it is experienced, is not simply the absolute "thing" which "flows equably, of itself" as in Newton's linear model of the universe. Newtonian time is but one way among countless ways of knowing and being "in time." Indeed, most historians of Western conceptions of time agree that three interrelated phenomena were especially important in the growth of the modern obsession with mathematical, impersonal time: The emergence of capitalism in the 14th century, the growth of towns, and the invention of the mechanical clock. Our linear, algebraic view of time is a historical arti-fact (Aguessy, 1977; Boorstin, 1985; Mayes, 2005b; Whitrow, 1988).[1]

There is a politics of the modern privileging of Newtonian time, one that may be blinding us to many other patterns and rhythms in life, other "temporal possibilities," that relate to other ways—vegetative, biological, familial, cultural, and mythic—in which events "happen." Each of these types and tempos of experience may be seen as a different archetypal embodiment of a central "archetype of time," which, as Kant argued, can not be known absolutely, as a thing-in-itself. Recog-nizing and even attempting to "enter into" other images and experi-ences of time can be an exciting element in a wide range of curricula—from chemistry to cultural studies, from math to myth.

Even in the sciences, then, which have not traditionally been seen as being as amenable to archetypal approaches, there are indeed various ways in which science teachers might approach their subject matter archetypally. The great curricularist Duane Huebner (1999) wrote:

> The creation of scientific knowledge requires participation in the transcendent and a responsiveness of the other. In one sense, the one who is a scientist is one who lets the object, the phenomenon which is other, love her. She is one who gives up her present ways that she may be formed anew by that strangeness, that otherness before and beyond her. The scien-tist accepts this incomplete relationship with the world and gives of herself to be drawn out, to be educated or trans-formed by that which is before her. Scientific knowledge, a symbol system which describes a dance of love with other phe-nomena, is also a conversation, a dialogue, with human be-ings. It is a consequence of meeting someone else and of say-ing, "This is the way I dance with the world. Is it also the way you dance with it? If so, can we dance together?" (1999, p. 367)

Teachers in any field can access this archetypal realm when study becomes an occasion for delving into deep and universal ways in which

---

1 The rise of guilds signaled the emergence of early capitalism in Europe (Marx, 1978 [1844]). At the same time, villages, growing larger and more complex in their means and relations of pro-duction, were supplanted by towns, some of which would soon become the great industrial cen-ters of Europe (Gurevich, 1976). And it was the clock—created in this proto-industrial context—that, perhaps more than any other single invention, best symbolized and advanced early capitalism (Whitrow, 1988).

people experience nature, others, and self. Indeed, a great teacher must do this in order to make the subject-matter come alive. When the science teacher presents her subject-matter in this manner, then she is filling the archetypal role of the teacher as a prophet of science, whose vocation it is to reveal and announce the existence of eternally durable truths, fundamental patterns, and ongoing human significances beneath the dizzying flux of otherwise disconnected data.

The Teacher as a Dialogical Prophet

Another image of the prophet-teacher is the teacher as philosopher. Here, the teacher is a prophet of the pedagogical possibilities of rich dialogue—a way of seeing the teacher that goes back to Plato's portrayal of Socrates. The goal is to draw students on to ever higher levels of procedural competency and cognitive insight in any given field of study. This approach to education has been characterized as interpretive-procedural, academic-rationalist, intellectual-academic, and cognitive-procedural (Eisner & Vallance, 1974; Mayes, 2003; Miller & Seeler, 1985, Ornstein & Hunkins, 1988). Whatever name it goes by, it assumes that the teacher's role is the prophetic one of announcing, demonstrating, and even embodying the intellectual, civic, and ethical riches to be gained through: (1) the appreciation of canonical texts in the traditional disciplines and (2) the mastery of the ways in which experts in various fields pose and answer questions.

Although such a traditional pedagogy may be dismissed as ethnocentric (Banks, 1997) or patriarchal (Kristeva, 1989; Cixous, 1991), the fact is that students who do not have access to such knowledge and skills will inevitably be at a disadvantage in a society that will always prize such things. This is a point that has been forcefully made by conservative educators and theorists from W.E.B. Dubois in the early 20th century, to the educational theorist Boyd Bode in the heyday of American educational Progressivism, to the educational historian Diane Ravitch recently. Certainly, education in a multicultural society must be sensitive to psychosocial differences among various groups of students (Mayes et al., 2007). However, any approach to teaching and learning that does not give children from disempowered groups full access to the knowledge, skills, and dispositions that make for socio-economic success ultimately does those groups much more harm than good—and is, indeed, a sort of liberal paternalism that, by catering down to marginalized people, keeps them marginalized (Sowell, 1993). The teacher-as-philosopher-and-dialogical-partner is thus an archetype that is personally compelling to many teachers, and one that—when effectively embodied in the classroom by a teacher—is not only intellectually enriching but politically empowering for students from across the socioeconomic spectrum.

Jung affirmed the importance of philosophical/procedural adeptness, not only to education, but to thinking in general when he wrote: "Differentiation is the essence, the *sine qua non* of consciousness" (1953, p. 206). In their archetypal analysis of the Grail Legend, Emma Jung and Marie-Louise von Franz (1986, p. 80) said that the phallic symbol of the sword wielded by the hero in quest of the Holy Grail symbolizes this discriminating function of consciousness—an archetypally masculine function, an embodiment of the principle of *Logos*, reason. The teacher as philosopher is thus rightly considered an archetypally male figure—although that teacher who is actually incarnating and enacting this archetypal energy in a given classroom may, of course, be either a man or woman. "He" serves as a balance to the opposite, archetypally feminine function of the teacher as nurturer and great mother. I once had a dream in which I was standing in front of a class teaching about Aristotle (and his archetypally male emphasis on *Logos*) but I was wearing pink (the traditional color of the female principle). "How do you remain intellectually rigorous with your class while at the same time nurturing them?" was obviously the question I was posing myself in the dream.

As important as this *Logos*-rich vision of teaching and learning is, it carries with it a danger, for every archetype has a shadow. By overidentifying with this masculine archetype, the teacher runs the risk of concentrating so much upon propositional, "official," and syllogistic truth that he or she loses touch with deep transpersonal and transrational images and energies. There is no denying the importance of propositional truth, but, equally, there is no denying its contingency upon deeper psychospiritual factors. Thus, Jung felt that any approach to education "that satisfies the intellect alone can never be practical, for the totality of the psyche can never be grasped by the intellect alone" (Jung, 1953, p. 119). Taken to extremes, intellectualism leads to intellectual pride which has lost sight of the fact that every system of thought is, in the last analysis, "the product of a certain personality living at a certain time and in a certain place, and not the outcome of a purely logical and impersonal procedure" (Jung, 1978, p. 106).

Jung thus went so far as to claim that overreaching intellectualism —rationalism that sets itself up as an end-in-itself rather than a means of transcending itself in higher forms of knowing and interrelating—is "in point of fact...nothing more than the sum total of all [a person's] prejudices and myopic views" (1968b, p. 13). Jung would undoubtedly agree with Fairbairn's appraisal of excessive intellectualism as a schizoid position. Teachers may avoid fostering such an unhealthy perspective in themselves as well as in their students by reflecting deeply on both the power and limitations of the archetype of the teacher as philosopher—as dialogical prophet.

The Teacher as a Prophet of Democracy

The image of the teacher as a prophet of democracy is clearly delineated in Lawrence Cremin's (1977, p. 77) definition of prophecy in pedagogical terms as "the calling of a people, via criticism and affirmation, to their noblest traditions and aspirations. Prophecy, I would submit, is the essential public function of the educator in a democratic society." In Cremin's portrayal of the teacher, she is a federal minister. She calls a people to repentance "via criticism and affirmation," which have ever been the two sides of the prophet's rhetorical sword. She criticizes her culture for not living up to its foundational democratic principles; she affirms those principles by embodying and proclaiming them to her students.

This vision of the teacher as a minister of democracy has been an important one in the history of U.S. education. From at least the late 18th century on, it was widely felt that education—either formal or informal—would be a primary means, if not indeed the primary means, of carrying the American experiment in democracy forward. Certainly, this was the political and spiritual warrant for public schooling in the eyes of Horace Mann—one that invested his *Reports to the Massachusetts Legislature* with numinous energy and poetic power (Messerli, 1972). Nor was Mann alone in his insistence that public schools would be the essential tool in both democratizing and spiritualizing the people. Catherine Beecher, Emma Willard, Zilpah Grant, and Mother Mary Seton shared this vision. These extraordinary (yet still insufficiently celebrated) women believed that it was females who could best fulfill the historically crucial function of educating children into the ethos of democracy. Here we see a fascinating merger of two archetypes—the Great Nurturing Mother and the teacher as a Prophet of Democracy, in which it was women who would purify the Republic by purifying its children—lovingly and tenderly educating them into lofty moral and civic virtues and thereby preparing them for the Millennium, of which America would be the site (Jones, 1980; Messerli, 1972; Sklar, 1973).

The vision of the teacher as federal prophet is alive and well today although it manifests itself in different ways—all of which are essentially variations on the same archetypal theme. For instance, on the political Right, teachers are currently enjoined to instill in their students a commitment to the foundational Judeo-Christian beliefs that are the "pillars of the republic" (Kaestle, 1983). These pillars have (it is believed) fallen into disrepair because of a secular humanism that has infiltrated the schools, leading to ethical relativism and moral decay. Teachers must teach students how to repair and revere those Judeo-Christian pillars of the Republic.

On the political Left, the teacher is asked to be a prophet and agent of radical cultural change. Typically basing its program on those secular-humanist views of society and psyche that the conservative Right abhors, the Left points out that America has never even remotely approximated a perfect democracy. It has consistently marginalized people who do not conform to the White, Anglo-Saxon, Protestant, middle-class standards of what it means to be "a real American." Both in what they teach and how they teach it, the job of these teacher-prophets is to resist and change unfair, anti-democratic ideas and practices in the schools (McLaren, 1998).

These two views of the teacher's political function—as disparate as they are—both draw on the archetypal energy of the teacher as a prophet of democracy. Both envision the teacher as the Wise Political Elder who reveals to the Hero/Student on the archetypal path of intellectual and moral awakening the decadence of the present order of things (symbolized in many fairy-tales by a dying, corrupt king) so that the Hero/Student may ideologically overthrow the corrupt king and then ascend the throne as the new, redemptive king who will usher in a saner moral and social order. One hears this archetypal call to teachers throughout the history of American education—in the towering prose of everyone from Horace Mann in the 1830s arguing for the establishment of public schooling to George Counts' (1933) demand in *Dare the Schools Build a New Social Order?* that entreated teachers to help their students catch the vision of America as not only a political democracy but also as an economic democracy in the form of socialism.

This same archetypal energy infuses the writings of such contemporary educational scholars as Wexler (1996), Purpel and Shapiro (1995), and Kozol (1991) with their call for educators to be political change-agents. However, nowhere is the archetypal image of the teacher as a world-historical agent of democratic empowerment so powerfully presented as in the work of Paolo Freire. Freire advances the notion that the politically prophetic teacher finds her own psychological and ethical redemption in dedicating herself to the conscientizacion (or "consciousness-raising") of disempowered people. In a process that is intensely individual yet inevitably political, Freire shows how the teacher works out her own individuation by promoting that same process in her students (Freire, 2001). Education, revolutionary social change, and the teacher's and student's individuation are inseparably interwoven threads in the wonderful tapestry of Freirian pedagogy.

Of course, the teacher, in performing certain prophetic functions, must be careful not to become inflated with this archetype, believing that she is a prophet and that every word that falls from her mouth is fraught with timeless meaning! Such a teacher—whether on the Right or Left—soon becomes an insufferable ideologue, insisting that her message embodies all that is true, good, and beautiful, and must be completely accepted and obeyed. Or she becomes a martyr, spending herself beyond all reasonable limits to insure that her students find "salvation" by converting to the gospel of her redeeming message. These are both paths that lead the teacher to emotional depletion and professional burnout—and lead the offended student to disengage from classroom discussion or even withdraw from school. In other words, the archetype of the teacher as federal prophet also has its shadow side as any archetype does—one which the archetypally wise teacher will avoid even as she draws on the power of the archetype. By reflecting deeply upon both the bright and dark sides of the archetypal images and narratives that are meaningful to them in their work, teachers can learn to tap archetypal energy in ways that further their own and their students' psychosocial growth—without becoming classroom demagogues! Such teachers can harness archetypal energy instead of being harnessed by it.

Hopefully these assorted archetypal images of teacher have offered the reader a few clues about the nature of and need for archetypal reflectivity among teachers.

Part 2: Eve, *Eros,* and Education

According to some feminist critics of public education, the disproportionate focus in the schools on rule-governed, technically-oriented, and quantifiably assessable means and goals is symptomatic of a larger cultural practice of undervaluing "women's ways of knowing" (Belenkey, 1986), which tend to be more intuitive, poetic, organic, and interactional (Chodorow, 1978; Gilligan, 1982). In Jungian terms, what has been lacking in official education is the influence of the archetypally feminine *Eros* to balance the archetypally masculine *Logos* (Jung, 1956, pp. 185–186). This is not *Eros* in the Freudian sense of merely erotic libido—a picture of *Eros* which, although "true and factual" up to a point, according to Jung, is ultimately "one sided and exclusive" because it "commits the imprudence of trying to lay hold of unconfinable *Eros* with the crude terminology of sex" (Jung, 1953, p. 28). Rather, this is *Eros* as Freud began to sense it in his later writings but which it would take Jung to fully articulate in all its psychological and ethical subtlety.

In this view, *Eros* encompasses the passions that not only make life physically possible but emotionally meaningful. *Eros* includes *Sexus* but goes well beyond it (Goldbrunner, 1965, p. 20). Although *Eros* is a sort of "pleasure principle," it is pleasure that has been transformed into the psychospiritual passion for deeper communion with others, the universe, and the divine. It is "the principle of relatedness" and the hunger for "intensity of experience" that is so "pronounced in the consciousness of women and usually present more unconsciously in men" (Ulanov, 1999, p. 13). What *Logos* wants to measure and master with the streamlined tools of detached analysis, *Eros* wants to embrace and affirm with the arms of intuition and involvement. Education under the sign of *Eros* does not aim at "perfect performance" on the standardized test (the numerically "ideal" 100%) but at engagement with others and their ideas in a facilitating environment. "Perfectionism always ends in a blind alley," Jung warned, for it "excludes the principle of relatedness" (1958, p. 620).

EVE AND EDUCATION

Jung believed that the archetypally feminine is epistemologically prior to the archetypally masculine, a point that must have profound educational consequences. Nowhere does he make this point more clearly than in his reading of the story of Adam and Eve in the Garden of Eden.

The traditional Christian view of the genesis of human consciousness is quite different from Jung's. According to the traditional view, humanity lost its pristine state of consciousness because Adam and Eve ate the fruit of the Tree of Knowledge of Good and Evil, thus necessitating an atonement to restore consciousness to its fullness. Jung held that this view of the fall of human consciousness from a so-called primal purity in the Garden was deficient for one simple reason—namely, that it was not really about consciousness at all.[2] Eve's so-called "transgression" in the garden should not be interpreted as the descent of pure consciousness into something lesser, but rather as humanity's ascent into consciousness in the first place—on the wings of Eve's intuition.

Eve in the Garden intuited that hers and Adam's rudimentary form of proto-consciousness was not enough—and that humanity must pass through opposition in order to grow. She wisely sensed—as her literalistic, legalistic husband did not—that the only way to achieve full, and fully human, consciousness was in eating the fruit of opposition, the knowledge of "good and evil." She thereby started a phenomenological process whereby the secondary discriminative and judging processes of analytical consciousness would ultimately evolve from the primary intuitional processes of the subconscious and unconscious.

Furthermore, intuition was central to the evolution of consciousness because it is the basis of the transcendent function. As we saw earlier, the transcendent function is the primarily intuitive capacity to reconcile the primary processes of the unconscious with the secondary processes of consciousness in order to achieve individuation. This reconciliation of the primary and secondary processes results in a higher perspective, a "transcendent third," that typically finds expression in a poetic image—one that, in turn, forms the basis for a new system of thought. Stated differently, we could say that logic arises out of poetry.

Eve's dynamic moral intuition, as opposed to her husband's static and statutory obedience, thus emerges as psychologically profound and morally heroic. As in such 2nd and 3rd century Gnostic texts as The Gospel of Philip and The Gospel of Mary (Magdalene)—which were of

2 Blackwell-Mayes and I have written about many of the parallels between Jungian psychology and Mormon theology—especially regarding the view of the feminine principle—and their implications for therapy (Mayes & Blackwell-Mayes, 2005).

intense interest to Jung—Jung pictured Eve as "the mother of all living" (the meaning of her name, Havah) in a psychological sense.[3] She is our mother not only because she gave birth physically but because Adam's *Logos*-centered cognition emerged from the womb of her *Eros*-rich intuition. In terms of consciousness, therefore, Eve is as much Adam's mother as his wife. The rationalistic languages and procedures of *Logos* must gestate in and be born from the poetic womb of *Eros*. *Logos* speaks in the language of equations and propositional logic, but this is a discourse that rests upon Eve's more fundamental poetry.

The great aesthetician Bendetto Croce also believed that the analytical languages of *Logos* come from the poetic womb of *Eros*:

> The relation between knowledge or expression and intellectual knowledge or concept, between art and science, poetry and prose, cannot be otherwise defined than by saying that it is one of double degree. The first degree is the expression, the second the concept: the first can stand without the second, but the second cannot stand without the first. There is poetry without prose, but not prose without poetry. Expression, indeed, is the first affirmation of human activity. Poetry is "the mother tongue of the human race"; the first men "were by nature sublime poets." (in Vivas & Krieger, 1953, p. 86)

One thinks of the great scientific discoveries that began as a poetic image in the scientist's mind. For instance, von Stadonitz's dream of the ends of swirling molecules bending and touching to form a ring (similar to the image of intertwining snakes—an archetypal picture of psycho-spiritual energy that appears in sources as diverse as Kundalini Yoga, Gnostic Christianity, and the modern physician's caduceus) set the imagistic stage for the empirical discovery of the double-helix in biology. Einstein—who proclaimed that imagination is more important than knowledge—reported that his first inklings of the theory of relativity occurred when he fantasized as a boy what it would be like to ride on a beam of light. *Eros* is the muse of science. Science is one of *Eros's* languages.

The educational consequences of the epistemological primacy of *Eros* are many. We can only look at a few of them here.

---

3 There is even an important ancient Gnostic manuscript that has been named after Jung himself—the Jung Codex.

Symbol, Intuition, and the Aesthetic Curriculum

To be emotionally attractive, to capture the student's heart as well as her mind, to make of learning a heroic adventure rather than a grade-grubbing exercise in deception and alienation, pedagogy must pay homage to the fact that there is a "poetic basis to mind" (Hillman, 1996, p. 40). "The greatest and best thoughts of man shape themselves upon [the archetypes] as upon a blueprint"—a blueprint whose symbols only the intuitively sensitive eye can decipher (Jung, 1953, p. 69). A culture whose educational system inordinately stresses analysis and technology needs reminding that technical rationality, despite its great importance, is secondary to the ability to grasp those timeless symbols and archetypal truths that let us know where we came from, why we are here, and where we are going. Mere "technical rationality" spurns Eve's wisdom and turns a deaf ear to her symbolic incantations.

Not only is such exclusion of the feminine principle morally indefensible, it is simply unwise in practical terms. For poetic intuition, the "noblest gift of man," lies at the heart of truly creative thought in any field—often producing "a superior analysis or insight or knowledge which consciousness has not been able to produce" (Jung, 1938, p. 49). Jung practiced what he preached in this regard. Risking—and frequently getting—the contempt of his contemporaries, for whom anything "less" than the ideal of "clinical detachment" and "scientific objectivity" was a scandal, Jung was very open and clear about the fact that his own scholarship and clinical practice grew primarily out of intuitive insights—the "irruption into consciousness of an unconscious content, a sudden idea or 'hunch'" (Jung, 1960, p. 132).[4] Certain critics, past and present, caught up in *Logos*-obsessed discourses that provide little if any room for the feminine, and unhappy with how Jung privileges the intuitive capacity, have therefore unwisely dismissed him as just a fuzzy-headed mystic. Mystical he was. Fuzzy headed he was not.

A Jungian approach to curriculum thus aims to excite and expand in students their natural desire to find archetypal truths—those universal ideas, motifs, and narratives—that are at the spiritual core of any

---

4 This is what makes Jung so rewarding to read for some and so frustrating for others, for his writings have that multifaceted, constantly evolving, and spiritually suggestive power that only the intuitive mind can produce or appreciate. This is also what makes it so difficult to fit Jung's ideas into conventional psychological categories—and what makes his books so exasperating to readers who come looking for a simple, straightforward, and therefore inevitably limited model of that most infinitely complex of all things—the psyche.

discipline, and it does this by helping students intuitively engage with their inner and outer worlds in richly symbolic terms. With its emphasis on the curriculum as a means of bringing the student into closer contact with the psychosocial wellsprings of her own being, a Jungian pedagogy shares with a good deal of postmodern educational thought a focus on the individual's ultimately subjective experience of external and internal existence (Doll, 1993). This is what Eisner and Vallance characterize as the *aesthetic curriculum*, arguing that virtually any discipline or topic, from physics to physical education, is *aesthetic* if it is being used to promote the goal of helping students achieve "expressive outcomes" at the archetypal level. For,

> any activity — indeed, at their very best, activities that are engaged in to court surprise, to cultivate discovery, to find new forms of experience — *is expressive in character*. Nothing in the sciences, the home or mechanical arts, or in social relationships prohibits or diminishes the possibility of engaging in expressive outcomes. The education problem is to be sufficiently imaginative in the design of educational programs so that such outcomes will occur and their educational value will be high. (Eisner & Vallance, 1974, p. 134. Emphasis added.)

Of course, as things play out practically in the rough-and-tumble of the day-to-day life of the school, where teachers are called upon to perform so many tasks and make so many decisions in the course of an hour, it is sometimes difficult to be "sufficiently imaginative." Indeed, it is precisely "institutionalized time" that frequently makes imagination and creativity impossible. Luckman is surely correct in his observation that "inner time...cannot be adequately segmented into equal units without doing violence to its intrinsic articulation" (1991, p. 154). I have written elsewhere (2005b) how this "temporal violence" occurs in many classrooms, where the institutional division of time into unforgiving and anonymous "periods" of mechanical instruction and standardized assessment — the tools of corporate capitalism in it relentless press to maximize "the bottom line" — threaten the teacher's and student's psychological health and creative potential by repressing their personal, cultural, and spiritual experiences and uses of time.

A particularly poignant example that I encountered in that study of the violation of teacher's time and student's time by institutional time, came from a creative writing teacher:

Those creative moments are the ones I live for as a teacher and they make the clock seem pretty darn irrelevant! In fact, I see the clock as my enemy at those times. Getting your students into the frame of mind—and heart!—where they can, say, write a poem, or begin the first paragraph of a short story... well, you just can't cut and dry that kind of thing up into these neat little 45-minute periods. So that's always been my challenge! How to get that special kind of experience *going* with kids who stumble into my class after a day of moving to bells and hall monitors, and then, oh my!—how to *sustain that creative mindset* in my class. And then always comes the part I *don't* like—how to ease my kids back into the so-called real world when I see by the clock on the wall that we've only got five or ten minutes left before their next bell. I mean, I look at the clock. Fifteen minutes left. And then I look at them—most of them so intent, chewing their pencils, furrowing their brows, smiling to themselves because they just found the right word or just the right image! But I know that in five minutes or so I'm going to have to "wake them up gently" before the bell does it rudely! And I just look at them and think, "What the heck are we doing to these kids! It sure doesn't have anything to do with why *I* became a teacher!" And now there are all these new testing requirements being pushed down our throats with *No Child Left Behind*. I call it *No Child Left Breathing*! These new tests just make it all that much harder for me to do what I want to do, what I *need to do,* as a teacher. Maybe it will make it impossible. I don't know. I don't like to think that way because, you know, I'm a pretty positive person. I have to believe that there will be some kind of corrective in the collective consciousness of this nation.

The violation of "creative time"—which is the repression of an archetypal experience of time—forecloses the teacher's and students' ability to produce archetypally rich images. The hegemonic institutional time of standardized instruction and testing runs roughshod over the various archetypal times that engender rich classroom conversation. I am convinced that most teachers want their classroom to be places where such conversations happen. I am also convinced that most teachers, working against great odds, often do make such things happen—even in the most rigid institutional circumstances. Certainly, this is no easy thing to accomplish in any classroom—whether it is a large public school classroom or a small university seminar—but it is always worth aiming at. My years of working with both prospective and practicing teachers have shown me time and again that most teachers long for moments when such intellectually, emotionally, and morally vibrant discussion takes place. And it is always awe-inspiring for me to see how immensely creative teachers can be—in acts of educational commitment that are nothing short of heroic—in finding ways to accomplish these "expressive outcomes."

Of course, because of the premium placed on intuition in "aesthetic knowing," an archetypal approach to education is a stumbling block to corporate education. Because there is simply no way to statistically quantify or fiscally assess psychological depth, emotional subtlety, moral clarity, or spiritual commitment, such things are typically pushed to the margins or even ignored in capitalism-obsessed reforms for education. This is ironic, of course, since the ability to think creatively and act ethically is vital to the long-term viability of any business—as the number of classes dealing with creativity and ethics at places such as the Harvard Graduate School of Management shows. Thus, wherever there is an educational agenda that revolves around standardization of the curriculum and the objectification of students, the archetypally oriented educator must resist it not only because of its psychological, political, and moral violence against students and teachers but also because of its ultimate impracticability—whatever its short-term, bottom-line advantages may be.

The archetypal educator also resists standardized approaches to education for the simple reason that they commit one of the worst and most unforgivable of all educational sins. They are boring! They have no sense of the delight that the play of intuition and imagination bring. Jung was well aware that, to the devotee of norm-referenced approaches to education, the spontaneity, unpredictability, and idiosyncrasy of the intuitive spirit will always seem to be mere "tomfoolery" (Jung, 1963, p. 58). Yet, a wise pedagogy will not submit to the dull demands of a joylessly statistical, fiscal view of the world—a world that discourages creativity. The intuitive, symbolic, poetic capacity is the mother lode of creativity in any field.

> Not the artist alone, but every creative individual whatsoever owes all that is greatest in his life to fantasy. The dynamic principle of fantasy is play, a characteristic also of the child, and as such it appears inconsistent with the principle of seri-

ous work. But without this playing with fantasy no creative work has ever come to birth. The debt we owe to the play of imagination is incalculable. It is therefore short-sighted to treat fantasy, on account of its risky or unacceptable nature, as a thing of little worth. It must not be forgotten that it is just in the imagination that a man's highest value may lie. (Jung, 1921, p. 63) [5]

Where Eve's *Eros*-saturated phenomenon of play is squeezed out of the classroom by the fist of standardization, the result is that the classroom will inevitably be dominated by the archetype of the decrepit *Senex*. Who is he? He is the dry and dreary old man who can see no farther than his rules and regulations. He is Scrooge, to whom any vital exercise of the imagination is mere humbug. He is Darth Vader (that is, the Dark Father), a parody of the healthy paternal principle of *Logos*, scarred and scared underneath the shiny black helmet of his imperialist organization. Indeed, he is the male principle of *Logos* that has degenerated because it has divorced itself from the balancing principle of *Eros*. (Of course, when divorced from *Logos*, *Eros* can also go mad, degenerating into sloppy sentimentalism, unchecked emotionalism, and suffocating over-protectiveness. Examples of that are provided in some of the following chapters.)

Clearly, the aesthetically oriented approaches to education are psychologically enriching. What is more, they also have the potential to be socially transformative. Jung agreed with the English Romantic poet Shelley that "the poet is the unacknowledged legislator of the world." "The great secret of art...and the creative process," Jung said,

> consists in the unconscious activation of an archetypal image, and in elaborating and shaping this image into the finished work. By giving it shape, the artist translates it into the language of the present, and so makes it possible for us to find the way back to the wellsprings of life. Therein lies the social significance of art: it is constantly at work educating the spirit of the age, conjuring up the forms in which the age is most lack-

---

5 This Jungian critique of standard education also applies to the Montessori Method and its goal of discouraging "mere fantasy," which Montessori saw as pedagogically and developmentally unsound. See Crain (1992) and Gutek (2000) for more on this conflict between Montessori and a Jungian perspective. On the other hand, Montessori's idea of "sensitive periods" in a child's maturation, in which certain skills and topics can best be introduced, is consistent with a wide range of psychodynamic views of learning, including the Jungian one.

ing. The unsatisfied yearning of the artist reaches back to the primordial image in the unconscious which is best fitted to compensate the inadequacy and one-sidedness of the present. The artist seizes on this image, and in raising it from the deepest unconsciousness, he brings it into relation with conscious values, thereby transforming it until it can be accepted by the minds of his contemporaries according to their power. (1966, pp. 82–83)

Of a classroom that prizes and protects intuition and passion, students will still say many years later: "I remember that class. I felt alive in that class. I truly learned in that class. I loved and was loved there. It changed my life." On the other hand, where nurturance and nuance have been banished, the classroom becomes an educational gulag in which students must either strategically gag their souls in order to survive the next report card—or be forced into submission through pharmaceutical means of chemically "normalizing" them, keeping them quiet, obedient, uniform, and fixated on the only thing that really matters in the archetypally impoverished classroom: the scores on the next test. The dark Senex is triumphant whenever children are psychologically and ethically degraded, the heroic journey of teaching and learning is scrapped, and *Eros* lies bleeding to death on the steps of a schoolhouse that she is forbidden to enter.

THE THERAPEUTIC CLASSROOM

Education in a therapeutic mode also exists under the sign of *Eros* for its focus is upon nurturance, which is in the domain of the archetypally feminine. Indeed, this maternal impulse is often strong in men and women whose work centers around service to others. Thus, it will come as no surprise that an image frequently used by "spiritually called" teachers in describing their work—and one that has already figured prominently in this study—is of the teacher as Great Mother. Although in my own experience as a teacher and researcher, this image is most commonly employed by female elementary school teachers, it is by no means rare among female secondary school teachers. In many research interviews which I have done with teachers over the years, I have often heard them referring to their students as "my kids," "my children," and even "my babies." A poignant example of this comes from a former student of mine—an African American woman from the projects of an East-Coast city—who was preparing to become a public-school principal. During an interview for a study that I was doing of teachers who wished to explore the spiritual dimension of their work, she tearfully related:

> I've had so many experiences with my kids. My life has been so touched by them. I once lost a student because she was murdered. I let my feelings show in class—just like now. I thought it was important for her classmates to know that people care. I've taken in a child because his mother didn't want him. And there are other things, too, that I've done in my life for my students.

Such images evidence what Valli has called "the relational approach" to teaching—one that resembles "the natural relation of mothering" that therapists often feel towards their clients (1990, p. 43; see also Woodman, 1990, 1995). The maternal, therapeutically inclined teacher believes that, above all else, it is her role to help the student find emotional stability, existential safety, and sometimes even a degree of spiritual awareness in her classroom (Roberts, 1979, 1981, 1985; Roberts & Clark, 1975; Whitmore, 1986). That this view of teaching closely parallels the way in which many therapists picture their roles follows from the fact that teaching and therapy both attract nurturing people who wish to be of service.

Not all students in a classroom or clients in therapy will immediately "buy into" an intuitive approach, of course. Sometimes a little gentle persuasion is required. An example of this that has become quite famous in Jungian lore involves a young woman of "excellent education," a student of philosophy, who, with her "highly polished Cartesian rationalism" and "impeccably 'geometrical' idea of reality" had hermetically "sealed herself" inside her intellectualism to such a degree that she was "psychologically inaccessible" (Jung, 1960, pp. 525–526). Jung reports:

> After several fruitless attempts to sweeten her rationalism with a somewhat more human understanding, I had to confine myself to the hope that something irrational would turn up, something that would burst the intellectual retort into which she had sealed herself. Well, I was sitting opposite her one day, with my back to the window, listening to her flow of rhetoric. She had just had an impressive dream the night before, in which someone had given her a golden scarab—a costly piece of jewelry. While she was still telling me this dream, I heard

something behind me gently tapping on the window. I turned round and saw that it was a fairly large flying insect that was knocking against the window-pane from outside in the obvious effort to get into the dark room. This seemed to me very strange. I opened the window immediately and caught the insect in the air as it flew in. It was a scarabaeid beetle, or common rose-chafer..., whose gold-green color most nearly resembles that of a golden scarab. I handed the beetle to my patient with the words, "Here is your scarab." This experience punctured the desired hole in her rationalism and broke the ice of her intellectual resistance. The treatment could now be continued with satisfactory results. (Jung, 1960, pp. 525–526)

This synchronicity convinced the woman that, in the words of Hamlet to Horatio, "there are more things under heaven and earth than are dreamt of in your philosophy." Without forfeiting her reason, this woman was now able to begin to go beyond it, affirming deeper truths that could now manifest themselves as archetypally rich phenomena. By building up a previously atrophied intuitive capacity, she was increasingly fit to encounter, grasp, and deploy the psychospiritual energies at the core of her being.[6]

Jung's point in offering this example was the same as the one made by the psychoanalysts in Chapter 1: a merely cognitive approach to therapy or education, one that neither honors nor feeds the basic passions and commitments that are the irreducible alpha and omega of each person's life, is inadequate. It fails to touch those passions and commitments—much less embody them in psychically and socially transformative ways. When therapy and education do not extend beyond the realm of ego-consciousness, when they do not touch or draw upon what makes an individual unique at her deepest levels, they crucify any possibility of real creativity. Therapy and education then sim-

---

6 Main (2004) has argued that Jung put such stress on synchronistic phenomena not only because of their inherent interest and therapeutic value but primarily because they constitute a critique of Western culture's obsession with merely linear, materialistic views of the universe. In a Newtonian universe, synchronistic events should not occur. That they do occur represents a major challenge to conventional physics and requires that we look to post-Newtonian models of the universe. Moreover, these models may well be consistent with Jung's feeling that archetypes underlay not only psychological but physical reality, both of which realities stemmed from an even more ontologically primary field of being that Jung called the "psychoid realm"—a term which Jung began to use around 1946 (Wehr, 2002).

ply become another means of perpetuating the dull daily round of the personal, intellectual, and social status quo. Jung agreed with the psychoanalytic theorist Cornelius Castoriadis that therapy and education must be tools of psychological and political reformation.

> The aims of psychoanalysis and pedagogy [are], first, the instauration of another type of relation between the reflexive subject (of will and of thought) and his unconscious, that is, his radical imagination and, second, the freeing of his capacity to make and do things, to form an open project for his life and to work with that project. We can similarly define the aims of politics.... Democracy in the full sense can be defined as the regime of collective reflexivity. (Castoriadis, 1991, p. 8)

Archetypal reflectivity under the sign of *Eros* offers the teacher many ways to "go deeper" in understanding what is going on within both herself and her students. This means acknowledging and working with those insights that psychoanalysis offers the teacher, as discussed in Chapter 1. However, it also means more than that. For, just as there is an archetypal core to every neurosis, so there is usually an archetypal, transpersonal dimension to what might at first blush seem to be merely a psychodynamic, personal issue playing out in the classroom (Kirsch, 1995; Knox, 1998).

For example, a teenage girl who falls in love with her middle-aged male mathematics teacher may not simply be showing symptoms of an Electra complex regarding her father but may also be attempting to access her own animus, her inner male. She may even be projecting her desire for communion with the *Logos* principle embodied in the Father-God archetype onto this particular teacher who, for one reason or other, provides a particularly good "hook" for that projection to hang itself on. A teenage boy who nastily rejects the best efforts of a middle-aged female English teacher to get him interested in poetry may not only be symbolically breaking the Oedipal ties that bind him at home but may also be resisting the archetypal Great Mother's call to rest in receptivity and quiescence at precisely the time in life that he feels the stirrings of the Warrior archetype in his soul, calling him to either a literal or symbolic field of battle upon which he can display and test his potency.

Jung agreed with the psychoanalytic pedagogues that a teacher should have both general psychoanalytic knowledge of herself and her students (1954b, p. 93), but he also felt that in order for a teacher to be able to view her students' and her own psychic issues in a transpersonal light, "it is in fact highly desirable that the educator...should pay attention to the findings of [archetypal] psychology" as well as psychoanalysis (1954b, pp. 68, 93–94). In teacher education, such psychodynamic knowledge is much more important, in Jung's view, than a technical approach to "training" practitioners. "Psychotherapy has taught us," Jung observed, "that in the final reckoning it is not knowledge, not technical skill, that has a curative effect, but the personality of the doctor. And it is the same with education: it presupposes self-education" (1954b, p. 140).

Also like the psychoanalytic pedagogues, Jung warned the teacher not to believe that her deepened psychological knowledge qualified her to act as an actual therapist to her students. "The deepened psychological knowledge of the teacher should not, as unfortunately sometimes happens, be unloaded directly on the child; rather, it should help the teacher to adopt an understanding attitude toward the child's psychic life" in order to create a more intellectually, morally, and ethically compelling classroom (Jung, 1954b, pp. 50–51). Along with the psychoanalytic writers on education, therefore, Jung insisted that education has therapeutic dimensions but that the teacher is not a therapist (1954b, pp. 74–75).

The need for therapeutically sensitive teachers is probably greater now than at any other time in the history of American education because more students than ever are coming from dysfunctional and even abusive homes (Conger & Galambos, 1997). While providing psychologically sensitive, emotionally healing classroom environments will not solve all of these children's problems, it can be an important part of helping such children find some measure of emotional comfort and spiritual sustenance in the midst of their many challenges.

THE THERAPEUTIC POLITICS OF RESISTANCE TO TECHNICAL RATIONALITY IN THE CLASSROOM

I have already noted that education in any society includes certain technical means and goals. This is not a problem; it is a socio-economic inevitability. The problem arises when "technical rationality" so dominates a culture's view of education that it marginalizes, and sometimes even attempts to erase, the more humane views of schooling that should be psychologically, politically, and ethically central to how and why a culture educates its young (Schön, 1987). At such times, *Logos* has not only marginalized but eliminated *Eros* from the educational scene. Education, *Logos*-possessed, then becomes the mere "transmission" of facts and skills, where the emphasis is on "information" in the form of discrete and manipulable factoid-packets that are impersonally delivered and received (Kane, 1999). The curriculum becomes little more than a technical manual of instruction.

Michel Foucault's (1979) revealing analysis of the rise of technical manuals in the 16th and 17th centuries is relevant here. Used to train workers and soldiers about the institutionally "correct" ways of uniformly performing the tasks associated with their jobs, the technical manual was symptomatic of the rise of the cult of expertise — and the consequent empowering of a governing elite which declared certain ways of doing things "officially acceptable" and other ways clinically or legally "wrong," requiring medical or penal "remediation." Only the institutionally approved ways of polishing a shoe, loading a gun, making a chair, grooming an animal, or teaching a lesson would be permitted, for only those had been "scientifically" demonstrated to be worthy of licensure by the state.

A similar view of "good practice" dominates many colleges of education in the U.S. today, where teaching is seen as being composed of particular "competencies." These are the "elements" of "effective performance." These competencies are in turn reduced to measurable "units of behavior" that "pre-service" teachers are "trained" to "perform" under the institutionally watchful eye of an "expert" who will then "certify" them as either fit or unfit for the classroom. Student performance is also assessed in this behaviorist fashion — one laid out in all its chillingly sterile specifics in B.F. Skinner's (1956) *The Technology of Teaching*. Norm-referenced tests indicate in the anonymous jargon of statistical coefficients how well students have "mastered" (which usually means "memorized") unrelated bits of information in domains of knowledge that have themselves been dissociated from each other. The dream of a vibrant community of learning organized around an integrated curriculum must shipwreck on the jagged rocks of such a morally perilous approach to education.

Evidently, Thorndike's and Terman's positivistic faith, articulated early in the 20th century during the rise of the psychometric movement, that everything exists in some measurable amount, is still very much alive in mathematical definitions of human "intelligence" that dominate current educational discourse. This atomistic and molecular—as opposed to holistic and molar—approach to "assessing" the child is psychosocially egregious. It can do considerable damage to a child because it does not address the whole child in all of her physical, emotional, political, cultural, and ethical complexity. It fails to honor the fact that there are many kinds of "intelligence": mathematical and verbal proficiency, interpersonal and intrapersonal sensitivity, the ability to thrive in natural settings, artistic and spiritual intuitiveness, mechanical adroitness, athletic giftedness, and, probably, many others (Gardner, 1999).

When these multiple facets of what it means to be human are declared marginal, even irrelevant, by an educational system that prizes only what will serve corporate and military objectives, the effects spread beyond the schoolroom and into the culture at large. As Jung warned, not addressing children holistically results in psychic "disorientation and fragmentation" in them—and in the society whose adult citizens they will be. It contributes to that internal fracturing which psychoanalytic theorists from Anna Freud and Melanie Klein to Fairbairn and Winnicott have warned about—an overdevelopment of the merely ratiocinative aspects of the psyche to the detriment, and ultimate atrophy, of the other parts.

Jung never denied that "school is...a means of strengthening in a purposeful way the integration of consciousness" and that one of its most important functions is to promote the development of ego functioning in the form of technical and analytical abilities (Jung, 1954b, p. 52). However, this is only one of the many things education should do. Along with the psychoanalytic pedagogues, Jung insisted that school's pragmatic purposes should not blind us to the fact that "the integration of consciousness" cannot happen unless adequate attention is also paid to the primary processes of the unconscious—something that rarely happens in "our conventional system of education" which is guilty of a "devaluation of the psyche" (Jung, 1963, pp. 163–164). Like his psychoanalytic cousins, Jung declared that it was of the first importance educationally to bear in mind that the unconscious is the matrix out of which consciousness grows (1954b, p. 52). If the subconscious and unconscious infrastructure of the child's conscious mind is ignored, then it will wreak its vengeance in the form of the psychologically based learning disorders that were discussed in Chapter 1. And even when it does not result in obvious disorders, it will still hamper creativity.

When education is "confined to precise techniques learned and applied [in the service of] the workplace," the neo-Jungian theorist Andrew Samuels (2001) has argued, it is "psychologically demeaning" to students and teachers (p. 139). Such things impoverish the classroom—transforming it from a potentially enchanted zone of deep moral encounter into a corporate cubicle of emotional deadening and social engineering. Corporate education "blots out" the individual—a dehumanization that "begins in school [and] continues at the university" (Jung, 1953, p. 153). Jung judged such approaches to education as nothing less than grossly immoral, for they spawn the "mass man" of technocratic society by dulling the teacher's and student's sense of existential identity and interpersonal connectedness. Violating the archetypal relationship between teacher and student, the technical-rationalist approach to teaching and learning is both a cause and symptom of a deeper psychological, social, and moral malaise (Jung, 1954a, p. 48; 1954b, pp. 14–15). This explains Jung's warning that an overemphasis on "technique" in therapy and education is politically dangerous.

On the other hand, the good therapist and teacher, by helping their clients and students discover their own psychospiritual depths, empower, them to resist both the seductions and threats of a morally vacuous political order. By promoting psychospiritual health in order to resist the dehumanizing status quo, therapy and education are inevitably political. They foster psychospiritual health in the service of resistance and freedom in what the British sociologist Anthony Giddens (1990, 1991) has called "lifestyle politics." Because psychoanalysis and archetypal psychotherapy are two of the 20th century's greatest tools of "lifestyle politics," a pedagogy that is grounded in these therapies can serve politically liberatory functions in the classroom (Castoriadis, 1991; Samuels, 1997). What I am arguing, then, is that the classroom —under the sign of *Eros*—can become a site of lifestyle politics through pedagogical resistance to the unreality and dehumanization of the corporate state. The teacher who employs the curriculum to develop not only cognitive and technical skills in her students but also to promote psychological and spiritual growth is in the temenos (the "sacred precinct") of the archetypal classroom—pedagogically engaged in lifestyle politics. Education for individuation is a revolutionary act.

Of course, not everyone has the ability or resources to engage in the therapeutic or "therapy-like" process of individuation. However, as Giddens (1990, 1991) has argued, the world-historical significance of "therapy" is not that everyone can now enter therapy but that the growth of the therapeutic movement, indeed its "triumph" (Rieff, 1987), reflects the growing tendency throughout Western history—at least since the Renaissance—for individuals to explore and expand the limits of their unique psychospiritual identity. That tendency has reached a world-historical climax at this time, Giddens argues, which means that, whether or not a person is formally "in therapy," she is probably more or less engaged in quasi-therapeutic projects involving self-exploration and self-creation. This is what he calls the "self-reflexive project of late modernity." A psychoanalytically and archetypally rich pedagogy—by promoting such "self-reflexivity" in teachers and students—adds an educational dimension to the lifestyle politics of reflexivity and resistance.

Another reason that it is now more important than ever to promote therapeutically sensitive classrooms has to do with the fact that late modernity is a historically unique time for individuals in the technologically advanced nations. To a degree unknown before, people are experiencing the dilemmas and opportunities of defining and maintaining a coherent sense of self in a cultural environment in which there are fewer and fewer moral certainties shared by all people. These dilemmas and opportunities for self-creation are the very stuff of lifestyle politics. "In the post-traditional order of modernity," writes Giddens,

> and against the backdrop of new forms of mediated experience, self-identity becomes a reflexively organized endeavor. The reflexive project of the self, which consists in the sustaining of coherent, yet continuously revised, biographical narratives, takes place in the context of multiple choice as filtered through abstract systems. (1991, p. 5)

In other words, with more and more options about how to interpret and carry on their lives in an environment that has fewer and fewer traditional certainties to guide them, it becomes increasingly difficult for some people to create a coherent narrative about their lives—one that tells the where they came from, the significance of where they presently are and what they are doing, and where all of this is all leading. A therapeutically sensitive pedagogy can help a student create such a narrative for herself. How can it do this? To answer that question, it is necessary to look in greater depth at Giddens' idea of the life-narrative in late-modernity.

Giddens lists four major problems that an individual must negotiate in creating a satisfying life-narrative in late modernity. First is the problem of "unification versus fragmentation." By this, Giddens means that a person in our increasingly multicultural society generally has many different ways and contexts in which to see herself: as a parent and spouse or a single person; as a member of a particular socio-economic group; as a member of a political party or a racial, ethnic, regional, or national group; as a member of various clubs or other types of voluntary organizations; as one who chooses to identify herself—through dress, linguistic mannerisms, musical preferences, spending habits, and even food choices—with a particular sub-cultural group; and as a person whose form of spirituality may range from an affiliation with a traditional religious institution, to a combination of various different traditions (Zen-Catholic, Jewish-Buddhist, and so on), to a completely individualistic and idiosyncratic form of spirituality. With so many "lifestyle" options, how does the individual overcome a sense of fragmentation in order to create a more or less integral self-narrative?

Second is the problem of "powerlessness versus appropriation." Giddens describes this dilemma, which is similar to the previous one, thus: "the lifestyle options made available by modernity offer many opportunities for appropriation, but also generate feelings of powerlessness" (1991, p. 201). The third dilemma has to do with "authority versus uncertainty." "In circumstances in which there are no final authorities," Giddens points out, "the reflexive project of the self must steer a way between commitment and uncertainty" (1991, p. 201).

Fourth is the problem Marx (1978 [1844]) also wrote about —namely, that of "personalized versus commodified experience." As people get more addicted to things, they become more like things—and less like people. This issue is exacerbated by the new media, which work very hard to convince us that we should be just like the characters we see on television and DVDs or hear on our iPods® and CDs—people who are painted in glitzy, slick, and salacious hues, encouraging us to become mindless consumers of everything from beer and trucks to personal computers and impersonal sex. The purveyors of these media images of "desirable" people and things want the individual to buy into those images that they have so slyly designed to lure the individual into ever deepening addiction to consumption—in order, of course, to maximize their profits. Giddens concludes: "The narrative of the self must be constructed in such circumstances in which personal appropriation is influenced by standardized influences on consumption" (1991, p. 201).

A therapeutically sensitive, archetypally rich education can help teachers and students deal with these issues by aiding them in the construction of psychologically and socially healthy narratives. Abraham Maslow (1968, p. 693) set the tone of this therapeutic-educational enterprise several decades ago when he wrote:

> if we want to be helpers, counselors, teachers, guides, or psychotherapists, what we must do is to accept the person and help him learn what kind of person he is already. What is his style, what are his aptitudes, what is the person good for, not good for, what can we build upon, what are his good raw materials, his potentialities?... Above all, we would care for the child, that is, enjoy him and his growth and his self-actualization.

The key phrase here is "self-actualization," which was for many years the highest level in Maslow's famous "hierarchy of needs."

The educational philosopher Maxine Greene (1974) also said that the curriculum should offer the student the "possibility for him as an existing person [to make] sense of his own life-world." "Making sense" of one's "life-world," is, of course, equivalent to creating a coherent life-narrative and to the existentialist project of living in "good faith." Greene was arguing that the most important educational project in late modernity is to create classrooms in which students may appropriate what they learn in order to forge a unique and morally rich self-narrative, one which challenges the corporate capitalist status quo. This late-modern educational goal also is the purpose of Noddings' (1992, 1995) "teaching as care," where the teacher nurtures the student into a unique apprehension of her own life-world.

Many of the best teachers seem to intuitively understand and practice the therapeutically sensitive principles of narrative construction. When, for instance, teachers say (as they so often do) "I teach students, not subjects," they are underlining the fact that their pedagogy is dedicated above all to helping students define and refine themselves as politically, ethically, and spiritually integrated individuals. In teaching in this mode, subject-matter is important, but it is secondary to the teacher's deeper moral concern for her students' general existential well-being— their "coherent life-narrative."

In interviewing a high-school art teacher for another study several years ago, for example, I found that her primary goal was not to make an artist of every student but rather to use art as a medium for helping her students make sense out of their lives—particularly in times of crisis, by "just trying to let them know I'm there for them to talk to, if they need something, a shoulder to cry on, whatever.... 'Just come to me if you have a problem!'" She went on to explain that her ultimate objective as an art teacher was

> to get to a more personal level with my kids—their artwork—because sometimes they are using it as therapy to get through a hard time—or to deal with a past experience. They don't even realize why they are doing certain pictures or certain sculptures a certain way. And you get to really know the kids deep down. Sometimes you live with them from crisis to crisis..., and you're trying to put them back together. Sometimes it's just crazy, but it's just so neat to see them respond to you. A light goes on inside them: "Oh, now I see!" It's wonderful!

A gifted painter, this teacher saw her students' paintings as secondarily a technical exercise but primarily as an attempt to "know the kids deep down," to help "put them back together," "living with them from crisis to crisis" so that, finally, each student can begin to create not only an image on canvas but a holistic inner picture of her life—one that vibrates with direction, purpose, and insight. "Oh, now I see!"

Like a good therapist, then, the therapeutic teacher is a good listener whose empathic responses to her student encourages the student to forge a powerful self-narrative.

> [T]he teacher, to participate in a young person's emerging or unfolding story, must be an able listener, one who "listens" the young person into an articulate consciousness, and a narrator who has the necessary language to fit an episode into the young person's story line. This narrative function has been left to instruments of evaluation, the language of which is severely limited, reductive, and often distracting. These instruments do answer the question, "where are you?" but the answers which come back in terms of impersonal groupings or structures cannot inter-relate the young person's past, present, and future. In contrast, the language of the person who is called to teach can become poetry in Heidegger's sense—naming "what is" in new ways. The poetry can recollect old life, redirect it, and renew it for the future. (Huebner, 1999, p. 383)

In sum, the therapeutically sensitive teacher helps the student respond to Giddens' four dilemmas of late modernity and construct a viable narrative by fostering in the student (1) a sense of unity in her personality, (2) the conviction that she can personally appropriate what she discovers in class (3) the belief that she has some degree of authority about the direction of her life, and (4) the knowledge that this teacher recognizes and honors her as a unique person—one whom she can trust to never reduce her to a category, to just one of many students on a computerized list, or to a statistical coefficient on a standardized test. The therapeutically sensitive teacher—richly endowed with the wisdom of *Eros*—stands as an advocate and "narrative guide" for the student-hero or heroine in his or her intellectual, emotional, and moral journeys in the classroom.

Part 3: Teaching from the Spirit, Teaching to the Spirit

A deep and rich life-narrative must deal with what T.S. Eliot called "the overwhelming questions"—those issues that revolve around the experience of morality and mortality (Ricoeur, 1976). What does it mean to lead a good life? Am I doing so right now? Do I continue to exist as a person after I die? If so, what is the nature of that existence—and will my ways of living during this life affect the nature of my life on the other side of the mortal veil? What is the best thing to do with the portion of time, talents, and energy that have been allotted to me in this life? These questions are central to any serious life-narrative. In addressing these issues, such a narrative will naturally draw upon the archetypal realm, for these issues are themselves archetypal. The very impulse to find moral direction in life is itself an archetype, said Jung,

> a function of the human soul, as old as humanity itself. Morality is not imposed from outside; we have it in ourselves from the start—not the law, but our moral nature without which the collective life of human society would be impossible. That is why morality is found at all levels of society. It is the instinctive regulator of action.... (1953, p. 27)

The most compelling life-narratives are those that grapple with these questions as authentically as possible. They are also narratives that are always more or less in a state of flux as the self-narrator is constantly revisiting and refashioning her narrative in light of more complex experience and deeper wisdom. This recursive process—in which narrative deliberation engenders action, which in turn leads to deeper forms of narrative deliberation—results in those "exemplary" life-narratives that inspire other individuals to imagine their own narratives in principled freedom.

Some of these life-narratives are actually written down, and a few of them receive popular acclaim. Most of them are simply lived out in quiet dignity among one's circle of family and friends. But in all cases, these life-stories are (narrative theorists assure us) infused with and informed by a moral purpose. Indeed, a life-narrative aims at nothing less than "creating, negotiating, and displaying the moral standing of the self" (Linde, 1993, p. 123), which is why such texts are both made and interpreted in an ultimately "ethical spirit" (Booth, 1972, p. 62). White (1980, p. 27) poses the rhetorical question, "Could we ever narrativize without moralizing?"; for, the very idea of a narrative, on one hand, and the necessity of establishing meaning (that quintessentially moral endeavor) on the other hand, cannot be separated.

The fact that our narratives are inevitably "moral" does not necessarily mean that they encode a particular religion's or culture's view of the Good—although they can do that, and can do it with great passion and sincerity, as the autobiographical accounts of everyone from St. Augustine to Mother Teresa show (in exemplifying religious virtues), and of everyone from Marcus Aurelius to Winston Churchill demonstrate (in exemplifying civic virtue).

Without excluding this more conventional sense of "morality," I am using the term in the broader psychospiritual sense that the modern Existentialist theologian Paul Tillich (1959) did in his famous pronouncement that everyone, whether or not they are aware of it, has a set of fundamental assumptions and commitments that define their "ultimate concerns." Those "ultimate concerns," which are the moral infrastructure of a person's "life-narrative," are her "morality." There are doubtlessly better and worse "moralities"—even in this more liberal sense of the term. Gandhi's "ultimate concerns" are not merely different from Hitler's; they are infinitely better than Hitler's—truly and objectively, not just relatively and subjectively. I am not arguing for moral relativism in my use of Tillich's "ultimate concern," for that would run quite contrary to my own beliefs. I simply want to point out that any life-narrative—to even qualify as a life-narrative—rests upon concerns that are ultimate and therefore ethical in nature.

A mature life-narrative must deal not only with questions of morality but with questions of mortality, for the two sets of questions are quite intertwined. What may or may not await us on the other side of death, on one hand, and how our actions here may or may not affect all of that, on the other hand, are issues that typically weave in and out of each other. According to Dunne (1973, p. 37), our stories are the judgment we render on our own lives in search of the eternal—a narrative of our journey "with an unknown God and to an unknown God." As the greatest narrative theorist of our time, Paul Ricouer (1991), has concluded, our life-narratives echo with the longing for eternal truth—something that is durable and reliable beyond our mortal limitations.

What is more, it is not only our individual narratives (as existential beings) but also our collective narratives (in the foundational stories that we call our myths and religions) that embody our ultimate hopes and fears about life and death, for

> every human society is, in the last resort, men banded together in the face of death. The power of religion depends, in the last resort, upon the credibility of the banners it puts in the hands of men as they stand before death, or more accurately, as they walk, inevitably, toward it. (Berger, 1967, p. 52)

Tillich (1956, p. 103) eloquently captured this interaction of psyche, culture, and spirit in his famous statement that "religion is the soul of culture and culture the form of religion." Self, society, and spirit form an inseparable whole. Jung also believed in this indivisibility of religion, community, and soul. He wrote that any adequate psychology must realize that there is both a cultural component to consciousness and a religious foundation to culture; for, every culture has "a highly developed system of secret teaching, a body of lore concerning the things that lie beyond man's earthly existence, and of wise rules of conduct" (1966, p. 96). A society's foundational narratives grow out of this "body of lore," which in turn rests upon that society's unique apprehension and "living out" of the archetypes.

Thus, both personal and cultural narratives are typically and inextricably involved with issues that are spiritual—a term which, for the purposes of this book, I would define as the pursuit (either institutional and formal or personal and informal) of a transpersonal and transtemporal reality which entails a code of behavior based upon compassionate service to others. Or as one of the most beloved passages of scripture in my faith community puts it quite simply: "When ye are in the service of your fellow beings, ye are only in the service of your God" (Mosiah 2: 17, The Book of Mormon). And as we have already discussed, many sociologists of religion stress that spirituality is as important now to most people as it ever was, and perhaps even more so (Greeley, 1974; Johnstone, 1997; Marty, 1987; Wuthnow, 1994).

Given the psychological and cultural importance as well as the narrative centrality of spiritual commitments, any education that does not honor spirituality is at best hollow and potentially destructive. "The ultimate goal of education," Huebner reminds us, "is the journey of the soul" (1999, p. 20). We, as theorists and teachers, must not foreclose our own or our students' journeys of the soul. If schools are not places where these journeys can take place, and where stories can be made and told about them, then education becomes morally irrelevant and psychologically alienating to teachers and students alike. Sadly, the message conveyed in most colleges of education today is that spirituality is and should be taboo in the classroom, especially the public school classroom (Kniker, 1990; Nord, 1990; Warshaw, 1986).

Yet, as pedagogically and personally problematic as such a message to our teachers and students is, how can we, after all, introduce spirituality into the classroom without crossing some very healthy legal and institutional prohibitions on religion in the public education? I want to suggest that an archetypal approach to education provides an important way to answer this question.[7]

EDUCATION FOR INDIVIDUATION

I believe that by promoting individuation in students, schools can help each student discover her own ultimate truths in legally appropriate ways that neither prohibit nor promote religion in the classroom—as provided by the First Amendment (also see Lemon v. Kurtzman, 403 US 602 [1971]). Individuation is a process that, although inherently spiritual, neither requires nor forbids specific spiritual beliefs or religious commitments. This makes an archetypal pedagogy well suited for

---

7 The reader who is interested in exploring in greater depth than the present study allows how to introduce explicitly spiritual themes and activities in public school classrooms in legally and institutionally appropriate ways should consult Brown et al., 1976; Kniker, 1990; Marsden, 1997; Mayes & Ferrin, 2001; Nord, 1994, 1995; Warshaw, 1986; and Whitmore, 1986.

achieving a fair and balanced approach to spiritually oriented topics in the public school classroom. Education as individuation accomplishes this balance because, in archetypally oriented forms of teaching and learning, the teacher and students can, in authentic and mutually respectful dialogue, archetypally examine the structures and images that underlie their own and each other's personal spirituality and cultural traditions.

Jung (1954a, p. 80) wrote that "the highest dominant always has a religious of philosophical character." This "highest dominant" is what Tillich meant by "ultimate concern." Any pedagogy that aims at the revelation and cultivation of students' "ultimate concerns" personally and culturally is necessarily spiritual—yet doctrinally neutral. Naturally, such discourse in the classroom must adhere to the basic legal requirements of any classroom discussion that involves such issues: (1) the student's expressions of belief or non-belief in a higher spiritual reality must be directly relevant to the topic under discussion in the classroom and appropriate to the age of the students; (2) all the other students must also be given a chance to express their beliefs; and (3) teachers must not endorse or in any other way privilege the religious or non-religious opinion of any student in the classroom (Nord, 1994). Happily, these are precisely the kinds of conditions that should, in any case, naturally exist when students are examining the archetypal images and ideas that underlie their own and their classmates' deepest beliefs relative to a topic under discussion in the classroom.

An archetypal approach to teaching and learning, in other words, accommodates the expression of diverse cultural and spiritual perspectives in a legally and pedagogically appropriate way by (1) tapping into those dominant archetypes that inform a student's individual and cultural life, and (2) offering various opportunities for her to study those of her classmates (Jung, 1954a, p. 80). In this kind of open educational environment, students can become "ethnographic detectives"—Heath's (1983) felicitous phrase for students engaged in multicultural classroom activities where they explore and honor the foundational principles and practices of each others' ways of seeing, being, and acting in the world. In this way, a true "community of learning" (Brown et al., 1989) can be created and maintained—one that is never trivial because it deals with matters of ultimate concern, and yet one that is multiculturally rich because it genuinely honors the foundations of a wide variety of other perspectives, experiences, and traditions. This approach to the discussion of cultural/spiritual commitments in the classroom allows passionate involvement while also fostering genuine tolerance—worthy goals for a truly democratic society.

Jung believed that there are many ways to access the Divine because there are many archetypal images (i.e., individual beliefs and cultural traditions) that emanate from and embody the God-archetype (Jung, 1964, p. 667). In the Jungian view, the search for the Self is so deeply involved in the search for the Divine that it is difficult, and perhaps impossible, to separate the two quests.[8] Thus, when education is promoting the student's individuation and the discovery of her innermost Self, it is thereby encouraging her to engage in various forms of spiritual inquiry into her own and her classmates' ultimate concerns, and it is doing so in legally appropriate ways that revolve around the exploration and sharing of archetypal images and motifs that can be examined as such and not as doctrinal statements. Moreover, such education for individuation is well suited to our psychologically oriented times. As the great Jungian psychiatrist and student of religion Edward Edinger (1973, p. 104) wrote, "For the modern man, an encounter with the autonomous archetypal psyche is equivalent to the discovery of God."

When education leads in this manner to diverse experiences of various foundational cultural and spiritual truths, then the classroom becomes a Jungian temenos, an enchanted precinct, in which the teacher and her students individually and jointly engage in the project of individuation through the vehicle of the curriculum. In profound and respectful dialogue, they individually and jointly explore and celebrate that which is culturally rich and spiritually revelatory in themselves and each other. They do not preach at each other; they edify each other —and in this way, grow as individuals and as a class. This is truly democratic dialogue in the service of the spirit. It is also spiritual inquiry that serves pluralistic democracy by encouraging deep knowledge of each other. Teachers and students discover themselves as cultural and spiritual beings at the deepest archetypal levels—and they do it through the curriculum, in relationship, and for themselves and each other.

---

8 It is necessary to bear in mind, however, that whether or not Jung believed that individuation and the search for the Self were "spiritual" depends on the phase of Jung's career to which one is referring. As Palmer (1997), Shamdasani (2003), and Homans (1985) have pointed out, Jung's view was increasingly spiritual from the middle to later phase of his career. However, in the earlier phases of his career, Jung was probably more inclined to believe that the subjective variability of religious experience served to cast doubt on the ontological validity of those experiences. See Mattoon, 1985; Palmer, 1997; Ulanov, 1999; and White, 1982 [1952] on the idea that the search for the Self is ultimately religious in nature.

Not only do we dare to educate our children in these terms; we dare not do so in any other terms. Education that does not originate in and aim at the ultimate concerns of the individuation process must ultimately fall short of its full potential, for "the journey of the self is short circuited or derailed by those who define the ends of life and education in less than ultimate terms" (Huebner, 1999, p. 404). An approach to subject-matter that encourages archetypal explorations in teachers and students provides a "transcendental ideology of the curriculum" (Macdonald, 1995) that neither favors nor excludes the personally or culturally important spiritual beliefs (or lack of beliefs) of any student. Education for individuation continually and creatively attempts to incarnate the various personal and cultural manifestations of the *Spirit of Ultimacy* in the classroom as teachers and students — archetypal heroes and heroines in search of ever greater knowledge of self, others, and the divine — meet and come to know each other with increasing depth and goodwill in the sacred space of the living curriculum.

CHAPTER FIVE

THE TEACHER AS SHAMAN

As the first example of archetypal reflectivity, I would like to mine the archetypal image of a shaman—a First-Nation medicine man, many of whose functions revolve around teaching—to see what gold it may yield in telling us about the deeper spiritual nature of a teacher's calling and practice.

WHAT IS A SHAMAN?

Before looking at the teacher as shaman, let us first look at the traditional definition of a shaman.

Mircea Eliade, who after almost half a century probably remains the most authoritative source on shamanism, informs us that the shaman, being a doctor, is able to heal. Furthermore, "the shaman, and he alone, is the great master of 'ecstasy'" (Eliade, 1954). Here Eliade is using the term "ecstasy" in its classic sense as "ex-stasis"—transcending oneself—in this case to travel to other realms of existence. Because he (most shamans are males) regularly journeys to both the underworld and the heavens, the shaman is able to serve as a *psychopomp*. A psychopomp is someone who has gained sacred knowledge, mastered certain spiritual techniques, and has otherworldly experiences which enable him now to guide others in their own mystical journeys to either the heavens or the underworld.

Most important of all is the fact that the shaman receives his calling in the form of a wound. In many cases, shamans have been rescued from their initial crises by agreeing to learn to shamanize and help others. In other cases "the shaman must first cure himself and his initiatory sickness and only afterwards can cure the other members of the community" (Walsh, 1990, p. 205). Like most archetypal heroes, the shaman must experience a period of separation from his people because of this wound, forsaking the comfortable confines of his community in order to enter the forest or desert of tribulation and transfiguration. There, he learns crucial lessons which prepare him for his ultimate heavenly ascent. Then, and only then, is he in a position to bring back saving knowledge to his people (Campbell, 1949).

The Call as a Vocative Wound

Several years ago, I had a student named Larry (the names of all the informants in this chapter have been changed) who was in his mid-thirties while in our educational leadership program at Brigham Young University, preparing to become a principal. He shared with me an epiphanic moment that had happened some fifteen years previously, resulting in his decision to become a teacher. It exemplifies in dramatically shamanic terms the *vocative* dimension of teaching—a term which I am using in the classic sense of a "vocation" or spiritual calling.

"I think I have a fair idea of why you want to be a principal, Larry," I said one day during a conversation in my office, for we had often discussed this. "But I'm interested in how you first decided to be a teacher." "Well, I was in my sophomore year," he said as he leaned back in his chair. "I was cutting weight for the wrestling team, and it's amazing what sacrificing food can do to clarify your vision. I'd been fasting quite a while, and it was winter and I couldn't sleep, so I went out and ran for a couple of hours. The snow was coming down. And I lay down in the snow and I looked up at the sky. A clear Iowa sky with no lights around! It was beautiful. And I just thought, 'I'm so confused. I don't know what to do. I don't know what I need to do—what God wants me to do!' And then," Larry continued, "it came to me, like a flash out of that clear cold sky, that I wanted to affect people, especially children, and help them believe in themselves and have confidence. That bolt from the blue that night in the field—that's when it all started."

The imagery Larry used to describe the moment of his calling is not only compelling but also suggestive for our purposes here, for as Eliade notes, "sometimes one becomes a shaman after a divine election...; for example, the gods choose a future shaman by striking him with lightning.... The role of lightning in designating the shaman is important; it shows the celestial origin of shamanic powers" (Eliade, 1954, p. 19). And thus had my student experienced his calling—as a metaphorical lightning bolt which issued from another realm and sought him out on a snowy Iowa farm at midnight.

Of course, not all calls issue so suddenly. Often, the vocative dimension of a call to teach occurs more gradually—but no less definitively. But whether the call is instantaneous and dramatic, as in Larry's case, or unfolds in a less "jolting" fashion, the sense of spiritual calling to any life-work typically partakes of the "mystery of transfiguration..., a spiritual passage, which, when complete, amounts to a dying and a birth" (Campbell, 1949, p. 51). Is it any wonder, then, that we often resist a call because of the momentous changes that it will certainly entail, often dragging us kicking and screaming out of our comfort zones? And this is all the more true when the call is beckoning toward a profession which is so emotionally demanding, politically complex, culturally misunderstood, and generally undervalued as is teaching in the contemporary U.S. In these cases, the call to teach is what I identify as the first of the three wounds of the shamanic teacher—*the vocative wound.*

I was speaking to Peg, a woman in her mid-thirties at a small university in the Northwestern part of the United States. She told me the story of her journey to the blackboard.

> My mother was a teacher, and I saw how much work she put into teaching. It made me angry, and not only for her sake but also because I felt it robbed me of her attention. And I thought, "I'll never be a teacher! Never!" So I spent many years avoiding that calling, even though I think I knew from the time I left high school that it's what I was meant to do. But boy, did I ever try to deny it! It's been within the past five or six years (now that my children are out of elementary school) that I have seen that I can't avoid it any longer. So a few years ago I became an aide and got into the classroom with the children. I've struggled a lot with depression, but when I am in the classroom with the children, I don't think about myself. I'm just always thinking about the children. I love it! I just feel like, "Finally, I'm where I'm supposed to be!"

It was clear to me in our conversation that vocative wounding had been key in Peg's taking on the mantle of the teacher. At the same time, she was certain that being a teacher had aided greatly in dispelling her depression. This is a constant theme in the shamanic literature: one becomes ill if one denies the call. I sensed that at least some of Peg's depression may have been due to her long standing refusal to accept the call to teach. I recalled something Walsh (1990, p. 38) had written in his Jungian interpretation of shamanism.

> The call to shamanism may be received with considerable ambivalence, and those who receive it may be regarded as "doomed to inspiration...." [If the shaman-elect continues to refuse the call,] the spirits, symptoms, or dreams may be distressingly persistent and eventually win out. Indeed, many shamanic traditions, like many hero traditions, hold that refusal of the call can result in sickness, insanity, or death.

Certainly, in my own case, I find that after more than six or seven weeks of just researching and not teaching, I begin to get a little "squirrelly," as my wife aptly puts it. I *need* to teach, and I know that the gods get quite cross with me when I do not. Like my students, I cannot refuse the call—or rather, cannot refuse it for very long without paying emotional and spiritual costs.

The question and consequences of refusing the call to teach are especially poignant and paradoxical for young people in the U.S. today. Virtually every message that they receive about teaching has the cynical subtext that becoming a teacher is a betrayal of one's "full potential." To choose the classroom instead of the more glamorous and lucrative courtroom, operating theater, or stock exchange as the site of one's lifework is to become a second-class citizen in the eyes of many. For young women as well as members of traditionally marginalized racial and ethnic groups, the conundrum is doubly difficult, I believe, because they may further be accused of betraying their group by falling into a line of work that members of their group once occupied in great numbers before other professional avenues began to open as a result of those equal opportunity programs that got under way in the late 1960s and early 1970s.

A female student of mine last year shared with me an instance of the vocative wound that she had experienced in choosing teaching instead of law. A bright young woman with high grades, she told me once during office hours, "I always wanted to be an attorney. I love the law and politics. And, of course, everybody gave me all kinds of kudos because I was going to be 'Lesley Holt, Attorney at Law'! Impressive-sounding, right? And it was a great plan—it really was. Just one problem. It was all wrong! I felt that God did not intend that path for me." "Did this realization come to you all at once or gradually?" I asked. "It was a series of moments," she replied with a thoughtful furrow of her brows. "It started to dawn on me that pre-law classes weren't bringing me the kind of satisfaction or growth that I was looking for. I felt that I needed to do more, to give more, to help others with the talents that I had. And I felt that I couldn't really do that as a lawyer. I needed to figure out what God wanted me to do. It wasn't an easy process to figure it out! Especially because everyone would say to me, 'You mean that you're giving up being a lawyer in order to become a teacher? You can't be serious!' But," she concluded, grinning broadly, "it felt really good when I finally did come to this conclusion. I felt that I was finally listening to that still, small voice inside me."

We have just seen how in some instances the call to teach *is* a wound. It can also *result from* a wound. The most dramatic example of this type of vocative wound which I have ever seen came from a woman in her early forties. During an interview for another study, she very generously shared with me the following galvanizing story about her decision to leave a highly remunerative position in the business world to become a teacher. "About a year and a half ago, God slammed me in the face and said in effect, 'This is what you are going to do with the rest of your life. You're going to teach!' See, my husband was diagnosed with AIDS, and I found out that I was HIV positive too. It turns out that he'd been messing around with prostitutes near [an overseas military base], where we had been stationed. We decided to stay together—we had been together seventeen years when we found out about the AIDS. I came to understand that I was supposed to stay with this man."

Interestingly, it was at precisely this juncture of maximum psychospiritual intensity that Jill began to experience a steady stream of synchronistic events that "showed me that I was meant to be a teacher. People I hardly even knew started coming up to me and suggesting out of the blue that I be a teacher, 'You *need* to be a teacher,' they all said. They didn't know my history. They didn't know my husband was so ill. Even my mom said I should be a teacher. This was really amazing to me because she said that she had known her entire life that I didn't want to be a teacher. She had been one for twenty years and I had often talked about what a hard job it is. And I mean, now, here's my mom saying, 'Jill, why don't you think about going into teaching?' It was a complete reversal! Suddenly I started getting all these offers from teachers to be a paid aide in their classroom. All of this happened within a year. God was making a point, and I finally got it!" Like a bolt out of the blue.

THE WOUND AND THE VOCATION,
THE WOUND AS THE VOCATION

In *Four Quartets,* T.S. Eliot (1971, p. 27) wrote,

> The wounded surgeon plies the steel
> That questions the distempered part.
> Beneath the bleeding hands we feel
> The sharp compassion of the healer's art
> Resolving the enigma of the fever chart.

I have always felt that Eliot's Christological imagery in this stanza is also a poetic acknowledgment of all great healers, guides, and teachers who have become compassionate and wise in their calling due to their own suffering. In my own experience as a teacher of teachers and as a student of teaching, I have come to believe that the teachers who touch one most deeply are also those who seem to have suffered the most. Of course, in some, and perhaps many cases, suffering simply embitters and may even destroy a person. But when it does not do this, pain engenders a more mature and tender knowledge of self, others, and subject matter. Certainly I know that the more I confront, survive, and am shaped by life's trials and tragedies, the better I become as a teacher. But how is it that travail can come to play such a crucial role in one's calling and growth as a teacher? Archetypal psychology provides a clue to answering this question.

We can understand pain archetypally as that creatively destructive process of breaking down and then transcending the naïve and solipsistic limitations of mere ego-consciousness. This purifying process grants us access to the domain of the archetypal. Or as Jung (1966, p. 140) averred, what is required for the prospective savior and guide is that she experience a "*katabasis,* a journey to the underworld," which results in her "soul [being] not only impressed by it but radically altered." In most shamanic ceremonies of initiation, therefore, the novitiate is taken apart and then put back together again.

> After a night of incantations, the old shamans take the neophyte to a room shut off by curtains. And there, as they assert, they cut his head open, take out his brains, wash and restore them, to give him a clear mind to penetrate into the mysteries of evil spirits, and the intricacies of disease; they insert gold dust into his eyes to give him keenness and strength of sight

powerful enough to see the soul wherever it may have wan-
dered; they plant barbed hooks on the tips of his fingers to enable him to seize the soul and hold it fast; and lastly they pierce
his heart with an arrow to make him tender-hearted and full of
sympathy with the sick and the suffering. (Eliade, 1954, p. 57)

I believe that Jill, my friend with AIDS, would resonate to these images as a psychologically and morally accurate representation of her experience of vocation and initiation as a teacher. The awareness of her
husband's infidelity and the potential presence of a lethal disease in her
own body obliterated her old ego-driven identity so that she might be
reshaped as a spiritually called teacher. As Jill put it, "it was a complete
reversal" — a shamanic rebirth which empowers the person as a teacher
to serve her students with special insight (because her eyes have been refined with the gold dust of affliction), to have a special power to hold
students who might otherwise stray (because her fingers are crowned
with the barbed wire of adversity), and to radiate a special kind of compassion for her students' suffering (because her heart has been pierced
with an arrow).

Now, I do not mean to imply that one must face a trauma of the
same life-or-death enormity as Jill's to undergo the transformations
that preface a spiritual call to teach. However, without fully and authentically experiencing, exploring, and learning to endure some sort of
significant existential wound that has led to higher insight and deeper
compassion, it is not, in my view, possible to attain full maturity as a
spiritually called teacher. For the spiritually called teacher — no less
than for the prospective shaman — the wound is the heart of the matter.

The Interpretive Wound:
Toward a Homeopathic Pedagogy

The second type of wound that shamanic teachers suffer and must
learn to recognize and treat in themselves and their students is what I
call *the interpretive wound*. Even in the most communally oriented visions of the classroom — where teachers are *not* pictured as the sole
source of knowledge and authority — they must still have access to certain bodies of knowledge and heuristic strategies that their students do
not possess. If teachers do not have this, it is hard to see what distinctive
purpose they serve. After all is said and done, the teacher must remain
— to some degree or other — the captain of her classroom ship.

But even such a healthily authoritative position has its limitations. Teachers' knowledge of their subject matter is always partial and contingent—and they must recognize it as such if they are to have that humility which is the sine qua non of growth. No matter how well informed they are, how profound their insights or how broad their reading, teachers know only so much. Beyond that point, they become learners themselves—fellow travelers with their students in a journey of discovering more about their subject matter and, not incidentally, about themselves and their students. True, they must see a farther horizon than their students do, but their scope is still foreshortened. This epistemological limitation is what I am calling the interpretive wound. And as is always the case with a shamanic figure, it is a wound leading not only to death but also to new life. By frankly facing and even publicly acknowledging their interpretive limitations, teachers become susceptible to change. They can evolve—and in that evolution bring their students along with them to a higher plane of understanding. By being willing to die, to outgrow paradigms and points of view, teachers can then be reborn. Hence, Socrates proclaimed in *The Phaedo* that "true philosophers make dying their profession." And perhaps it is more than just coincidence that when Jesus says that one must die and be reborn to understand the mysteries of the spirit, he is addressing his comments to a "teacher of Israel" (John 3: 9).

But how difficult this paradoxical process is for teachers! On one hand, they must assume some sort of authoritative role in their classrooms. Yet they must also know themselves (and sometimes show themselves) to be fallible. Is it any wonder, then, that so many of us, occasionally unable to reconcile these conflicting demands, attempt to deceive others and ourselves by donning a "teacherly" mask of omniscience (Shaker, 1982)? Like frightened magicians, we hide behind our dark academic gowns, brandish our degrees like maleficent wands, and then threaten our students with the evil potion of a bad grade if they dare to suggest that we are less miraculous, our knowledge less godlike, than we would like to believe and have others believe. All it takes on our part is a withering bit of irony directed at a student, a barely concealed grin after one of her comments, or a seemingly innocuous mention of grading policy, to maintain our tyrannical sway in the classroom. If we persist in denying and concealing our limitations, then those limitations will remain active in our personal shadows, which we will then cast onto our students.

As a classroom example of the teacher fleeing from her own shadow by projecting it onto another, take one who is so threatened by a student whose incisive questions and comments reveal the teacher's own interpretive limitations that she, the teacher, begins to assume a persona of omniscience in order to protect herself by casting her student in the role of the fool. In other words, the teacher projects her own interpretive limitations—her hermeneutic wounding—onto the student, who, as the less empowered member of the dyad, is being set up to internalize the teacher's shadow and see himself as the very clown that she needs him to be if she is to maintain her shaky authority. Denying the interpretive wound in herself, the teacher inflicts an ethical wound on her student.

An excellent way to prevent this is, I believe, to cultivate paradox and complexity in the classroom. This is a medicine that teachers, like the shaman, distill from the psychic material of their own wounds. In my teaching, I always try to stress that very little is clear in dealing with the philosophical, historical, social, and ethical quandaries that beset education in the U.S. today. I insist that every "solution" is a hydra-headed beast. Chop off one problem and seven new ones appear! Although I have wrestled with the Hydra myself for decades in my teaching, reading, and writing, I have not yet conquered the beast—and probably never will. All I can do is what I publicly invite my students to do—which is not to find the one "correct" answer that covers all cases but to identify the approach to a specific question that generates the kinds of problems that one is prepared to accept. I have found that this relativistic message is an especially hard one for students to hear, much less assimilate, in an institution such as the one where I teach—a conservative religious university in the United States. For me, the challenge is to explore with my students how those theological principles which we believe to be universally true can be variously, yet still validly, interpreted and applied by many different people in many different ways, each way depending upon the interpreter's emphasis, situation-specific issues, institutional and historical constraints, and practical goals.

Yet, even in more secular academic settings the same dilemma exists for the shamanic teacher. To take but one example from curriculum theory, which I teach, there is the perennial democratic question of whether the curriculum should emphasize equity or excellence, whether it should be egalitarian or meritocratic. Even if it were possible to achieve complete "equity" in public schooling (I tell my students), this would probably entail a certain overall decline in "excellence." Conversely, an absolute focus on "excellence" at the expense of all else would be unethical, running roughshod over the fact that many differences in student performance stem from socio-economic inequities which, as teachers, we are morally bound not only to acknowledge but to work to correct.

In my classes, we tug and pull at one after another of such Gordian knots. I believe that most of my students emerge from these academic and moral exertions with the curiously enlivening knowledge that there is not a single right answer. There are simply certain measures that generate certain problems. A measure that works in one site, district, or even historical epoch may not be as appropriate as in another—and it may even be wrong. Students often want the quick fix about how to handle a certain issue when they become teachers or principals. But as professors of education we must have both the humility and the courage to freely acknowledge that we do not have those panaceas. Barzun's wise warning regarding the study of history applies to any intellectual inquiry, "Whoever wants an absolute [answer] must gain access to the mind of God" (2000, xi). Here and now, caught in a nexus of epistemic and moral limitations, we can only hope to foster an ever richer sense of the complexity of things so that we may think, feel, and act as authentically and humanely as possible as we find ourselves in that ongoing series of existentially unique configurations that we call "experience."

By publicly sowing, cultivating, and harvesting the crop of complexity and paradox in her classroom—and by inviting her students to join her in this endeavor—the teacher dialectically demonstrates both the profundity and paucity of her knowledge. She thereby inflicts a wound on her students, who now, *a fortiori,* come to understand the limitations of their own vistas. But this is not the same kind of wound wrought by the teacher who casts her interpretive shadow onto her student-victim. Rather, it is a salutary injury wherein the teacher wounds students by awakening them to their existential limitations— and in this way subverts the students' self-serving assumption that they already knew the correct answer before they entered the classroom on the first day, or would in any case soon get it as a reward for a slavish obedience to a teacher-god. In other words, the teacher simply cannot give her students a clean bill-of-health epistemologically or ethically for the simple reason that she is also fevered with the multifarious infections of the human condition. What she can do is skillfully, lovingly inflict a rich wound, a fertile injury—one that (never completely cauterized) motivates her students to seek higher visions and more authentic experiences.

This, then, is the ultimate puzzle in the paradoxical classroom of the shaman-teacher. The boon that she gives is the wound that she lives. Her very pedagogy becomes a "paradoxical passage"

> because it sometimes proves to be an impossibility or a situation from which there is no escape. [C]andidate shamans, or the heroes of certain myths, must sometimes go "where night and day meet," or find a gate in the wall, or go up to the sky through a passage that opens but for an instant, pass between two constantly moving millstones, two rocks that clash together, through the jaws of a monster, and the like. (Eliad,e 1954, pp. 485–486)

Our interpretive wounds as teachers, unacknowledged and untended, fester and pedagogically maim both us and our students. However, with the curious balm of paradox, our wounds can yield a substance which—administered at the right time and in the right doses—will stimulate our students into higher forms of seeing and being, into their own more poignant and potent wounding. What I am arguing for, then, might be called a homeopathic pedagogy. In such a pedagogy, the product of the wound is the treatment for the wound. For in homeopathy, "like cures like."

THE TRANSFERENTIAL WOUND

Having already looked in earlier chapters at the transference in the classroom from various theoretical and practical angles, I offer only a few more examples here—speculating as I proceed about the wounds in which they originated and the wounds that they caused. I have culled these examples from the numerous stories that my students have shared with me over the years.

A particularly dramatic instance of an emotionally and physically hurtful mother-transference by a student onto a female teacher comes from a 45-year-old woman who had been a special education teacher at both elementary and secondary levels for eight years. After one of our group discussions on transference, she wrote later that night in her class journal the following words about one of her students named Warren.

> Warren, a very troubled young man, began our relationship by saying that he trusted me and felt safe with me. Then with-

out notice or reason, he would suddenly see me as the enemy. He would make all sorts of symbolic attempts to "assassinate" me as leader of the class. At first, I couldn't make heads or tails of this. I knew that Warren lived with his grandfather, whom he loved as much as he did his roosters [fitting symbols of the pugnacious male that the grandfather truly was]. We [teachers] strongly suspected that this grandfather was also Warren's father and that his mother was also his half-sister. This mother-sister had abandoned him to his grandfather-father and grandmother and was never seen again by the family. Warren came to our program after he had tried to kill himself because of his grandfather's recent death. He hated his grandmother and every woman, I suspect, because of his mother abandoning him. He made numerous threats to kill his grandmother, whose name, interestingly enough, was Margaret— the same as mine! Every time Warren would say my name his eye would twitch a little bit and he would grimace. He never smiled or laughed. One day during reading, Warren said, "Do you know why women have PMS?" Trying to keep things on an even keel, I answered calmly, "No. Why?" He replied with all the hate and biting contempt he could muster, "Because they deserve it!"

My student then went on to relate how she had been literally wounded by Warren because of what she had come to surmise were his mother-complex transferences onto her.

One day when I called him on something he had done wrong, he became angry at me. He threw a pen at me and it hit me in the shoulder. How he got it to go twenty feet across the classroom and hit my collar bone and shoulder with the impact of a heat-seeking missile I'll never know. But did it hurt! Immediately his eyes teared up and he could barely blubber under his breath, "F***ing grandma!" He would often call me, "Mom," and then follow it up with some negative remark. Most of the time he sought to remind me that I was a second-class person with PMS who was occupying space and who made his world unpleasant and crowded. Then he'd flip-flop and would quietly ask me if I could please get more gum for the classroom store and maybe some markers.

Margaret claimed that understanding the transference gave her a tool for beginning to interpret Warren's psychic wound—and begin to heal her own that she had incurred in her relationship with him.

A less dramatic but equally illustrative example of the classroom problems that can arise because of a negative transference from a student onto a teacher comes from a 28-year-old math teacher who had been at the junior-high-school level for six years. In her class journal, she recalled,

> Tom was a student who was very venomous regarding anything I did or said. I spoke to the counselor about this and he had been hearing similar things from other teachers about Tom. The counselor told me that Tom did fine with male teachers; it was female teachers he responded so negatively to. Well, parent–teacher conferences rolled around and it turned out to be only Mom who showed up because Dad had left the marriage a long time ago. Mom made it quite clear that she was doing me an extremely huge favor by showing up. She kept telling me how many appointments she had canceled or would not make because of our (ten-minute!) parent–teacher conference. Mom was very harsh, very critical of Tom and demanded better performance "or else." So I think Tom hated all women because he hated his mother. And I can't say that I blame him. She was a cold fish, a real witch, and definitely a taskmaster with him. As far as I could determine, she was never at all affectionate with Tom. Whenever I saw him with his mother, he was always quite submissive. That's why I believe he was lashing out at all the female teachers—it was an attempt to get back at his mother.

Another member of one of my graduate seminars reported a series of events involving not a student and a teacher but a supervisor and her superiors in the district office. Mike, a 47-year-old man who had been a secondary-school teacher for 20 years, wrote,

> My current supervisor, Betty, was an only child. Her father was a military man and a school teacher. He had high expectations for Betty, and from what she has told me, always demanded nothing less than complete excellence from her. She had worked hard to please him as a girl and young woman, jumping whenever he barked a command. Now, I see her showing this deference to her male superiors at the district of-

fice. She simply will not question male authority and is constantly seeking men's approval. She toes their party line to the tee. I've found that in our curriculum committee meetings, she allows me to take liberties well beyond what she permits the female curriculum members to take. I have more opportunities to speak up, and she often defers to my opinion on matters, but not when that opinion is likely to rock the boat with a male superior.

By the end of the term, Mike, after thinking, speaking, and writing about Betty in class and in his journal, had gradually come to the conclusion that her unresolved psychic wound, inflicted on her by a totalitarian father, caused her not only to continue playing out this possible Electra complex with her district superiors but also to inflict wounds on the female teachers in her charge. If his reading of the situation is correct, Mike's conclusions certainly square with those of Grumet (1988), who has examined a similar dynamic between female teachers and the male principals in certain schools, with the women teachers playing out Electra dynamics, searching for the "father's" approval and love in their interactions with the principals, and the principals relating to the female teachers on the basis of their Oedipal need for female attention and affection. I would add the archetypal dimension to Grumet's analysis and point out that these projections might also be infused with the transpersonal imagery and energy of the Great Wise Father and the Great Nurturing Mother (Neumann 1954).

A final example of a teacher wounded by a need for perfection that resulted from a troubled relationship with her mother comes from Annie—an extremely bright and engaging 30-year-old woman who had been an elementary school teacher for six years. Perhaps because she knew that I had a counseling practice, she had told me that she had been sexually abused throughout her childhood by both of her parents. Having spent many years in therapy, she was "therapy savvy" and quite conversant with the terms and mechanisms of transference. Of her wounded relationship with a past principal, she wrote,

> I have come to realize that I have applied my feelings about my mother to a previous principal—let's call her Vera. I viewed Vera as a mother and saw her real faults in a very unaccepting way. My reaction to her shortcomings was exaggerated and unfair. I was expecting perfection, protection, and attention from this person. When in my estimation she didn't perform

adequately, I felt intense disdain and dislike for her. I would then "repent" guiltily and try to make up for my often unexpressed feelings about her by being extra helpful. This relates to my past, having had a mother who failed to protect me from abuse. It is inappropriate in the present because of the extreme nature of my response to Vera's actions. She may have made mistakes and had weaknesses, but my reaction to them was overblown.

The rupture in Annie's relationship with both her personal mother and the archetypal Great Mother was, Annie believed, repeating itself in the form of her relationship with her female principal.

Finally, Brandy, a 30-year-old unmarried teacher, offers a good example of a syntonic (productive) counter-transference by her onto her students. Her counter-transferences, stemming from a wound, operated to her students' benefit, not harm—although they exacted a substantial cost from her in terms of time and energy. Passionately engaged with her work and students, she was pursuing a graduate degree in order to move into more influential roles in her school. In her journal, she noted that

when I taught at the junior high level, I spent a lot of time consciously and unconsciously trying to save young boys who were slowly falling away from the school and from society in general. I know that this directly relates to having had two brothers who left the public schools and, as a result, fell into really troubled life-styles for a time. I think that I came to view myself as the nurturing mother—going way beyond what a teacher is called upon to do—in order to save the boys in my classroom. Sometimes I would be a nurturing mother to them, sometimes a controlling mother, but my goal was always to make up for my loss of control over my own brothers' situation by making things alright for my at-risk students.

Brandy's counter-transferential wound empowered her and her students.

I hope these examples have served to convey to the reader some sense of how important it is for us as teachers to know whether we are involved in counter-transference with a student or students—and, if so, whether it is positive or negative. If the teacher recognizes this in a timely, sensitive, and sensible way, not only can the negative effects of the counter-transference be avoided, but its energy may be alchemically translated into a force for pedagogical good. By not merely facing but honestly embracing our wounding, we start to attain the psychic adroitness of the good shaman.

This has curricular implications for colleges of education. A course exploring the theory and practice of the transference, with special reference to its application to educational settings, should be a standard feature of the curricula of graduate educational leadership programs. Teacher education curricula might, with substantial modifications, also include some limited mention of these sensitive issues — always keeping in mind the relative lack of teaching experience and, in general, the limited life experience of most undergraduate students.

THE SHAMANIC TEACHER AS A PSYCHOPOMP

The climax of the shaman's calling is to be a *psychopomp*. In Greek mythology, a psychopomp is a person who has learned certain sacred lessons and techniques that have prepared him to serve as a guide of souls to other spheres of existence. He journeys through various realms of existence "in order to learn, to heal, and to help. He may seek knowledge and power either for himself or for his people. He may seek information for healing, for hunting, or to appease and petition the gods" (Walsh, 1990, p. 142). In a word, the shaman is a teacher. Nowhere is this mystico-pedagogical role clearer than in his function as psychopomp. He visits, interprets, and reconciles different levels and types of being in order to bring saving knowledge and healing power to his apprentices and community. It is true that his sacred vestments exhibit many triumphant symbols, but they also contain other symbols of the wounds that he has suffered — and must cause others to suffer. The shaman as teacher as well as the teacher as shaman thus personify what Kerenyi, in his study of Chiron, the wounded physician in Greek mythology, called the archetype of "the wounded healer."

> The tragic view was that Chiron's wound was incurable. Thus Chiron's world, with its inexhaustible possibilities of cure, remained a world of eternal sickness. And even aside from this suffering, his cave, the site of a chthonic subterranean cult, was an entrance to the underworld. The picture to which all these elements, religious and poetic, give rise is unique. The half-human, half-theriomorphic [in the form of an animal]

god suffers eternally from his wound; he carries it with him to the underworld as though the primordial science that this mythological physician, precursor of the luminous divine physician, embodied for the men of later times were nothing other than the knowledge of a wound in which the healer forever partakes. (1959, pp. 98–99)

Partly human, partly beast, the shaman has confronted and combined the conscious and unconscious aspects of himself, the light and the shadow, the intact and the torn. Similarly, spiritually called teachers are wounded healers. They have examined the delicate, living tissues of human knowing and feeling; they have pondered how complexly those tissues intertwine; they have come to know in their own bodies how easily and painfully the spiritual tissues rip, how laboriously they mend, and how inevitably they scar. But even more than this, they understand that these wounds breed existential possibilities. They are aware of all this because they have known it for themselves by having experienced it in themselves.

Finally, then, the shamanic teacher not only shares psychic, epistemological and ontological wounds with her students; she knows how to tend to them in herself and others, and this allows her to be acutely "caring" in her calling. If we are to explore all the compelling implications of Noddings' (1995) powerful notion of teaching as "ontological care," we can do so best in the context of the wound. Only in this way can we communicate with our students not only mind to mind, but heart to heart. This bestowal of ontological heart-knowledge is hauntingly symbolized in a shamanic practice in tropical South America, where "magical power is concretized in an invisible substance that masters transfer to the novices, sometimes from mouth to mouth," as well as in Sumatra, where "the initiatory master blows in the apprentice's ear through a bamboo tube to enable him to hear the voice of spirits" (Eliade, 1954, pp. 52, 96).

Indeed, like Jesus, whom I believe to be humanity's greatest Shaman, the shamanic teachers' wounds are the very evidence and instruments of grace. And this is the crowning paradox of the teacher as shaman. Having suffered the darkness of the vocative, interpretive, and projective wounds, she now wins the various bright tokens that symbolize her apotheosis as a light-bearer.

The rock crystals that play an important part in the initiation of the Australian medicine man are of celestial origin, or at least related—even if sometimes only indirectly—to the sky. Baiame [the Supreme Deity] sits on a throne of transparent crystal [and] throws the fragments of crystal, doubtless detached from his throne, down to earth.... The detached crystals from his throne are "solidified light." (Eliade, 1954, p. 137)

Teachers who understand their calling in spiritual terms may learn a great deal from the life of the shaman if they will but cultivate some of the patterns and possibilities of that life in their own reflectivity and practice. They must skillfully suffer their own wounds. Sometimes they must also tend to those of their students. They must be humble enough to admit their disciplinary limitations, and thus be able to grow. And finally they must suffer the wound of their misunderstood calling. But if spiritually called teachers are willing to tread this path of restorative pain, then they will be in a position to help others do the same—their archetypal wounds having distilled into the balm of a spiritualized vision of themselves, their students, and their curricula.

CHAPTER SIX

ARCHETYPE, CULTURE, AND GENDER

A Maori Professor Reflects on Her Academic Career
(with Debbie Hippolite-Wright)

In this chapter, a professor of social work (Debbie) and I reflect on her experience as a Maori psychotherapist, social worker, and academician in largely white patriarchal institutional environments. I facilitated Debbie in her "therapeutic" reflective processes.

The reflective processes often go most deeply and unfold most smoothly when the facilitator and reflecting practitioner share a "common vocabulary" in which to frame and pursue the processes (Mayes, 2001, 2002). For, in reflectivity (as in the psychotherapeutic processes generally) psychic energy must ultimately be "contained" by models and images that enable one to make sense out of one's inner and outer experiences, thereby enabling those experiences to promote the transformation of self, setting, and other. Since Debbie and I take a Jungian approach in our research and practice, it was natural for us to employ Jungian terms and models to inform her reflectivity, and this led to a host of compelling and transformative insights into Debbie's history, present situation, and future prospects as a female psychotherapist and academician of color.

We also used Jungian terms and techniques of reflectivity because of the sensitivity of Jungian psychology to cultural images, narratives, myths, and, in general, to the Jungian belief that any approach to the individual is incomplete unless it honors the sacred narratives and normative values that underlie the person's culture. Jung insisted that our personal identities are so interwoven with our individual and collective histories that we cannot know *ourselves* if we do not know *them*.

DEBBIE'S AND CLIFF'S DISCUSSIONS

In this presentation and analysis of some of the major Jungian themes that emerged in my discussions with Debbie, we see how framing her reflectivity in terms drawn from both psychoanalysis and from archetypal psychology was personally, professionally, and culturally empowering for Debbie.

Theme 1: The Midlife Transition

It will be recalled that Jung was thus the first great modern psychologist to look systematically at the developmental period in the lifespan from mid-life to death—from late noon to sunset.

Debbie, now in her mid-40s, certainly evidenced one of the prime psychological markers of this period of life—uncertainty as to her next major professional step in life. Indeed, it was not clear that her next step *would* be professional. It might instead entail dramatically reducing the scope of her academic career to spend more time with her teenage children. Because Debbie's career has been in the service of helping students of color find intellectual and professional empowerment—a calling that she feels has deeply spiritual dimensions—she said that she wanted "the Lord's confirmation and assurance" that moving from academia into a more domestic setting "would be where I would be of most value." This tug and pull between her sense of mission as a social worker and academic of color, on one hand, and a mother, on the other hand, was a theme throughout much of the interview.

> DEBBIE: I think that now is the time of my life that I want to be more of a mother.
>
> CLIFF: More of a mother. What would that mean?
>
> DEBBIE: I want to do something feminine. More womanly. I've only got a short time left before my children move on!

As we have already discussed, in the classical Jungian developmental model the second half of life is the time when one begins to get more in touch with the contrasexual inner-other—the man with his *anima* and the woman with her *animus*. The businessman who has worked tirelessly establishing a company, for instance, might, at 50 years old, want to spend more time nurturing his grandchildren, relaxing in nature, or working on his garden. At the same time of life, a woman who has dedicated herself to hearth and home might decide to go back to school to get a graduate degree, start a business, or run for public office.

For Debbie, on the other hand, whose life has been largely spent in the political fray of cultural and academic battle, the classical Jungian picture has been reversed: It is in the second half of life that she is now thinking with increasing urgency of how she has had to sacrifice something from her feminine side in order to steel herself for the work of breaking down the institutional bastions of white male privilege. Because of her role as a cultural activist, Debbie had to access her *animus* quite early in life. It is in the second half of life that Debbie—reversing the usual pattern—is more involved with issues involving her "femininity."

Theme 2: The Persona and the Animus

Another characteristic of the midlife transition is that the *persona* often becomes more problematic. The social masks that one has worn in order to succeed, or even just survive, in public contexts become less and less relevant to the increasingly pressing existential issue of one's own mortality, and of what to do with one's remaining years as those years become much fewer than those that have already passed. The most pressing life-narrative issues now revolve around one's ultimate purpose in having lived and the legacy one will leave behind.

The fact that Debbie has been a female academic of color has made this ethical and developmental issue even more complex for her. She often observed throughout the discussions how she had shaped her *persona* (sometimes consciously and sometimes not) to best fill her role as a powerful agent of cultural change. The question with which she struggled throughout the discussions was how much she had adopted white male postures and perspectives in order to be allowed to play in the white male arena of academia.

To be sure, the idea of being a powerful woman has never been a difficult one for Debbie, given her own innate strength and the Maori reverence of the woman as the *wharetangata*—that is, the child-bearer and life-giver, whose womb is "the house of humanity." In the Maori view, the woman's *mana* is inextricably tied in to her connection with the primal, eternal reality of Mother Earth, *papatuanuku*. In Debbie's experience growing up as a Maori girl, she had abundant evidence that the woman's mana is not merely a charming cultural relic but a very real psychosocial force. When a Maori woman has her mind fixed on something important and good, Debbie laughed, a man is well advised not to try to impede her but rather to "get out of her way!"

> CLIFF: As you were growing up, did you see many examples of people "getting out of the way" of feminine power?
>
> DEBBIE: Oh, lots and lots of examples—lots and lots of times. My great- grandmothers, grandmothers, and aunties all had tremendous mana. They were key to the welfare of their families, hapu (sub-tribe) and broader community which included Paheha (Europeans). So I'm talking about them having this deep sense of their own mana.
>
> CLIFF: And do you feel that mana within yourself as well?
>
> DEBBIE (laughing): Oh, yes! I have that power. I have tapped into and used that power—mana wahine (woman's power).

In Jungian terms, Debbie was deeply in touch with both the cultural archetype of the mana wahine, the powerful woman warrior, as well as with the universal archetype of the female as Amazon (de Castillejo, 1973). Indeed, anyone who has known Debbie for only five minutes cannot possibly miss the fact of her power!

Jung postulated that the second half of life is when it is most natural for one to access and express the contrasexual inner-other. Maori culture clearly evidences profound developmental wisdom in this regard.

> CLIFF: Deb, it seems to me that most of the examples that you've given of powerful women in your life are of older women. This is so different from standard American culture—you know, where a woman is only interesting if she's young and sexually desirable, and gets increasingly neglected as she gets older.
>
> DEBBIE: That's so true, Cliff. But a Maori woman only really comes into contact with her power after the child-bearing

years. So I'm more fully coming into my mana because I'm a middle-aged woman now. And that's the most powerful time.

Indeed, it is because of the potency and wisdom of the woman in the second half of life that, in the Maori ritual of approaching members of another tribe for the first time, it is the woman who stands at the head of her tribe's combined forces.

CLIFF: Debbie, a couple of times you've alluded to the Maori ritual of encountering another tribe, and you've said that women play an especially important role in that. Could you say more about that?

DEBBIE: Well, you see, Cliff, it's the older woman who is out there, full-on, as the approaching visitors or enemies come. She's standing at the very head of the group—everyone behind her. And she does the call to say, "Advance so we can see you. Come a little closer."

CLIFF: Sounds a tad on the dangerous side!

DEBBIE: Oh, yeah, most definitely. And not only that, but it's also that woman who can say, if necessary, "We're ready! We're ready to battle now!"

Clearly, Debbie has very little trouble accessing the power of her contrasexual inner-other—her animus! Nevertheless, Debbie struggled mightily throughout the discussions with the question of how much of her power was an authentic expression of the gender wisdom of Maori culture and how much of it was an aggressive white male persona that she had adopted in order to succeed in white patriarchal institutions. How much of her power came from her Maori roots—and how much from "playing white"?

CLIFF: What do you mean by that phrase, "playing white," Deb?

DEBBIE: Well, in order to, you know, overcome the roadblocks in the formal setting of academia and to deal effectively with my colleagues—my white, male, and middle-aged and older colleagues, I had to cultivate that formal academic identity.

CLIFF: I know that routine alright—the traditional credentials and tenure game.

DEBBIE: That's it. You know, "I have a Ph.D., I'm a professor, I even have full professorial rank" — just in order to be heard at all!

CLIFF: And did this get you "heard"?

DEBBIE: Oh, yeah. I was heard that way alright. And I have to admit that it was kind of exhilarating because I was, finally, being heard.

CLIFF: And that was both good and bad.

DEBBIE: Yep. Both good and bad. Because, what was happening to me, to my mana as a Maori person, as a Maori woman? And it just hit like a brick, and then I said to myself, "Wait a second! I'm running around, playing white, you know, with white ways of doing things, white management styles, and I'm leaving behind my Maori-ness, my true strength."

CLIFF: And what kind of personal, emotional cost did that entail?

DEBBIE: A big cost, I can tell you! I was becoming depleted, as a person. I had really gobbled up the "white perspective" of doing things, and I had moved so far away from my Maori culture. I was mimicking. I was "playing white."

Again, it is clear that Debbie's movement into middle age with its attendant persona and animus/anima issues has been rendered even more complex for her by the fact that this transition is overlaid with issues of cultural struggle. Not only does she have to wrestle with the strictly personal questions involved when critically examining one's own persona — which is a difficult enough task in any case — but she must also wrestle with the paradox of how that persona may represent both a betrayal of her fundamental cultural identity at the same time as it is a strategy to further her culture's political cause.

Theme 3: The Shadow

We tend to project our shadows onto others as a way of externalizing and disowning what is really unfinished internal business that we need to attend to ourselves. Those elements of Debbie's power that stem from having adopted an inauthentic white male identity are the unpleasant shadow side of those other bright elements of her power that are truly mana wahine—that genuinely emerge from her identity as a Maori woman. The internalized oppressor, in short, is part of Debbie's shadow.

As a very self-aware psychotherapist, Debbie recalled times when she projected that shadow onto colleagues. She recalled a time when she was working at an institution other than the one where she presently teaches.

DEBBIE: I had a colleague there who was a small, southeast Asian woman—very detail-oriented and sort of disconnected from her own emotions. And sometimes I felt that she was my shadow in some ways.

CLIFF: You felt that at the time or you see it now in retrospect?

DEBBIE: Well, I think I sensed it at the time but it's only now that I'm able to put it into words—you know, because of the kind of process you and I are engaged in right now.

CLIFF: Let's go back to how you felt about her at that time, alright?

DEBBIE: Sure. O.K. Well, let's see. I guess I was often very critical of her. But I also felt for her, too, because I think she was trapped. She was stuck. But that was just a feeling I had, really—nothing I particularly put into words.

CLIFF: And now?

DEBBIE: Well, now, as you and I discuss it, I suspect that many of my negative feelings about her at the time came from the fact that she was me, too—being trapped, being a kind of performing puppy for the institution, over and over. Yeah, she was my shadow. That's really it!

Of course, the shadow often appears as a person of color, or an ill or dwarfed person of some sort, and that this is true even in the dreams of people of color (Mattoon, 1985). Debbie reported that "in my dreams my shadow figures are usually small dark and very materialistic women." This is not a surprising form for the shadow to take for Debbie, who, in fact, is tall, powerfully built, and deeply devoted to the spiritual values affirmed by her church. Debbie's shadow (in both her waking, professional life, as well as in her sleeping, unconscious life) is often a diminutive woman of color who is susceptible to the lure of worldly rewards. This mirrors the threat to Debbie of being culturally and ethically diminished as a Maori woman by the seductive appeal of institutional power and largesse. Fortunately, Debbie's ability to reflect deeply on this subconscious dynamic and the images in which it expresses itself left Debbie feeling at the end of the conversations that she could now be better able to handle this shadow element in herself and not project it onto others.

Theme 4: The Cultural Politics of Sexual Domination

We noted above the idea that in both classical and neo-Jungian theory, racism is seen as a projection of the racist's own personal and cultural shadow onto another group. The multicultural Jungian psychotherapist Michael Vanoy Adams (1996) has even speculated that this idea helps explain why males from supraordinate groups often seem to feel so free to psychologically and physically violate women from subordinate groups. Such men, projecting their psychosocial shadow onto subordinate women, attempt to dominate (and thereby purge themselves of) their own shadows by violating the oppressed female. This act is rendered permissible in the mind of the "master" because he "sees" the slave woman only in terms of the shadow that he casts over her —that is, as a lusty sexual animal. The physical and psychological violation of women of color by their white overlords thus emerges as a psychosocial act of not only sexual aggression but primarily of cultural and political violence.

> CLIFF: I know this is sort of hard, Deb, but could you tell me more about that sexual harassment you experienced when you were working at that state hospital?

> DEBBIE: I was working as a social worker there. And a psychiatrist, during a case review, said out loud to everyone that was there—because I was presenting a report and I think he was wanting to diminish my mana—but he said, kind of off-handed, while I was talking about something serious, "Haha! I just have this fantasy of mud-wrestling nude with you on the floor of a grass shack!"

> CLIFF: Have you often gotten that kind of harassment from white male bosses?

> DEBBIE: Often enough....

To be sure, Debbie is an attractive woman. However, what was going on in this instance was more complex than just a male sexual fantasy. Note, for instance, that this psychiatrist—probably a product of the white male discourse of conventional medical models of the psyche—is "upstaging" Debbie in her more intuitive, relational, and archetypally feminine analysis of a patient's case. He thereby makes it clear that his white patriarchal view of the psyche will be the only institutionally acceptable one and that Debbie's view—which is a rich product of her experiences as a female of color from a First Nation culture—will not be tolerated. Indeed, if necessary, Debbie's views will even be ridiculed, symbolically "wrestled" and forced into "the mud." In this sense, then, the sexually degrading comments that constitute the interruption merely encode and reinforce the power that the head psychiatrist has already exercised by inappropriately and smugly interrupting (i.e., violating) Debbie's presentation, dismissing it with a vulgar, irrelevant comment.

Oppressive gender politics are certainly at play here, but even more salient perhaps is the culminating image in the psychiatrist's fantasy about Debbie. He is wrestling her not only in the mud (which symbolizes his own sexual shadow) but also in a "grass shack"—clearly a deprecating allusion to a Polynesian architectural structure, which now comes to symbolize the structure of the culture itself. It is not only Debbie the woman whom he is raping but Debbie the Polynesian woman. He enters and dominates the shack before going on to enter and dominate her. His salacious imagery betrays the fact that his fantasy is not only a personal psychosexual one but is also an archetypally cultural one. Maori culture is reduced to the stereotypical image of a "grass shack." In short, sexual oppression and cultural domination so intermingle in this man's discourse and fantasy that it is impossible to tell where one starts and the other leaves off. That is how Debbie made sense of this experience while reflecting on it in political, cultural, and archetypal terms.

DEBBIE: It's a white patriarchal view of powerful women of color.

CLIFF: That seems right to me—"right," I mean, in the sense that that interpretation uncovers a lot of what was going on that was a whole lot more than just sexual.

DEBBIE: Yeah. And now that I think of it in those terms, I think that memory of that psychiatrist sort of stayed with me because it was about more than sexual harassment—although it was certainly about that, too! But in general, I guess I see now how that incident explains so much about how white men in power have often treated me.

Reflecting on this experience in terms of both colonial politics and archetypal psychodynamics helped Debbie make sense out of the experience—and thereby grow from it both psychologically and politically.

Theme 5: The Archetype of the Great Mother

Throughout the interviews, it was clear that Debbie was trying to come to terms with the powerful archetypal energy of the Great Mother in herself as a teacher and therapist—a task made all the more poignant and complex by the fact that the energy and imagery of the Great Mother is so important in Maori culture. Debbie identified with the trans-generational archetype of the Maori Great Mother.

CLIFF: I can see how important all of the incidents that you recall and all the stories that you tell of older women in your life are deeply, deeply important to you. Seeing them has been pivotal in defining yourself. Would that be a fair way of putting it?

DEBBIE: Yes, it would. In fact, you could go so far as to say that my mother and grandmother and aunties—well, they are me!

Thus, Debbie's challenge is how to make this powerful archetypal energy operate in her life in ways that are appropriate to where she presently finds herself in her personal and professional development.

On one hand, of course, Debbie naturally embodies that archetype in her role as the mother of her four children. Yet, she often wondered aloud throughout the interview if she had adequately performed that role, or whether she had sacrificed it somewhat in order to pursue her career as a cultural worker and activist. Recall the section in the interviews when Debbie said, "I think I want to be more of a mother! I want to be involved more with my children. I actually just feel like I want to do something feminine. More womanly. I mean, I've got just a short time left before my children move on." The irony in all of this, Debbie noted, is that her "maternal" commitment to her students, clients, and their psychosocial struggles—a commitment that also draws upon archetypal energy of the Great Mother energy—is precisely what may have been interfering with expressing the same kind of archetypal energy in her familial life.

Debbie spoke of the program that she had created at her present university as something to which she had, in her words, given birth. This tender ethos of care was also evident in her description of her teaching style, which she rendered in imagery that was both highly feminine and highly Maori. For instance, she described how she uses elements of the female-led ritual of encounter (discussed above) to create more of a "family" environment in her classroom—one in which her students could access their own Polynesian roots.

CLIFF: Deb, as you know, one of my major research interests is how a person's cultural assumptions and practices affect how she sees herself as a teacher—affects how she actually teaches. Can you think of any examples of this in your own classroom practices?

DEBBIE: Oh, sure. Lots of them.

CLIFF: What's one that just comes to mind?

DEBBIE: O.K. Well, I could begin with what we actually do begin with at the beginning of each term. See, what I try to do is, establish a Pacific Islander perspective. I have all the students stand up together and move together as a whole—very organically interrelating—and then I call out the beginning of a chant "Hiki mai i na pua i ka Laie."

As the teacher, I model this. And then they—even if they're not Pacific Islanders but are even Asian or White—well, they then call back to me, "Hiki mai i na pua i ka Laie." If they don't get it, if it's not sounding right, I go again, "Hiki mai i na pua i ka Laie!" And in this way, they start relying less and less on the paper and books and more and more on each other, on these beautiful words that they're hearing and repeating. They have to stand closer together and hear from each other. Well, that's a metaphor for what happens in the classroom—for how the classroom becomes a family, a community, in a Maori way! I'm starting them off, from day one, this is what it is. You have to listen. You have to form a group, you have to help each other, you have to get in sync. And pretty soon the students really start getting it, and they start singing back, "Hiki mai i na pua i ka Laie...!"

Reflecting on the archetype of the Great Mother—indeed, the Great Maori Mother—Debbie was able to understand better how a major challenge for her at this stage of her life and career was to draw upon the psychospiritual energy available in this archetype—and to balance it between her domestic and academic responsibilities:

> I'm drawn to that—to the Great Mother archetype, to mothering, to putting my energies of birthing and mothering and assisting where, you know, I can see that it's of value. And I think it's of most value if I'm not putting it solely in one place or the other—but am striking a balance between both places. And, yes, I think that's possible. I'm coming to see that's possible!

THE ARCHETYPAL POLITICS OF PRACTICE

In this chapter, we have seen how Debbie's reflecting on the cultural aspects of her personal and professional life in Jungian terms was of great value to her. It helped her understand as a teacher, therapist, social worker, cultural activist, mother and wife where she has been, where she presently is, and where she plans to go. Armed with such knowledge, Debbie concluded the interviews feeling that she would now be able to better balance all of those different yet still interrelated parts of herself—and thus be of even greater service to her family, students, and culture.

Hopefully, this example of reflectivity will inspire other educators to engage in deeply reflective processes. In doing so, they may find, as Debbie has, that such reflectivity is a useful tool in their struggle to find greater personal balance, pedagogical effectiveness, cultural empowerment, and deepening spirituality.

CHAPTER SEVEN

ALCHEMY AND THE TEACHER

AN ALCHEMICAL PRIMER

In the last major phase of his career, Jung turned to the lost art and arcane texts of alchemy in his researches, claiming that alchemical processes symbolized the psychospiritual transformations that occur in the course of individuation. He asserted that "the world of alchemical symbols definitely does not belong to the rubbish heap of the past, but stands in a very real and living relationship to our most recent discoveries concerning the psychology of the unconscious" (1963, p. xiii). In this chapter, I show how alchemy in its psychotherapeutic contexts offers especially rich archetypal symbols for exploring oneself as a teacher. I do so by giving an example of how I guided a teacher through a deeply reflective process by means of a set of archetypal symbols that enriched our conversation. Since these symbols have to do with alchemy and Jung's psychological interpretation of it, it is necessary to say a few words about that ancient art.

A FEW HISTORICAL NOTES ON ALCHEMY

Contrary to the popular contemporary image of the alchemist as a quick-change artist trying to coax a *sub rosa* fortune in gold out of coal shards, the religious alchemists were, Jung claimed, engaged in a labor of high spiritual import. The gold that they aimed to produce—the Philosopher's Stone, the *lapis philosophorum*, the Philosophical Gold—represented nothing less than the actual spiritualization of matter, just as the wine of the Mass became the true blood of Christ. Thus, the religious alchemist insisted that the transformations of matter that he sought in both himself and his material were *tam moralis quam physica*—moral as well as physical. Little wonder, then, that the religious alchemist believed that he could bring his work to completion only if he achieved a *unio mystica*—a mystical union—with God, which could happen only if he purified his own psyche and spirit. Contained in each alchemical text, in other words, are archetypal projections of the individual alchemist engaged in a proto-chemical drama of psycho-spiritual integration. Psychologically interpreted, alchemy is "a treasury of analogies that corporify or embody the objective psyche and the process it undergoes in development" (Edinger, 1985, p. 100).

Each alchemist practiced and wrote about his craft in unique, even idiosyncratic terms, but there are nevertheless generalizations that we can make about the art of alchemy (Edinger, 1985). The alchemical project would almost always involve the differentiation of the *prima materia* (or the base starting material) into one of the four elements: earth, air, water, or fire. The *prima materia* was typically some disprized material: refuse, shards and stones, fecal matter, menstrual blood, even scabrous remnants. Looked at therapeutically, this rather shockingly symbolizes the beginning of the therapeutic process. We must begin with our primal wounds, sins, shames, dreads, and indeed all those shabby parts of ourselves that we desperately attempt throughout our lives to hide in the nooks and crannies of our psyches—in the shadow.

For the alchemist, each of the four elements answered to a particular alchemical process. Fire was at the heart of the alchemical operation called *calcinatio*—heating a substance. *Solutio,* corresponding to water, referred to any dissolving operation. *Coagulatio,* an earthy process, was coagulation—such as mud becoming a brick or an egg hardening on a frying pan. And finally, corresponding to air was *sublimatio.* For the alchemists and Jung, *sublimatio,* derived from *sublimis* or *high,* refers to changing a tangible material into any sort of gas, which, of course, tends to rise. Each element and its corresponding process have both a light, healthy side and a shadowy, problematic one. This should not by now surprise the reader. As we have seen throughout this book, any archetype (and the alchemical stages are archetypal images *par excellence*) has a bright and a dark side.

The Alchemical Life of the Teacher

I had a series of four conversations with Christy Ann, a 59-year-old secondary-school teacher of 30 years. Christy Ann had taught both regular and special education classes in public and private schools. A religious person, she is also a person of passionate political convictions that stem back to her days as a political activist in the 1960s. Divorced at an early age, she had single-handedly raised her daughter, Danielle. Christy Ann was now married. Before our interviews, I asked her to read the information on alchemy that I have just presented to the reader. This then formed the foundation of our mutual reflections on her life as a teacher.

Calcinatio (Fire)

Although any alchemical operation could serve as the starting point of the alchemical process, *calcinatio* was probably the most common. "The chemical process of *calcinatio* entails the intense heating of a solid in order to drive off water and all other constituents that will volatilize" (Edinger, 1985, p. 17). Water, naturally associated with the depths of the primordial ocean as well as the fluids of the womb, is a common archetypal symbol of both the unconscious and innocence. Because fire evaporates moisture, it therefore symbolizes those experiences that dispel innocence. Jung explained: "When a man is subjected to a great emotion, it means that he is subjected to the fire, and the contact with the fire can give him the nature of a subtle body; the fire can subtilize him or it can destroy him" (Jung, 1995, p. 144).

Christy Ann and the Calcinatio

We have already had occasion to note how there has been a good deal of discussion over the last several decades about the trials and traumas of the first-year teacher—and how those initiatory blazes may either temper and mold her or cause her to "burn out." The first year or so of teaching can result in either a "subtilizing" *calcinatio* of the novice teacher into a more psychologically and pedagogically mature person, or it can be a professional holocaust that psychologically chars her and turns her optimism into cinders (Bullough, 1989).

Christy Ann immediately identified with the imagery of initiatory blazes because as she put it, "I'm a fiery Irish woman!" Christy Ann was in a teacher preparation program in the early 1960s at an Arizona university. As with so many other prospective teachers of that time (and with still far too many today), Christy Ann's "training" consisted almost entirely of learning principles of behaviorism and applying them to writing up lesson plans. Christy Ann felt that the first years of teaching could be likened to a *calcinatio* blaze. This caused her to muse about how poorly her teacher education program had prepared her for those novitiate flames.

CHRISTY ANN: Having the idea of the initiatory blazes causing someone to either temper and mold or to burn out—well, I was certainly unprepared by my teacher training to know what in the world I was getting into. When I went to do my student teaching I came to a classroom in which the teacher hardly let me do anything at all. I was 19, some of the students were 18, so he didn't want to leave me with the class. I didn't do anything but grade papers, basically. So I just had nothing—no preparation, and then I was hired at a junior high school where the discipline was to take children out into the hall and hit them with a paddle if they were out of line. This was in 1964. I knew how to calm the kids down with these harsh methods I'd been taught, but I wouldn't do it. The principal was just horrified that I would buck the system.

CLIFF: So one thing I hear you saying is that these fires were maybe especially intense because you weren't sufficiently prepared for them? That they would have been less intense had your teacher preparation been better?

CHRISTY ANN: Absolutely. If someone said to me in my teacher education program, "You're going to have to take children out and hit them with a board," it might have given me pause about whether or not I even wanted to be a teacher.... The other part was that no one ever taught me how to put units together. I know that teacher education isn't that way anymore. It's much more enlightened. But back then, I had no clear goals. So, when I got finished with that year, I thought, "You know, I did a pretty good job considering I just made up much of it." I guess that, having gone through those fires, I ultimately came out the other side thinking, "I want to be a teacher, and I'm going to have to be the Lone Ranger in terms of getting help from other people, but I want to go on with this." Anyway, because I refused to paddle students and was vocal about it, that year they did change the policy and they got rid of the boards.

CLIFF: You responded with some fire of your own.

CHRISTY ANN: Yes, that's exactly what I did. I'm a fiery Irish woman! But then there was a new problem: The students figured out that I wasn't going to hit anybody, which made the classroom even more raucous. Finally, I just sat down with them early in the morning when they were still half-asleep and said, "You know, you have to go to school and I have to teach. I have some really fun and interesting things I want to do with you guys, but I can't do anything the way things are now. So let's work out a system together of what we can agree upon." So we set up classroom rules which we put on the board. There were certain consequences, the final one of which was I was going to call the person's parents, which nobody in the school did. I ended up calling more than one of the children's parents and had them come in and had the child sit with me and just say what was going on in front of their parents so that we all became part of the solution. So I got past all the discipline issues, but I thought that if I didn't make it past that, that I would quit. I was just miserable.

CLIFF: Would it be fair to say that the fires that you were passing through helped you to hammer out your own system of classroom management that was emotionally productive and fair?

CHRISTY ANN: That's true! And not only that but it kind of became a model because I talked about this a lot with other teachers in the school who were faced with some of the same issues. I know I affected the fact that there was no more hitting of children after that school year and that several teachers did take on my approach. So I guess you could say that these fires helped me forge some tools that other teachers could use, too.

Even in light of how painful the initiatory flames were, Christy Ann strongly disagreed with what she felt was an excessive emphasis that I had placed on teacher burn-out.

CHRISTY ANN: You wrote about the teacher's optimism turning to cinders. Well, I don't agree! My optimism didn't turn to cinders. I felt that I had come upon something that really was a calling for me and I was mean and ornery (or Irish!) enough to take on an administration—an old man who just sat in his office and just didn't want anyone to bother him, basically—to force him to change some things there. I found that I had to be combative and I took pleasure in the fact that I had taken him on and that there were changes as a result of it.

CLIFF: The fires of your teaching experience spread to the new territory of political commitment—and you found that you liked it!

CHRISTY ANN: Uh huh. I think that I often saw the administration as adversarial. I was surprised at that—I thought that they were going to be the good guys who would understand and give me support and take care of the bad kids for me. None of that happened. So the fire of that awareness started me to believing that I would have to fight for anything I hoped to get from the administration. That was a bit of an extreme position, but then I wasn't continually disappointed when I didn't get support.

It emerged in our talks that Christy Ann had become increasingly radicalized politically throughout the 1960s, eventually winding up at Berkeley in the anti-war movement and after that at the Esalen Institute in Big Sur, where she studied massage and psychotherapy. As she reflected more and more deeply on how the *calcinatio* of her first year of teaching had shaped her professionally, she also began to explore how it had been the furnace in which her evolving political ideology was being forged in ways that she was only partially aware of at the time. This was particularly true, she said, when it came to challenging male authority—something that a woman born in 1942 had not been culturally primed to do.

CHRISTY ANN: I'm sure that the principal, who probably had just a year or so left to retire, just did not know what to do with this uppity first-year teacher, because in those days before the social revolution women were expected to be obedient, seen and not heard. I did get involved politically, and years later during Vietnam—which I thought was a huge social injustice—I took that sense of righteous indignation that I'd felt (and expressed!) against the principal to a higher level.

CLIFF: So, what happened to you in your confrontations with the school administrator—that was a step on the road of your radicalization?

CHRISTY ANN: Yep. Because I was successful at that level and forced the principal to make some changes, I think I felt emboldened to take it up to the next level.

The evocative imagery of fire also stimulated Christy Ann to speculate on some of the psychodynamic roots of her need to challenge unreasonable authority figures.

CHRISTY ANN: We were just discussing the political part of resisting the abusing of children by hitting them with a paddle. It was so important to me because I came from a family where my father, after returning from WWII when I was about four years old, became an erratic, abusive man who sometimes hit me with a belt or his hands. He was explosively abusive verbally, too, and so by the time that I was a teenager, I just wouldn't put up with it, and I just stood toe-to-toe with him and if he started shouting and cursing at me, I didn't curse at him, but I shouted back at him! I grew tall very quickly—I was about 5' 5" in the 6th grade—so by that time he stopped hurting me. I left home when I was 17 to go to college and was 21 when I started teaching, and now here was another older man ordering me to be physically abusive to the kids, which was horrifying to me. I had worked my way out of a situation in a family and then was being told to come back into it again. I was horrified that anyone would think of treating children that way.

CLIFF: Part of the flames that you were being forced to confront in your school situation were, in a sense, extensions of flames you had to face as a child, then?

CHRISTY ANN: Yeah, exactly! It's like the fire had spread—like I was even being asked to make it spread! So [in confronting the principal] I just went into the automatic mode which I had used in dealing with my father, which was just to confront him.

Solutio (Water)

Of *solutio,* the dissolving process that corresponds to the element of water, Edinger (1985) says, "for the alchemist, *solutio* often meant the return of the differentiated matter to its primal undifferentiated state—that is, to *prima materia.* Water was thought of as the womb and solutio as a return to the womb for rebirth" (p. 43). According to Jung, "Water in all its forms—sea, lake, river, spring—is one of the commonest typifications of the unconscious, as it is also the lunar femininity that is closely associated with water" (Jung, 1995, p. 272). Water is the alchemical symbol of *Eros* in the classroom.

Furthermore, water often symbolizes the dynamics of the transference. Whether it is a matter of subconscious psychosexual projections or archetypal supra-sexual ones, the patient's consciousness symbolically and symbiotically "flows" into the analyst, who must now "contain" it. If the analyst is able to healthily contain the patient's watery projections—that is, if the analyst can interpret them as information that she can use in furtherance of the patient's growth—then the transference becomes an invaluable therapeutic tool. Sometimes, however, the analyst cannot contain that torrential energy but is flooded by it. Falling under the seductive sway of the projections, the analyst comes to inappropriately see himself or herself as the all-wise archetypal Great Father or the all-nurturing archetypal Great Mother. Being flooded by an archetypal image is another way of characterizing what it means to become possessed or inflated by that archetype.

One of the most common archetypal transferences in the classroom is the solutio, or "dissolving" of the student into the archetypal womb of the teacher, who, as we have seen in previous chapters, thus takes on—and sometimes inappropriately acts out—the primordial role of The Great Mother. This archetypal regression to the waters of the primordial womb is called *uroboric incest,* defined as "a desire to be dissolved and absorbed; passively one lets oneself be taken in....The Great Mother takes the little child back into herself" (Neumann, in Edinger, 1985, p. 49).

However, nurturance can go too far; and when it does, it depletes. We have already come across in this study Wolstein's characterization of the therapist who nurtures beyond healthy limits as "the overprotective therapist" (Wolstein, 1988, p. 225). There are also overprotective teachers (Mayes, 2002). If care overflows healthy limits, not only the teacher but also the student can emotionally drown in the personal and archetypal waters of a failed solution. We see this in the following passages from Christy Ann's reflections.

Christy Ann and the Solutio

CHRISTY ANN: What kept coming into my mind while reading the water section on transference was the year after I taught at the junior high school—you know, my first year teaching. During the second year, I took a job as a home teacher. I went to the homes of students who could not come to school. In those days they did not let pregnant girls come anywhere near the campus, so most of the people I went to were pregnant girls. I found myself having a personal relationship with these students because I saw them twice a week and I felt bad for them—well, you know, they were mostly pregnant, unmarried girls in the early 1960s, so you can imagine, right?

I had a couple of girls who were in a terrible psychological state. And that aroused in me—well, I guess you could call it a counter-transference, a desire to help them beyond just bringing them English lessons or the like. I didn't know what I wanted to do about that, but I knew that it was very meaningful for me to have one-on-one encounters with students. Because I was just a few years older, they seemed like younger sisters to me and it was hard sometimes to stay on the subject matter. [After these experiences, Christy Ann returned to the classroom.] My teaching began to take an entirely different direction, which was away from public schools. I found that whenever I was in a classroom, that I couldn't go home without worrying about the one or two kids in my classes who I knew were in pain. It would almost stop the flow of what I was doing in a classroom if they didn't come to school that day. At one school I taught at I had 150 kids a day; you can ask what happened to Johnny or ask friends, but it's just a huge blur of processing people....

CLIFF: As you as a therapist know, there are two different kinds of transference: productive and unproductive ones. Sounds to me like what you're saying here is that this transference, with you in an older-sister or mother role, started out to be productive but was now getting to the point where it was consuming you—becoming unproductive.

CHRISTY ANN: To some degree, yes. The other part of it, of course, is that students transfer the bad mother onto me and I saw myself in the role of the good sister. I wanted to be the cheerleader or the good guy—you know, "When you come to my class you have fun!" But there were those students who constantly stopped the process because anything I said was taken as negative and disruptive. We would have to stop the class (and it was usually boys) and because I had high school kids I learned to be sarcastic, which is terrible, but I found that it was effective....

CLIFF: In terms of your teaching style, then, this solutio process also contributed to your style of teaching by forcing you to deal with a negative transference onto you?

CHRISTY ANN: Absolutely! Because, see, I was forced into being a parent [to these students] when I still was thinking that I was fairly young because I was in my late 20s. I was confronted with 14- and 15-year-olds who almost could have been my children. I realized that I didn't share the same music or the same fashion anymore and that they were pushing me into a parental authoritative role. I had to struggle with how I would parent teenagers, even though I was young, I think that you can only be the good guy/girl for a time, because it doesn't work after a while because you are then growing and changing and they don't see you anymore as an older sibling, they see you as a parent.

Christy Ann reported that her most painful experience of receiving negative parental projections from students happened during her time as a special education teacher. As she did so, I was reminded of what Aichhorn had written over 60 years ago. It still seemed relevant: "[With a neurotic child] with symptoms of delinquency...the tendency to transfer his [negative] attitude toward his parents to the person in authority is immediately noticeable" (1990, p. 97).

CHRISTY ANN: After years of teaching in typical public school classrooms—you know, with 30 or 40 students a class back then, I realized that I really missed working with kids one-on-one, so I went back to school and got a special ed teaching certificate working with emotionally disturbed kids. I felt that I would have small classes. This was in the 1980s, when special ed was still kind of a new thing. I did have smaller classes alright! But I found that the students were angry and so disenfranchised from the system that almost nothing I did had an impact on them or on our learning relationship. The classroom was really just a holding cell. I did do some innovative things, but they had projected so much onto me—from the system, from their parents, from whatever!—that I was just "the teacher," and that was the hated object, so I had almost no wiggle room to change their perceptions.... They projected "the enemy" onto me, and I just couldn't get out from under that projection.

In stark contrast to this negative solutio and Christy Ann's resulting emotional engulfment, she reported a quite different teaching experience several years later when she had returned to teaching again.

CHRISTY ANN: Five years later, I moved to Hawaii. I went back to teaching with great trepidation. I found a job teaching at a boys' school in Hawaii. I taught lower SES kids, and what I found was that I could go back to playing a role for them that they had projected onto me. I was a "haole"—that is, a white woman —in an all-boys school with mostly male teachers, and fortunately I was not seen as the bad mother-type but rather as a good mother. I was able to use this projection very effectively to give them some social capital that they would not have had otherwise. This was a group of boys that liked me. They opened up their hearts to me and as a result I was able to just move into that space. What I did there that I found so satisfying was that I could bring them information that they could use to better themselves. Mine was a very inviting classroom because the school was run by strict Catholic monks and I provided opportunities for them to speak and perform and display their poetry, etc. There was such severe discipline set up in the school that I could be the one who "freed" them when they came to my classroom.

CLIFF: So you were not only the nurturing mother, you were the liberating mother, too?

CHRISTY ANN: Yes. And a bit of a Peter Pan type. You know, "Let's-go-to-Neverland-for-the-hour-that-you-are-in-my-class" type of thing. I taught literature and creative writing, and because of the Polynesian cultural tendency to want to take flights of fancy and "talk story," they were very grateful to me for the opportunity to really get into the literature. They would draw it and write poems about it. It was the most re-invigorating thing for me as a teacher! I mean, to come into a setting with people who were somewhat naive and highly appreciative of what I did for them.

CLIFF: To me, this sounds like a great example of a healthy counter-transference. You're using information you're getting from them through their transference to find out who they are, what they need; you're containing it in such a way that you're meeting some of your needs, too, and are not being overwhelmed by it, not drowning in any illusions—you know, becoming so much of a mother to them that you try to displace their own mother, or begin to drown in your emotions for them so much that you couldn't take care of Danielle [her teenage daughter]. So you're getting your needs met, but you're also then using what the kids are projecting onto you as information about their needs. This shows you ways to help them grow. It seems like the model of good transference/counter-transference.

CHRISTY ANN: Thanks! Yeah, I think it was! A lot of these boys were affected by me because I took them to places that they couldn't go—I arranged for them to be on television, their works were published and we won a national award for our little poetry magazine—I could do things as a white woman who had power and social status for them. And I did play out that role of being the savior, the great mother for them. But it was just with pleasure; it never took on a negative aspect. I had my own teenage daughter at the time, and it wasn't always a bed of roses with her, but I could look forward to going to school and meeting a chorus of people who were actually happy to see me! I think that's the power of the positive projection: you find a role that you're playing in this play with your students. I got great pleasure playing the role of the one who releases them from their captivity. Of course, it all fit into my 60s stuff as well—you know, my years at Berkeley. "Power to the People!" We were playing out roles—they were doing it unconsciously, I was doing it consciously.

For me, another maternal part of all this was that it was also an obvious birth process for them, and that's where I could take great pleasure. I mean, boys who had a 200-word vocabulary (I'm not exaggerating) found their voice through poetry or a poet (for example, Dylan Thomas). They understood the poems, and when they would get up to present them to the class (and remember, they had fathers who had given up and were fishermen and just sat around and stared and drank) it had great meaning for them. I gave them somebody's words through which they could express their own feelings. My honors class wrote 50-page novellas, which we published and they were able to take home and proudly put on nearly empty bookshelves.

CLIFF: So there was definitely an element of political empowerment as well.

CHRISTY ANN: Oh totally. These boys, for the most part, came from West Oahu, where they would certainly be considered in the lower one-third of the social caste system, and most of them never gave any thought to going off-island, going to school anyplace else; they didn't think that they could get into colleges. I went through the process with a number of my boys of getting them into Catholic boys' schools on the mainland, which opened up their lives tremendously. So there was a social and political activist role there—wanting to make a difference in people's lives beyond teaching them the curriculum.

CLIFF: So because of how they empowered you through what they transferred onto you, you were then able to empower them by letting them know that a powerful person like you thought these things were possible for them—and then made it happen for them.

CHRISTY ANN: Yes, that's probably a pretty good way of putting it. And talk about going from negative to positive projection—going from the utter blackness of some public schools on the mainland—to a completely different type of place like Hawaii! I almost had to go out of white culture to be able to find the students I was looking for. I went back a year later to teach on the mainland in an affluent school, and none of them wanted what I had to offer....

CLIFF: So there is a cultural aspect to this transference as well. Because you were in such a "heartful" culture where women play such a dominant nurturing role, this transference could happen in a way that wouldn't be nearly so likely back here, especially with middle-class white kids.

CHRISTY ANN: Boy, you've said it! That's exactly correct.

Sublimatio (Air)

The sublimation process corresponds to air—*sublimis* meaning "sublime"—and refers to the process of transforming something low into something high. Although exhilarating, the potential danger in sublimatio experiences is that they may cause one to lose touch with concrete reality. The sublimatio should be in a healthy dialectical relationship with the grounded *coagulatio*. The ability to circulate between the concrete and the spiritual is what is called the alchemical process of the *circulatio*. Indeed, as we saw in the introduction to Jungian psychology, this harmony of the spiritual and mundane, the universal and specific, and the realms of archetype and ego, is the essence of individuation.

Christy Ann and the Sublimatio

I chose to examine the circulatio by questioning Christy Ann about possible ways in which her daily life as a teacher might have affected her spiritual development over the years, and about how that spiritual growth might in turn have influenced her pedagogical practice.

CHRISTY ANN: In the information you gave me to read about alchemy, you talk about the circulatio—the possible ways in which the teacher's daily life may have affected her spiritual development through the years, or how that spiritual growth may have influenced her pedagogical practice. Well, I was teaching in a Catholic school, so even though I'm not a Catholic, this gave me the freedom to openly teach my love of Jesus Christ.

CLIFF: So here, in this school on both the geographical and social margins of conventional American society, you find yourself positioned to be more open about your basic religious commitments?

CHRISTY ANN: Yeah. It was like a breath of fresh air!

CLIFF: That's an interesting image to use, you know, because this sublimatio process of spiritualizing your practice can be likened to the element of air. In Greek and Hebrew, for instance, the word for "breath" and "spirit" are the same. Could you give me an example of how this sublimatio, this turning the curriculum into spiritual air, happened with the Oahu boys?

CHRISTY ANN: Sure. I had to teach British literature to these boys who were poor and had never been off the island of Hawaii; in fact, no one in the class could find England on a map of the world. So the challenge was to make all this stuff relevant and interesting, while at the same time I was always looking for ways of infusing my own spirituality into the curriculum. So when we got to Chaucer and the Middle Ages, I decided that I would throw in the Grail Legend, which really is all about the knight's quest to come to the presence of Jesus Christ, and getting into the Grail Castle, where Christ himself serves them the sacrament from the Holy Chalice—or Grail. Nobody ever tells that story. I showed them *Monty Python* when it was over.

CLIFF: You mean, *Monty Python and the Search for the Holy Grail?* But that's kind of a parody of the whole thing, isn't it?

CHRISTY ANN: I wouldn't call it a parody. That's negative! It was just funny! We had a fabulous time with it—you know, a sort of comic relief after everything serious we'd learned about the Holy Grail Legend. Another thing I did was—we had discussions about their own beliefs and how they are knights too, and what their grail quest was, all from a mythical point of view: who they were, who they wanted to be, how they planned to accomplish it. *Monty Python and the Holy Grail* had the positive effect of showing these kids that spirituality didn't have to be grim—that it has a light, easy side too! All of this comes to my mind when I think about genuinely putting an obvious spiritual spin on the curriculum.

CLIFF: Can you think of some other examples—in other teaching settings?

CHRISTY ANN: Some years later I taught at a community college, and I would always include a section on psychospirituality and inform them about meditation and higher states of consciousness. I wanted them to absolutely encounter a spiritually devoted person who really sought to bring my spiritual beliefs into concrete action. I tried to present them with a possible model of psychological and spiritual evolution beyond, probably, what they had thought about before.

Christy Ann then spoke about how she had been able to infuse her classrooms with spiritual energy—and in a way that she found legally acceptable—through adopting an archetypal pedagogy.

CLIFF: Have you taught in the public schools at a time in your life when you have been passionately devoted to your present religious beliefs?

CHRISTY ANN: Sure. Lots.

CLIFF: I ask this because, in the other teaching settings you've mentioned—a Catholic school, a community college—it's easier to be explicit about your own spiritual commitments than in the public schools. In the terms we're using here, the public schools are not a very friendly environment for the sublimatio process. So, let's say you were teaching in, for instance, 10th grade in a public high school in Stockton, California? Would you try to engage in a sublimatio process in that kind of setting? Would you try to spiritualize your teaching there?

CHRISTY ANN: I probably would do the same thing; probably not to the same degree, because I don't think that the kids could follow it, but I think that if it came up, I would include the transpersonal element and lay down models of people who I think are "saints." I would obviously not go into specific religious doctrines. But I think that as long as we're having a discussion in which I'm having them talk about how they see things at very deep levels and what they believe, that I can do the same thing without feeling that I am crossing any sort of legal lines.

Anyway, I've got to say that this sublimatio is my favorite alchemical idea—it really catches me! That I can take this base matter—unformed adolescent minds—and begin acting like the sorcerer and begin the process of weaving their hearts, minds, and souls and get them to be excited about something that is at least a culturally high idea; to be able to talk about Dante or Goethe and see that that is exciting—that it also has some cultural capital to it. That's the excitement of being a teacher—taking something that is just clay, base material, and squeezing and squeezing it until you bring the students up and make them subtler or more refined. You hope that even for just one hour out of a year that you can hold them up so high so that they have been there once and remember it. That is my most favorite thing that I do! Maybe it's because I'm a product of the 60s, when getting high was the dogma—to get out of the ordinary and into the transcendent. So getting them high got me high as well, which was the fun of it. Pure energy!

CLIFF: As you know from the information I gave you to read, the second part of the sublimatio picture has to do not so much with how you are affecting your students' spiritual growth, but how they are affecting yours. This spiritual give-and-take is the circulatio, the circulating back and forth of spiritual influences.

CHRISTY ANN: Right. And as I read the alchemy stuff you gave me, the circulatio image made a lot of sense to me, because it's rarely, if ever, the case, that you just have this one-sided effect on someone without being changed by them too. And boy is this ever true in the classroom!

You know, people talk about the "aloha spirit" in Hawaii and it sounds like it's a canned thing that you get in downtown Waikiki. But it really is an incredibly beautiful Polynesian approach to life. Encountering all these kids every day whose first way of relating is a heartfelt, intuitive excitement about things —this allowed me to open up that part of myself, so that I found that when I left school that at the end of the day I was still feeling very open and could relate on a heartfelt level that allowed me to trust my intuitive self a lot more.

Actually, when I was in Hawaii I had a number of quite unique spiritual experiences that really changed me big-time, and I think they were the direct result of spending 60 hours a week with students whose culture valued ways of being that grew out of feeling and intuition. Teaching them sort of forced me to relate to them in those ways because that was their best way of learning. And as a woman, my ways of "being spiritual" probably relate more naturally to feeling and intuition—particularly intuition. But in orthodox religion, there is a tendency to focus more on discussion, doctrine, church meetings. I'd done all those things. But I'd never really been able to let my spirituality rip like I could in Hawaii, and that changed me and my spirituality—and my teaching!— forever.

Mortificatio (Earth)

The alchemists associated the *mortificatio* (or "mortification") with chthonic matter and destructive chemical processes. Jung saw the mortificatio as a projection of the alchemist's own shadow. This had therapeutic implications:

> Psychologically, we can say that [the mortificatio] has thrown off the conventional husk and developed into a stark encounter with reality, with no false veils or adornments of any kind. Man stands forth as he really is and shows what was hidden under the mask of conventional adaptation: the shadow. This is now raised to consciousness and integrated with the ego, which means a move in the direction of wholeness. Wholeness is not so much perfection as completeness. (Jung, 1963, p. 142)

Matter must decompose into the *prima materia* before it can ultimately be spiritually reconstituted as the Philosopher's Stone. To the Christian alchemists, Paul seemed to be referring to the mortificatio when he wrote of the glorified eternal body that "it is sown in corruption; it is raised in incorruption.... It is sown a natural body; it is raised a spiritual body" (1 Corinthians 15: 42-44). Eternal life grows out of the compost of our fallen natures. This is also the paradox of "individuation," which emerges out of therapeutic confrontation with our darkest secrets and complexes.

Christy Ann and the Mortificatio

CLIFF: Can you think of some times (that you'd be willing to talk about!) when some of your own issues, or wounds, or shadows have helped you to become a better teacher?

CHRISTY ANN: Well, I have a couple of things that I can think of right off the bat. The first has to do with the urge I had for flight. I grew up in a small town outside of Denver with a mother who was definitely a small-town girl. I had gone to Canada when I was 15; when I was 17 I went to Cuba, and there was always this urge that I had to get out of wherever I was. I think part of it had to do with being young and wanting adventure and believing that any job was a constriction. I was partly drawn to teaching because I would only have to work 185 days a year and that left me some freedom to travel and go and do.

CLIFF: I don't really see how traveling and freedom are a problem....

CHRISTY ANN: Well, see, I think that I was really running away from the shadow parts of myself, and the problem was that I didn't stay anywhere for more than a couple of years. With teaching, you can pretty much go wherever you want to go and people will hire you if you're halfway decent. The problem was that I never took the time to really refine my curriculum, never really got to know the staff that I worked with, never had as large an impact on school policies or curriculum as I could have had if I'd stayed. I think I was running away from getting old, running away from being my mother (who I saw as small and limited), from being lonely, and I think that I did myself and my students a disservice by not staying. But see, that would have meant owning up to this shadow, and that's what I was completely unwilling to do then.... I think the other thing the shadow image reminds me of has to do with my idealism, my perfectionism.

CLIFF: Perfectionism as a wound? Perfection seems exactly the opposite of a wound.

CHRISTY ANN: Yeah, but nothing ever is perfect! But that's what I had to have! I wanted the perfect administrator. Look, I was still a very young woman then, so I guess what I was really wanting was the perfect father. This was a shadow. This was a wound.

I thought as Christy Ann said this of Madeline Grumet's (1981) assertion that there is sometimes an Oedipal/Electra dynamic at play in school sites. The male administrator looks to the accessible and supportive female teacher to get maternal nurturing, while the female teacher sees the male administrator as a father figure whose approval and love she seeks. Christy Ann also went on to give a splendid example here of the Jungian notion that accessing and harnessing the energy of one's shadow can have positive effects.

CHRISTY ANN: But, of course, I never found an administration that I thought I could work with. After a while of being bothered by the principal or the rules or the unfairness of the situation, I think that rebellious adolescent part of me kicked in (by its jumping out of the shadows, right?), making me take on or otherwise just plain be unhappy with the adults or the authority figures. I think what I did in my classroom appealed to teens because I complained about those in authority, and adolescents love to have somebody who wants to complain with them about what's going on.

So, see, I think that my shadow parts not only had negative effects but also resulted in me, after all, doing a pretty darn good job of setting up a classroom environment that was, well, first of all, exciting—because I half-knew that I wasn't going to be there for more than a couple of years, so I could give it my all and not burn out.

CLIFF: Because you knew that fleeing your shadow would limit your time at any particular school, you could actually commit more in the short time you'd be there? And because of your "shadow rebel," your kids could identify with you more.

CHRISTY ANN: I guess so, huh? And I think that I did good being an ally with my students, empowering them (there's that word again! I do use it a lot, don't I?) to question authority and insist on making things fair. So, I guess—you know, looking at it in these terms—I did good as a result of being the wounded teacher. I did good in spite of myself.

Then, almost as if to confirm my silent musings about Grumet's psychoanalytic interpretation of certain teacher/administrator relationships, Christy Ann, after a long pause in which I knew she wanted to say something but was trying to find just the right words, let out a long sigh:

CHRISTY ANN: One more thing about the wound—I just want to say again that I had a very poor relationship with my father—or I guess my father had a very poor relationship with me. I really wanted one who showed that he cared about me, talked to me, came to see me in plays, stuff like that, you know—and stuff that lots more fathers do today than when I was a teenager in the 1950s! But my father's attitude was (and it was typical at the time): "Children are raised by the mother, and I do the work, and when I come home they're supposed to be quiet, and when I need a break from the rat-race, I go fishing." I know that that part of me, particularly that adolescent girl, is still harmed, still in the shadows. In fact, she still is a shadow. It's the part of me that wants a father's attention, someone to take me into the world and explain how it works, show me how cars work, you know, and just do a number of things so that I could survive in the world.

Maybe that's part of the reason that I had no patience with male principals—and back then almost all of them were men! And I can see now, after talking about all this, that that "Shadow-Me" also identified with some of the kids who came into the classroom who obviously were having a poor time with their parents. I think I was more aware of those troubled kids and more nurturing to them, and that I looked for more ways to educate those kids perhaps than kids who I saw as functioning adolescents.

THE ALCHEMICALLY TEMPERED TEACHER

The archetypal image of the calcinatio proved a highly generative metaphor for Christy Ann in reflecting on some of the most important dilemmas that she had had to confront as a novice teacher, and how little and poorly she had been prepared for those experiences in her teacher education program. Furthermore, exploring the calcinatio metaphor caused her to speculate on some of the psychodynamic origins of her political commitments. Fire imagery also helped both of us come to see that, taken together, the family dynamics that had first sparked her resistance to authority, her early growth as a teacher, and her ultimate emergence as a political person, were a growing flame which had, over almost forty years, taken the *prima material* of that first-year teacher and turned her into the Philosopher's Stone of a wise and tempered educator.

The watery images and motifs of the solutio also flowed quickly and naturally for Christy Ann into a wide range of recollections of how maternal transferences and counter-transferences had both served and hampered her in her teaching—depending upon the site, the cultural context, and her personal and professional stage of development.

Christy Ann was most gripped by the images of the sublimatio and cirulatio, for they seemed to allow her a very immediate and intimate access to the wellsprings of her calling—namely, to provide her students with cultural capital and political insights that would "lift" them into higher academic, political, and even spiritual spheres.

Finally, using the metaphor of the morificatio, Christy Ann probed some of her psychic wounds. She saw that one's shadow, if carefully questioned and respectfully handled, could paradoxically be a source of appropriately used power.

Near the end of our last interview, Christy Ann said:

These discussions have helped me catch a vision of how complex my reasons for teaching are—and also how those factors (personal, political, spiritual, the whole deal!) have molded my teaching in so many different ways. They've also helped me see how certain stages and issues throughout my life tie into things I was going through as a teacher. But most of all, I guess, this whole process has helped me see a bigger pattern in my teaching—one that relates to some really interesting alchemical images and practices that are hundreds—maybe even thousands—of years old. Teachers have to feel that kind of significance in what they're doing, that they're making a difference, that they're on a mission that matters—'cause, Heaven knows, that's not the message we get from society most of the time!

Alchemy offers a potent set of archetypal images to help teachers understand themselves, their sense of calling, and their ways of teaching with greater political sensitivity, heightened psychospiritual acuity, and a deeper sense of ethical significance.

CONCLUSION

THE CASE FOR A PSYCHOSPIRITUAL APPROACH TO PEDAGOGY

Teaching is a complex, delicate act involving the whole person. Anything less than a complete existential engagement of the teacher in her practice will render her performance mediocre at best—and, at worst, psychologically, socially, and ethically damaging to her and her students. My purpose throughout this book has been to show how depth psychology, in both its psychoanalytic and archetypal forms, can help a teacher rise to the full measure of her calling through insight into her own interior life and that of her students in the critical contexts of the classroom.

The need for, and difficulty of, depth pedagogy has become increasingly pronounced over the last century of American educational "reform." Financial, institutional, and legal threats and enticements are deployed with increasing force and fury to get teachers to submit to standardized approaches to curriculum and instruction (Kliebard, 1986). Such approaches run quite counter to most teachers' sense of calling as well as to their convictions and intuitions about what makes good teaching (Cuban, 1993). There are many socio-historical causes of this perennial project to both homogenize and trivialize what teachers teach and how they teach it (Tyack, 1974).

Lawrence Cremin, probably the greatest of all American educational historians, captured the essence of the problem when he wrote in 1988 that the grip of the military–industrial complex on education had become so tight that the primary challenge to public schooling in the United States during the rest of the 20th century would be to resist becoming part of a military–industrial–*educational* complex. This challenge grew even more intense in the United States as the 21st century dawned, bringing with it documents such as *No Child Left Behind*— representing, despite its rhetoric of "empowerment" of teachers and students, the most vicious institutional assault to date in the war against the autonomy and integrity of teachers and students. One of the reasons that I have argued for a psychospiritually informed pedagogy is that by fostering deep teacher reflectivity and existentially sensitive teaching practices, it can go a long way in helping teachers create and maintain classrooms that are vibrant zones of personal, cultural, and ethical encounter. Such classrooms become sites of pedagogical lifestyle politics: holdouts of resistance to the corporate threat to teachers' and students' humanity.

A Jungian approach to education can be an important part of this resistance, for such an approach reveals that, above all else, there is a certain *sacredness* in the teacher–student relationship, which, rooted in emotionally rich archetypal soil, is both fundamental and transcendental. Of course, teaching will invariably have certain technical aspects and goals in any culture. That is not a problem. However, when a culture comes to believe that the mechanical transmission of information is *all* or *most* of what there is to teaching, then that minimalist view of education *is* a problem, and one that bespeaks of even more fundamental problems in the culture in general. A culture that takes such a depleted, spiritless view of educating its young is already so psychologically and spiritually impoverished that it probably has little if anything of enduring importance to communicate to its children in the first place.

On the other hand, a culture that honors and fosters psychospiritual growth in its teachers and students would allow them to use the curriculum as a means of making sense out of their lives as emotional, political, cultural, and spiritual beings. Such a culture would settle for nothing less than classrooms in which teachers and students were engaged in the construction of psychically fulfilling, socially rich, and ethically profound narratives about their own and each other's lives. Such a culture would not shackle teachers, but liberate them so that they could do what most teachers passionately want to do—and that is to relate to their students and the curriculum in ways that are personally, politically, morally, and spiritually vibrant and fruitful. What is needed, in short, is *depth pedagogy*. This book has been an attempt to explore—and to stimulate other scholars and teachers to explore —what some of the essential elements of depth pedagogy might be and what some of its basic contours might look like.

First, depth pedagogy must understand the transference—how we all project the energy and imagery of personal and archetypal hopes and fears, experiences and expectations, onto each other. It must help the teacher learn how to cultivate the possibilities and avoid the quagmires of the transference in the classroom.

Second, by giving the teacher tools for deep reflectivity on both her sense of calling and the nature of her classroom practices, depth pedagogy must help her to refine herself not only as a teacher but, indeed, as a holistic being for whom teaching is an integral part of her life. In this fashion, depth pedagogy aids the teacher in her lifelong project of coming into more existentially complete and constructive encounters with her students in the course of their shared academic inquiries and activities.

Third, a viable psychospiritual pedagogy must aim for a curricular and instructional balance between the archetypally male principle of analysis and abstraction, on one hand, with the archetypally female principle of intuition and interrelatedness, on the other hand. The poetics of play must have equal sway in the classroom with the rigors of ratiocination. *Eros* and *Logos* are equally honored in depth pedagogy—which thereby becomes an alchemical marriage of the two great cosmic principles, one which produces the Philosopher's Gold of the holistic classroom. Psychosocially rich forms of "subjective time" are thus synchronized more delicately with the inevitable, but also inevitably impersonal, strictures of "institutional time." In this manner, the school can do its "business" more humanely and creatively for both teachers and students. A balance between *Eros* and *Logos* in the classroom is vital for another reason, too: an imbalance in favor of *Logos* creates a classroom climate that is dry and dull, while an imbalance in favor of *Eros* leads to sloppy sentimentalism and shoddy thinking.

And finally, psychospiritual pedagogy opens up institutionally and legally acceptable spaces in the classroom for examining the cultural and spiritual dimensions of what is being studied. It provides conceptual frameworks and concrete techniques for a student to use in clarifying, articulating, and developing her own intertwined cultural and spiritual commitments relative to the curriculum. It also provides ways and means for a student to explore and be edified by her classmates' cultural and spiritual perspectives.

I am convinced that, despite the various political and social forces lined up against them, most teachers continue to be successful at doing what led them to the art and craft of teaching in the first place: to examine a subject that they love, with students whom they wish to nurture, in ways that are deeply meaningful to those teachers and students at all levels of their being. Teaching from their depths to their students' depths allows teachers to find deeper satisfaction in their vital work as they foster psychodynamic and ethical growth in their students. Hopefully, this book will be of service to some of those teachers in their noble endeavors.

BIBLIOGRAPHY

Adams, M. (1996). *The multicultural imagination: "Race," color, and the unconscious.* London: Routledge.

Aguessy, H. (1977). Sociological interpretations of time and pathology of time in developing countries. In P. Ricoeur (Ed.), *Time and the philosophies* (pp. 93–105). Paris: UNESCO.

Aichhorn, A. (1951 [1925]). *Wayward youth: A psychoanalytic study of delinquent children, illustrated by actual case histories.* New York: Viking Press.

Aichhorn, A. (1990). The transference. In A. Esman (Ed.), *Essential papers on transference* (pp. 94–109). New York: New York University Press.

Anthony, E. (1989). The psychoanalytic approach to learning theory (with more than a passing reference to Piaget). In K. Field, B. Cohler, & G. Wool (Eds.), *Learning and education: Psychoanalytic perspectives* (pp. 99–126). Madison, CT: International Universities Press.

Appel, S. (1996). *Positioning subjects: Psychoanalysis and critical educational studies.* New York: Bergin and Garvey.

Banks, J. (1997). *Teaching strategies for ethnic studies.* Boston: Allyn & Bacon.

Barford, D. (Ed.). (2002). *The ship of thought: Essays on psychoanalysis and learning.* London: Karnac Books.

Basch, M. (1989). The teacher, the transference, and development. In K. Field, B. Cohler, & G. Wool (Eds.), *Learning and education: Psychoanalytic perspectives* (pp. 771–788). Madison, CT: International Universities Press.

Belenky, M. (1986). *Women's ways of knowing.* New York: Guilford Press.

Berger, P. (1967). *The sacred canopy: Elements of a sociological theory of religion.* New York: Doubleday.

Bernstein, H. (1989). Self-organization as a fundamental psychological need. In K. Field, B. Cohler, & G. Wool (Eds.), *Learning and education: Psychoanalytic perspectives* (pp. 143–158). Madison, CT: International Universities Press.

Block, A. (1997). *I'm only bleeding: Education as the practice of social violence against children.* New York: Peter Lang.

Blos, P. (1940). *The adolescent personality: A study of individual behavior for the commission on secondary school curriculum.* New York: D. Appleton–Century.

Boorstin, D. (1985). *The discoverers: A history of man's search to know his world and himself.* New York: Vintage Books.

Britzman, D. (2003). *After-education: Anna Freud, Melanie Klein, and psychoanalytic histories of learning.* Albany: State University of New York Press.

Britzman, D. (1999). Between "lifting" and "accepting": Observations on the work of Angst in learning. In S. Appel (Ed). *Psychoanalysis and pedagogy* (pp. 1–16). London: Bergin and Garvey.

Brown, G., Phillips M., & Shapiro, S. (1976). *Getting it all together: Confluent education.* Bloomington, IN: Phi Delta Kappa Educational Foundation.

Brown, J., Collins, A. & Duguid, O. (1988). Situated cognition and the culture of learning. *Educational Researcher,* 18, 32–42.

Bullough, R., Jr. (1989). *First-year teacher: A case study.* New York: Teachers College Press.

Bullough, R., Jr., & Gitlin, A. (1995). *Becoming a student of teaching: Methodologies for exploring self and school context.* New York: Garland.

Bullough, R., Jr., Patterson, R., & Mayes, C. (2002). Teaching as prophecy. *The Journal of Curriculum Inquiry,* 32(3), 310–329.

Campbell, J. 1949. *The hero with a thousand faces.* Princeton, NJ: Princeton University Press.

Castillejo, I.C. de. (1973). *Knowing woman: A feminine psychology.* New York: Harper & Row.

Castoriadis, C. (1991) Time and creation. In J. Bender & D. Wellerby (Eds.), *Chronotypes: The construction of time* (pp. 38–64). Stanford, CA: Stanford University Press.

Chapman, J.H. (1988). *Jung's three theories of religious experience.* Lewiston, NY: Edwin Mellen Press.

Charet, F.X. (1993). *Spiritualism and the foundations of C.G. Jung's philosophy.* Albany: State University of New York Press.

Chodorow, N. (1978). *The reproduction of mothering: Psychoanalysis and the sociology of gender.* Berkeley, CA: University of California Press.

Cixous, H. (1991). *"Coming to writing" and other essays.* Cambridge, MA: Harvard University Press.

Clift, W. (1982). *Jung and Christianity: The challenge of reconciliation.* New York: Crossroad.

Cohler, B. (1989). Psychoanalysis and education: Motive, meaning, and self. In K. Field, B. Cohler, & G. Wool (Eds.), *Learning and education: Psychoanalytic perspectives* (pp.11–84). Madison, CT: International Universities Press.

Conger, J., & Galambos, J. (1997). *Adolescence and youth: Psychological development in a changing world.* New York: Longman.

Cozzarrelli, L., & Silin, M. (1989) The effects of narcissistic transferences on the teaching–learning process. In K. Field, B. Cohler, & G. Wool (Eds.), *Learning and education: Psychoanalytic perspectives* (pp. 809–824). Madison, CT: International Universities Press.

Craig, R. (1994). *The face we put on: Carl Jung for teachers.* The Clearing House. March–April, 189–191.

Crain, W. (1992). *Theories of development: Concepts and applications.* Englewood Cliffs, NJ: Prentice-Hall.

Cremin, L. (1964). *The transformation of the school: Progressivism in American education, 1876–1957.* New York: Vintage Press.

Cremin, L. (1977). *Traditions of American education.* New York: Basic Books.

Cremin, L. (1988). *American education: The metropolitan experience.* New York: Harper & Row.

Cuban, L. (1993). *How teachers taught: Constancy and change in American classrooms, 1890–1990.* New York: Teachers College Press.

Doll, W. (1993). Teaching a post-modern curriculum. In J. Sears & D. Marshall (Eds.), *Teaching and thinking about curriculum: Critical inquiries* (pp. 42–57). New York: Teachers College Press.

Dourley, J. (1984). *The illness that we are: A Jungian critique of Christianity.* Toronto, Canada: Inner City Books.

Dourley, J. (1987). *Love, celibacy, and the inner marriage.* Toronto, Canada: Inner City Books.

Dunne, J. (1973). *Time and myth.* Garden City, NY: Doubleday.

Edinger, E. (1973). *Ego and archetype: Individuation and the religious function of the psyche.* Baltimore, MD: Penguin Press.

Edinger, E. (1985). *Anatomy of the psyche: Alchemical symbolism in psychotherapy.* La Salle, IN: Open Court Press.

Eisner, E., & Vallance, E. (Eds.). (1974). *Conflicting conceptions of curriculum.* Berkeley, CA: McCutchan Publishing Corp.

Eisner, E., & Vallance, E. (1985). *The educational imagination: On the design and evaluation of school programs.* New York: Macmillan.

Ekstein, R. (1969). Psychoanalytic notes on the function of the curriculum. In R. Ekstein, & R. Motto (Eds.), *From learning for love to love of learning: Essays on psychoanalysis and education* (pp. 47–57). New York: Brunner/Mazel.

Ekstein, R., & Motto, R. (1969). *From learning for love to love of learning: Essays on psychoanalysis and education.* New York: Brunner/Mazel.

Eliade, M. (1974). *The myth of the eternal return or, Cosmos and history.* Princeton, NJ: Princeton University Press.

Eliot, T. (1971). *T.S. Eliot: The complete poems and plays: 1909–1950.* New York: Harcourt, Brace and World.

Ellenberger, H. (1970). *The discovery of the unconscious: The history and evolution of dynamic psychiatry.* New York: Basic Books.

Elson, M. (1989). The teacher as learner, the learner as teacher. In K. Field, B. Cohler, & G. Wool (Eds.), *Learning and education: Psychoanalytic perspectives.* Madison, CT: International Universities Press.

Epstein, M. (1995). *Thoughts without a thinker: Psychotherapy from a Buddhist perspective.* New York: Basic Books.

Fairbairn, W.R.D. (1992). *Psychoanalytic studies of the personality.* London: Routledge.

Fairbairn, W.R.D. (1992 [1940]). Schizoid factors in the personality. In W.R.D. Fairbairn, *Psychoanalytic studies of the personality* (pp. 3–27). London: Routledge.

Fairbairn, W.R.D. (1992 [1941]). A revised psychopathology of the psychoses and psychoneuroses. In W.R.D. Fairbairn, *Psychoanalytic studies of the personality* (pp. 28–58). London: Routledge.

Fenichel, O. (1945). *The psychoanalytic theory of neurosis.* New York: Norton.

Ferrer, J. (2002). *Revisioning transpersonal theory: A participatory vision of human spirituality.* Albany: State University of New York Press.

Field, K. (1989).Some reflections on the teacher-student dialogue: A psychoanalytic perspective. In K. Field, B. Cohler, & G. Wool (Eds.), *Learning and education: Psychoanalytic perspectives* (pp.851–926). Madison, CT: International Universities Press.

Field, K., Cohler, B., & Wool, G. (Eds.). (1989). *Learning and education: Psychoanalytic perspectives.* Madison, CT: International Universities Press.

Forbes, S. (2003). *Holistic education: An analysis of its nature and ideas.* Brandon, VT: Foundation for Educational Renewal Press.

Fordham, M. (1994). *Children as individuals.* London: Free Association Books.

Fordham, M. (1996). In S. Shamdasani (Ed.), *Analyst-patient interaction: Collected papers on technique.* London: Routledge.

Foucault, M. (1979). *Discipline and punish*. New York: Vintage Books.

Fox, S. (1975). *Freud and education*. Springfield, IL: Charles C Thomas.

Frankl, V. (1967). *Man's search for meaning*. New York: Washington Square Press.

Franz, M.-L. von. (1984). Meaning and order: Concerning meeting points and differences between depth psychology and physics. In R. Papadopoulos & G. Saayman (Eds.), *Jung in modern perspective: The master and his legacy* (pp. 268–286). Lindfield, Australia: Unity Press.

Franz, M.-L. von. (1974). *Number and time: Reflections leading toward a unification of depth psychology and physics*. Evanston, IL: Northwestern University Press.

Franz, M.-L. von. (1978). *Time: Rhythm and repose*. San Francisco: Sigo Press.

Frazer, J. (1935). *The golden bough: A study in magic and religion*. New York: Macmillan.

Freire, P. (2001). *Pedagogy and freedom: Ethics, democracy, and civic courage*. New York: Rowman and Littlefield.

Freud, A. (1930). *Introduction to psychoanalysis: Lectures for child analysts and teachers, 1922–1935*. New York: International Universities Press.

Freud, S. (1910). *Totem and taboo: Resemblances between the psychic lives of savages and neurotics*. London: Kegan Paul, Trench, Trubner, and Co.

Freud, S. (1939). *Moses and monotheism*. New York: Knopf.

Freud, S. (1957 [1914]). On narcissism: An introduction. In J. Rickman (Ed.), *A general selection from the works of Sigmund Freud* (pp. 104–123). New York: Doubleday Anchor Books.

Freud, S. (1957 [1920]). Beyond the pleasure principle. In J. Rickman (Ed.), *A general selection from the works of Sigmund Freud* (pp. 141–168). Garden City, New York: Doubleday Anchor Books.

Freud, S. (1957 [1923]). The ego and the id. In J. Rickman (Ed.), *A general selection from the works of Sigmund Freud* (pp. 210–235). Garden City, NY: Doubleday Anchor Books.

Freud, S. (1970 [1915–1917]). *A general introduction to psycho-analysis*. (Trans. J. Riviere). New York: Simon and Schuster.

Freud, S. (1988). The future prospects of psychoanalytic therapy. In B. Wolstein (Ed.), *Essential papers on counter-transference* (pp. 16–24). New York: New York University Press.

Freud, S. (1990). The dynamics of transference. In A. Esman (Ed.), *Essential papers on transference* (pp. 28–36). New York: New York University Press.

Frey-Rohn, L. (1974). *From Freud to Jung: A comparative study of the psychology of the unconscious*. New York: G. P. Putnam's Sons.

Frye, N. (1957). *Anatomy of criticism: Four essays*. New York: Antheneum.

Fuller, R. (1986). *Americans and the unconscious*. New York: Oxford University Press.

Hall, G. S. (1904). *Adolescence: Its psychology and its relations to physiology, anthropology, sociology, sex, crime, religion, and education*. New York: D. Appleton and Co.

Gardner, H. (1983). *Frames of mind*. New York: Basic Books.

Gardner, H. (1999). Are there additional intelligences? The case for naturalistic, spiritual, and existential intelligences. In J. Kane (Ed.), *Education, information, and transformation* (pp. 113–131). Columbus, OH: Merrill/Prentice Hall.

Gellert, M. (2001). *The fate of America: An inquiry into national character*. Washington, DC: Brassey's.

Giddens, A. (1990). *The consequences of modernity*. Stanford, CA: Stanford University Press.

Giddens, A. (1991). *Modernity and self-identity: Self and society in the late modern age.* Stanford, CA: Stanford University Press.

Gilligan, C. (1982). *In a different voice: Psychological theory and women's development.* Cambridge, MA: Harvard University Press.

Goldbrunner, J. (1965). *Individuation: A study of the depth psychology of Carl Gustav Jung.* Notre Dame, IN: University of Notre Dame Press.

Gray, R. (1996). *Archetypal explorations: An integrative approach to human behavior.* London: Routledge.

Greeley, A. (1974). *Unsecular man: The persistence of religion.* New York: Delta Books.

Greene, M. (1974). Cognition, consciousness, and curriculum. In W. Pinar (Ed.), *Heightened consciousness, cultural revolution, and curriculum theory* (pp. 69–83). Berkeley, CA: McCutchan Publishing Corp.

Greene, M. (1995). Care and moral education. In W. Kohli (Ed.), *Critical conversations in the philosophy of education* (pp. 176–198). New York: Routledge.

Greenson, R. (1990). The working alliance and the transference neurosis. In A. Esman (Ed.), *Essential papers on transference* (pp. 150–171). New York: New York University Press.

Greenspan, S. (1989). Emotional intelligence. In K. Field, B. Cohler, & G. Wool (Eds.), *Learning and education: Psychoanalytic perspectives* (pp. 209–244). Madison, CT: International Universities Press.

Grossman, B. (1975). Freud and the classroom. In T. Roberts (Ed.), *Four psychologies applied to education: Freudian, behavioral, humanistic, transpersonal* (pp. 43–69). Cambridge, MA: Schenkman.

Grumet, M. (1988). *Bitter milk: Women and teaching.* Amherst, MA: University of Massachusetts Press.

Gutek, G. (2000). *American education: 1945–2000.* Prospect Heights, IL: Waveland Press.

Hall, A. (2002). Psychoanalytic research on learning: An appraisal and some suggestions. In D. Barford (Ed.), *The ship of thought: Essays on psychoanalysis and learning* (pp. 17–40). New York: Karnac Books.

Heath, S. (1983). *Ways with words: Language, life, and work in communities and classrooms.* Cambridge, England: Cambridge University Press.

Henderson, A., & Kegan, R. (1989). Learning, knowing, and the self: A constructive developmental view. In K. Field, B. Cohler, & G. Wool (Eds.), *Learning and education: Psychoanalytic perspectives* (pp. 267–304). Madison, CT: International Universities Press.

Henderson, J. (1967). *Thresholds of initiation.* Middletown, CT: Wesleyan University Press.

Hilgard, E. (1987). *Psychology in America: A historical survey.* San Diego, CA: Harcourt Brace Jovanovich.

Hillman, J. (1996). *The soul's code: In search of character and calling.* New York: Random House.

Homans, P. (1985). C.G. Jung: Christian or post-Christian psychologist? In L. Martin & J. Goss Eds.), *Essays on the study of Jung and religion* (pp. 26–44). Lanham, MD: University Press of America.

Homans, P. (1989). *The ability to mourn: Disillusionment and the social origins of psychoanalysis.* Chicago: University of Chicago Press.

Huebner, D. (1999). *The lure of the transcendent: Collected essays by Dwayne E. Huebner.* Mahwah, NJ: Lawrence Erlbaum Associates.

Isaacs, S. (1932). *The children we teach, seven to eleven years.* London: University of London Press.

Jacoby, M. (1984). *The analytic encounter: Transference and human relationship*. Toronto, Canada: Inner City Books.

Jaffe, A. (1975). *The myth of meaning: Jung and the expansion of consciousness* (R.F.C. Hull, Trans.). New York: Penguin Books.

Jansz, J., & van Drunen, P. (2004). *A social history of psychology*. Oxford: Blackwell Publishing.

Jersild, A., & Lazar, E. (1962). *The meaning of psychotherapy in the teacher's life and work*. New York: Bureau of Publications, Teachers College.

Johnstone, R. (1997). *Religion in society: A sociology of religion*. New Jersey: Prentice-Hall.

Jones, J. (1980). *Soldiers of light and love: Northern teachers and Georgia Blacks: 1865–1873*. Chapel Hill: University of North Carolina Press.

Jones, R. (1968). *Fantasy and feeling in education*. New York: New York University Press.

Jung, C.G. (1921). *Psychological types* (R.F.C. Hull, Trans.). Princeton, NJ: Princeton University Press.

Jung, C.G. (1938). *Psychology and religion*. New Haven, CT: Yale University Press.

Jung, C.G. (1944). *Psychology and alchemy* (R.F.C. Hull, Trans.). Princeton, NJ: Princeton University Press.

Jung, C.G. (1953). *Two essays on analytical psychology* (R.F.C. Hull, Trans.). Princeton, NJ: Princeton University Press.

Jung, C.G. (1954a). *The practice of psychotherapy: Essays on the psychology of the transference and other subjects* (R.F.C. Hull, Trans.). Princeton, NJ: Princeton University Press.

Jung, C.G. (1954b). *The development of personality: Papers on child psychology, education, and related subjects* (R.F.C. Hull, Trans.). Princeton, NJ: Princeton University Press.

Jung, C.G. (1954c). *The symbolic life* (R.F.C. Hull, Trans.). Princeton, NJ: Princeton University Press.

Jung, C.G. (1956). *Symbols of transformation: Analysis of the prelude to a case of schizophrenia* (R.F.C. Hull, Trans.). Princeton, NJ: Princeton University Press.

Jung, C.G. (1958). *Psychology and religion: West and East* (R.F.C. Hull, Trans.). Princeton, NJ: Princeton University Press.

Jung, C.G. (1960). *The structure and dynamics of the psyche* (R.F.C. Hull, Trans.). Princeton, NJ: Princeton University Press.

Jung, C.G. (1963). *Mysterium coniunctonis* (R.F.C. Hull, Trans.). Princeton, NJ: Princeton University Press.

Jung, C.G. (1964). *Civilization in transition* (R.F.C. Hull, Trans.). Princeton, NJ: Princeton University Press.

Jung, C. (1965). *Memories, dreams, reflections*. New York: Vintage.

Jung, C.G. (1966). *The spirit in man, art, and literature* (R.F.C. Hull, Trans.). Princeton, NJ: Princeton University Press.

Jung, C.G. (1967). *Freud and psychoanalysis* (R.F.C. Hull, Trans.). Princeton, NJ: Princeton University Press.

Jung, C.G. (1968a). *The archetypes and the collective unconscious* (R.F.C. Hull, Trans.). Princeton, NJ: Princeton University Press.

Jung, C.G. (1968b). *Aion: Researches into the phenomenology of the self* (R.F.C. Hull, Trans.). Princeton, NJ: Princeton University Press.

Jung, C.G. (1968c). *Alchemical studies* (R.F.C. Hull, Trans.). Princeton, NJ: Princeton University Press.

Jung, C.G. (1978). *Psychology and the East* (R.F.C. Hull, Trans.). Princeton, NJ: Princeton University Press.

Jung, C.G., von Franz, M.–L., Henderson, J., Jacobi, J., & Jaffe, A. (1964). *Man and his symbols.* New York: Doubleday & Co.

Kaestle, C. (1983). *Pillars of the republic: Common schools and American society, 1760–1860.* New York: Hill and Wang.

Kane, J. (Ed). (1999). *Education, information, and transformation.* Columbus, OH: Merrill/ Prentice Hall.

Kelsey, M. (1984). Jung as philosopher and theologian. In R. Papadopoulos & G. Saayman (Eds.), *Jung in modern perspective: The master and his legacy* (pp. 182–192). Lindfield, Australia: Unity Press.

Kerenyi, C. (1959). *Asklepios: Archetypal image of the physician's existence.* Princeton, NJ: Princeton University Press.

Kilpatrick, W. H. (1925). *Foundations of method: Informal talks on teaching.* New York: Macmillan.

Kirman, W. (1977). *Modern psychoanalysis in the schools.* Dubuque, IA: Kendall/Hunt.

Kirsch, J. (1995). Transference. In M. Stein. (Ed.), *Jungian analysis* (pp.170–209). Chicago: Open Court.

Klein, M. (1975 [1932]). *The psychoanalysis of children* (A. Strachey, Trans.). New York: Delacorte Press.

Kliebard, H. (1986). *The struggle for the American curriculum: 1893–1958.* New York: Routledge.

Kniker, C. (1985). *Teaching about religion in the public schools.* Bloomington, IN: Phi Delta Kappa.

Knox, J. (1998). Transference and countertransference. In I. Alister & C. Hauke (Eds.), *Contemporary Jungian analysis: Post-Jungian perspectives from the society of analytic psychology* (pp. 73–84). London: Routledge.

Kohlberg, L. (1958). *The development of modes of moral thinking and choice in the years 10 to 16.* Chicago: Department of Photoduplication, University of Chicago Library.

Kohut, H. (1978). *The search for self: Selected writings of Heinz Kohut: 1950–1978,* P. Ornstein, (Ed.). Madison, CT: International Universities Press.

Kozol, J. (1991). *Savage inequalities: Children in American schools.* New York: Harper.

Kristeva, J. (1989). *Language—the unknown: An invitation to linguistics.* New York: Columbia University Press.

Kubie, L. (1967). The forgotten man of education. In R. Jones (Ed.), *Contemporary educational psychology: Selected readings* (pp. 61–71). New York: Harper & Row.

Kuhn, T. (1970). *The structure of scientific revolutions.* Chicago: University of Chicago Press.

Lasch, C. (1995). *The revolt of the elites and the betrayal of democracy.* New York: Norton.

Laux, D. (1968) A new role for teachers? In R. Jones (Ed.), *Contemporary educational psychology: Selected readings* (pp. 187–195). New York: Harper & Row.

Linde, C. (1993). *Life stories: The creation of coherence.* New York: Oxford University Press.

Littner, N. (1989). Reflections on early childhood family experiences in the educational situation. In K. Field, B. Cohler, & G. Wool (Eds.), *Learning and education: Psychoanalytic perspectives* (pp. 825–850). Madison, CT: International Universities Press.

Lortie, D. (1975). *Schoolteacher: A sociological study.* Chicago: University of Chicago Press.

Luckman, T. (1991). The constitution of human life in time. In J. Bender & D. Wellerby (Eds.), *Chronotypes: The construction of time* (pp. 151–166). Stanford, CA: Stanford University Press.

Macdonald, J. (1995). *Theory as a prayerful act: The collected essays of James P. Macdonald*, B. Macdonald (Ed.). New York: Peter Lang.

Main, R. (2004). *The rupture of time: Synchronicity and Jung's critique of modern Western culture*. New York: Brunner–Routledge.

Marsden, G. (1997). *The outrageous idea of Christian scholarship*. New York: Oxford University Press.

Marshak, M. (1998). The intersubjective nature of analysis. In I. Alister & C. Hauke (Eds.), *Contemporary Jungian anaylsis: Post-Jungian perspectives from the society of analytic psychology* (pp.57–72). London: Routledge.

Marx, K. (1978 [1844]). *The Marx–Engels reader*, R. Tucker (Ed.). New York: W.W. Norton.

Maslow, A. (1968). *Toward a psychology of being* (2nd ed.). Princeton, NJ: D. Van Nostrand.

Matoon, M. (1985). *Jungian psychology in perspective*. New York: The Free Press.

Mayes, C. (1998). The use of contemplative practices in teacher education. *Encounter: Education for Meaning and Social Justice*, 11(3), 17–31.

Mayes, C. (1999). Reflecting on the archetypes of teaching. *Teaching Education*, 10(2), 3–16.

Mayes, C. (2001). A transpersonal developmental model for teacher reflectivity. *Journal of Curriculum Studies*, 33(4), 477–493.

Mayes, C. (2002). Personal and archetypal aspects of transference and counter-transference in the classroom. *Encounter: Education for Meaning and Social Justice*, 15(2), 34–49.

Mayes, C. (2003). *Seven curricular landscapes: An approach to the holistic curriculum*. Lanham, MD: University Press of America.

Mayes, C. (2004). *Teaching mysteries: Foundations of spiritual pedagogy*. Lanham, MD: University Press of America.

Mayes, C. (2005a). *Jung and education: Elements of an archetypal pedagogy*. Lanham, MD: Rowman and Littlefield.

Mayes, C. (2005b). *Teaching and time: Foundations of a temporal pedagogy*. Teaching Education Quarterly, 32(2), 143–160.

Mayes, C., & Blackwell-Mayes, P. (2002). The use of sandtray in a graduate educational leadership program. *The Journal of Sandplay Therapy: The C.G. Jung Institute of Los Angeles*, 11(2), 103–124.

Mayes, C., & Ferrin, S. (2001). The beliefs of spiritually committed public school teachers regarding religious expression in the classroom. *Religion and Education*, 28(1), 75–94.

Mayes, C., Cutri, R., Rogers, P.C., & Montero, F. (2007). *Understanding the whole student: Holistic multicultural education*. Lanham, MD: Rowman and Littlefield.

McLaren, P. (1998). *Life in schools: An introduction to critical pedagogy in the foundations of education* (3rd ed.). New York: Longman.

Meissner, W. (1984). *Psychoanalysis and religious experience*. New Haven, CT: Yale University Press.

Messerli, J. (1972). *Horace Mann: A biography*. New York: Knopf.

Miller, J., & Seeler, W. (1985). *Curriculum: Perspectives and practices*. New York: Longman.

Montessori, M. (1978 [1956]). In E. Plank (Ed.), *On development and education of young children: Selected papers*. New York: Philosophical Library.

Nagy, M. (1991). *Philosophical issues in the psychology of C.G. Jung.* Albany: State University of New York Press.

Naumburg, M. (1927). *The foundation and technique of curriculum construction.* Bloomington, IL: National Society for the Study of Education.

Neumann, E. (1954). *The origins and history of consciousness* (vol. 1). New York: Harper Brothers.

Neumann, E. (1973). Depth psychology and a new ethic. New York: Harper & Row.

Neumann, E. (1985). *Anatomy of the psyche: Alchemical symbolism in psychotherapy.* New York: Lightning Source.

Noddings, N. (1992). *The challenge to care in schools: An alternative approach to education.* New York: Teachers College Press.

Noddings, N. (1995). Care and moral education. In W. Kohli (Ed.), *Critical conversations in the philosophy of education* (pp. 137–148). New York: Longman.

Nord, W. (1990). Teaching about religion in the public schools: A model for teacher education programs. *Religion and Public Education,* 17(2), 223–227.

Nord, W. (1994). Ten suggestions for teaching about religion. In C. Haynes & O. Thomas (Eds.), *Finding common ground: A first amendment guide to religion and public education.* Vanderbilt University, Nashville, TN: Freedom Forum First Amendment Center.

Odajnyk, V. (1976). *Jung and politics: The political and social ideas of C. G. Jung.* New York: Harper & Row.

Odajnyk, V. (1993). *Gathering the light: A Psychology of meditation.* Boston, MA: Shambhala.

Ornstein, A., & Hunkins, F. (1988). *Curriculum: Foundations, principles, and issues.* Boston, MA: Allyn and Bacon.

Pajak, E. (2003). *Honoring diverse teaching styles: A guide for supervisors.* Alexandria, VA: Association for Supervision and Curriculum Development.

Palmer, M. (1995). *Freud and Jung on religion.* New York: Routledge.

Palmer, P. (1997). The grace of great things: Reclaiming the sacred in knowing, teaching, and learning. *Holistic Education Review,* 10(3), 8–16.

Pauli, W., & Jung, C.G. (2001). *Atom and archetype.* Princeton, NJ: Princeton University Press.

Pauson, M. (1988). *Jung the philosopher: Essays in Jungian thought.* New York: Peter Lang.

Pearson, G. (1954). *Psychoanalysis and the education of the child.* New York: Norton.

Peat, F.D. (1988). *Synchronicity: The bridge between mind and matter.* New York: Bantam.

Peller, L. (1978 [1945]). Educational remarks. In E. Plank (Ed.), *On development and education of young children: Selected papers* (pp. 11–18). New York: Philosophical Library.

Peller, L. (1978 [1956]). The school's role in promoting sublimation. In E. Plank (Ed.), *On development and education of young children: Selected papers* (pp. 89–107). New York: Philosophical Library.

Peller, L. (1978 [1958]). The development of the child's self. In E. Plank (Ed.), *On development and education of young children: Selected papers* (pp. 55–88). New York: Philosophical Library.

Pfister, O. (1922). *Psycho-analysis in the service of education, being an introduction to psycho-analysis.* London: Henry Kimpton.

Piaget, J., & Inhelder, B. (1969). *The psychology of the child.* New York, Basic Books.

Piers, M. (1969). Play and mastery. In R. Ekstein, & R. Motto (Eds.), *From learning for love to love of learning: Essays on psychoanalysis and education* (pp. 99–106). New York: Brunner/Mazel.

Piers, G., & Piers, M. (1989). Modes of learning and the analytic process. In K. Field, B. Cohler, & G. Wool (Eds.), *Learning and education: Psychoanalytic perspectives* (pp.199–208). Madison, CT: International Universities Press.

Progoff, I. (1959). *Depth psychology and modern man: A new view of the magnitude of human personality, its dimensions and resources.* New York: Julian Press.

Progoff, I. (1975). *At a journal workshop: The basic text and guide for using the intensive journal.* New York: Dialogue House Library.

Polette, K. (2004). Airing (erring) the soul: An archetypal view of television. In J. Baumlin, T. Baumlin, & G. Jensen (Eds.), *Post-Jungian criticism: Theory and practice* (pp. 93–116). Albany: State University of New York Press.

Purpel, D., & Shapiro, S. (1995). *Beyond liberation and excellence: Reconstructing the public discourse on education.* Westport, CT: Bergin and Garvey.

Redl, F., & Wattenberg, W. (1951). *Mental hygiene in teaching.* New York: Harcourt, Brace, and Co.

Ricoeur, P. (1976). Introduction. In P. Ricoeur (Ed.), *Cultures and time* (pp. 13–33). Paris: UNESCO.

Ricoeur, P.(1991). *Freud and philosophy: An essay in interpretation.* New Haven, CT: Yale University Press.

Rieff, P. (1961). *Freud: The mind of the moralist.* Garden City, NY: Doubleday.

Rieff, P. (1987). *The triumph of the therapeutic: Uses of faith after Freud.* Chicago: University of Chicago Press.

Rizzuto, A–M. (1979). *The birth of the living God: A psychoanalytic study.* Chicago: University of Chicago Press.

Roberts, T. (1975). Introduction. In T. Roberts (Ed.), *Four psychologies applied to education: Freudian, behavioral, humanistic, tanspersonal* (pp. 3–9). Cambridge, MA: Schenkman.

Roberts, T. (1979). Consciousness counseling: New roles and new goals. *Elementary School Guidance and Counseling* 14(2), 103–107.

Roberts, T. (1981). Expanding thinking through consciousness education. *Educational Leadership* 39(1), 52–54.

Roberts, T. (1985). States of consciousness: A new intellectual direction, a new teacher education direction. *Journal of Teacher Education* 36(2), 55–59.

Roberts, T., & Clark, F. (1975). *Transpersonal psychology in education.* Bloomington, IN: The Phi Delta Kappa Educational Foundation.

Robertson, R. (1995). *Jungian achetypes: Jung, Gödel, and the history of archetypes.* York Beach, ME: Nicolas–Hays.

Rogoff, B. (1984). *Everyday cognition: Its development and social context.* Cambridge, MA: Harvard University Press.

Rogoff, (2003). *The cultural nature of human development.* New York: Oxford University Press.

Ross, D. (1972). *G. Stanley Hall: The psychologist as prophet.* Chicago: University of Chicago Press.

Salzberger–Wittenberg, I. (1989). *The emotional experience of learning and teaching.* London: Routledge and Kegan Paul.

Samuels, A. (1997). *Jung and the post-Jungians.* London: Routledge.

Samuels, A. (2001). *Politics on the couch: Citizenship and the internal life.* London: Routledge.

Sartre, J. (1956). *Being and nothingness: An essay on phenomenological ontology.* New York: Philosophical Library.

Schon, D. (1987). *Educating the reflective practitioner.* San Francisco: Jossey–Bass.

Schwartz, D. (1989). Implications of the infantile neurosis for learning problems in childhood. In K. Field, B. Cohler, & G. Wool (Eds.), *Learning and education: Psychoanalytic perspectives.* Madison, CT: International Universities Press.

Schwartz–Salant, N. (1995). Archetypal factors underlying sexual acting-out in the transference/countertransference process. In N. Schwartz–Salant & M. Stein (Eds.), *Transference/countertransference* (pp. 1–30). Wilmette, IL: Chiron Publications.

Schafer, R. (1980). Narration in the psychoanalytic dialogue. *Critical Inquiry* 7(1), 29–54.

Shaker, P. (1982). The application of Jung's analytical psychology to education. *Journal of Curriculum Studies* 14(3), 241–250.

Shalem, Y., & Bensusan, D. (1999). Why can't we stop believing? In S. Appel (Ed.), *Psychoanalysis and pedagogy* (pp. 27–44). London: Bergin and Garvey.

Shamdasani, S. (2003). *Jung and the making of modern psychology: The dream of a science.* Cambridge, UK: Cambridge University Press.

Sheldrake, R. (1981). *A new science of life: The hypothesis of formative causation.* Los Angeles: J.P. Tarcher.

Silberman, C. (Ed.). (1973). *The open classroom reader.* New York: Vintage Books.

Skinner, B.F. (1956). *The technology of teaching.* New York: Appleton–Century–Croft.

Sklar, K. (1973). *Catherine Beecher: A study in American domesticity.* New Haven, CT: Yale University Press.

Sowell, T. (1933). *Inside American education: The decline, the deception, the dogmas.* New York: Free Press.

Spiegelman, J. & Mansfeld, V. (1996). On the physics and psychology of the transference as an interactive field. In J. Spiegelman (Ed.), *Psychotherapy as a mutual process* (pp. 183–206). Tempe, AZ: New Falcon Publications.

Spring, J. (1976). *The sorting machine: National educational policy since 1945.* New York: David McKay.

Stein, M. (Ed.). (1982). *Jungian analysis.* Boulder, CO: Shambhala Publications.

Stevens, A. (1999). *On Jung: An updated edition with a reply to Jung's critics* (2nd ed.). Princeton, NJ: Princeton University Press.

Symonds, P. (1951). *The ego and the self.* New York: Appleton–Century–Croft.

The Holy Bible, King James Version. Salt Lake City, UT: The Church of Jesus Christ of Latter–Day Saints.

Tillich, P. (1956). *The essential Tillich.* New York: Macmillan.

Tillich, P. (1959). *Theology of culture.* New York: Oxford University Press.

Todd, S. (2003). *Learning from the other: Levinas, psychoanalysis, and ethical possibilities in education.* Albany: State University of New York Press.

Tyack, D. (1974). *The one best system: A history of American urban education.* Cambridge, MA: Harvard University Press.

Tyler, L. (1975). Curriculum development from a psychoanalytic perspective. In T. Roberts (Ed.), *Four psychologies applied to education: Freudian, behavioral, humanistic, transpersonal* (pp. 55–62). Cambridge, MA: Schenkman.

Tyler, R. (1989). Psychologically informed education: Historical foundations. In K. Field, B. Cohler, & G. Wool (Eds.), *Learning and education: Psychoanalytic perspectives* (pp.127–142). Madison, CT: International Universities Press.

Ulanov, A. (1999). *Religion and the spiritual in Carl Jung.* New York: Paulist Press.

Valli, L. (1990). Moral approaches to reflective practice. In R. Clift, W. Houston, & M. Pugach (Eds.), *Encouraging reflective practice in education: An analysis of issues and programs* (pp. 39–56). New York: Teachers College Press.

Vivas, E. & Krieger, M. (Eds.). (1953). The problems of aesthetics. New York: Reinhart.

Vygotsky, L. (1986). *Mind in society: The development of psychological functions.* Cambridge, MA: Harvard University Press.

Wade, J. (1996). *Changes of mind: A holonomic theory of the evolution of consciousness.* Albany: University of New York Press.

Walsh, R. (1990). *The spirit of shamanism.* Los Angeles: Jeremy P. Tarcher.

Warshaw, T. (1986). Preparation for teaching about religions in public schools. *Religious Education,* 81(1), 79–92.

Watson, G. (1975 [1956]). Psychoanalysis and the future of education. In T. Roberts (Ed.), *Four psychologies applied to education: Freudian, behavioral, humanistic, transpersonal* (pp. 32–38). Cambridge, MA: Schenkman.

Wehr, G. (2002). *Jung and Steiner: The birth of a new psychology.* Great Barrington, MA: Anthroposophic Press.

Wertsch, J. (1985). *Vygotsky and the social formation of mind.* Cambridge, MA: Harvard University Press.

Wexler, P. (1996). *Holy sparks: Social theory, education, and religion.* New York: St. Martin's Press.

Wheelwright, P. (1974). Poetry, myth, and reality. In W. Handy & M. Westbrook (Eds.), *Twentieth century criticism: The major statements* (pp. 252–266). New York: Macmillan.

White, V. (1982 [1952]). *God and the unconscious.* Dallas, TX: Spring Publications.

Whitmore, D. (1986). *Psychosynthesis in education: A guide to the joy of learning.* Rochester, VT: Destiny Books.

Whitrow, G. (1988). *Time in history: The evolution of our general awareness of time and temporal perspective.* Oxford: Oxford University Press.

Winnicott, C., Shepherd, R., & Davis, M. (Eds.). (1992). *Psychoanalytic explorations: D.W. Winnicott.* Cambridge, MA: Harvard University Press.

Winnicott, D.W. (1992 [1962]). The beginnings of a formulation of an appreciation and criticism of Melanie Klein's envy statement. In C. Winnicott, R. Shepherd, & M. Davis (Eds.), *Psychoanalytic explorations* (pp. 447–457). Cambridge, MA: Harvard University Press.

Winnicott, D.W. (1992 [1969]). The mother–infant experience of mutuality. In C. Winnicott, R. Shepherd, & M. Davis (Eds.), *Psychoanalytic explorations* (pp. 251–260). Cambridge, MA: Harvard University Press.

Wolf, E. (1989). The psychoanalytic self-psychologist looks at learning. In K. Field, B. Cohler, & G. Wool (Eds.), *Learning and education: Psychoanalytic perspectives* (pp. 377–394). Madison, CT: International Universities Press.

Wolstein, B. (1988). The pluralism of perspectives on countertransference. In B. Wolstein (Ed.), *Essential papers on counter-transference* (pp. 339–354). New York: New York University Press.

Woodman, M. (1990). *The ravaged bridegroom: Masculinity in women*. Toronto, Ontario: Inner City Books.

Woodman, M. (1995). Transference and countertransference in analysis dealing with eating disorders. In N. Schwartz–Salant & M. Stein (Eds.), *Transference/countertransference* (pp. 53–66). Wilmette, IL: Chiron Publications.

Wool, G. (1989). Relational aspects of learning: The learning alliance. In K. Field, B. Cohler, & G. Wool (Eds.), *Learning and education: Psychoanalytic perspectives* (pp.747–770). Madison, CT: International Universities Press.

Wuthnow, R. (1994). *Producing the sacred: An essay on public religion*. Chicago: University of Illinois Press.

Zachry, C. (1929). *Personality adjustments of school children,* with an introduction by William Heard Kilpatrick. New York: C. Scribner's Sons.

Zachry, C. (1940). *Emotion and conduct in adolescence. For the commission on secondary school curriculum*. New York: Appleton–Century.

INDEX